FROM RETRIBUTION TO RESTORATION

A Biblical Guide to Restorative Justice

Answering the Tough Questions on Crime, Punishment, and Healing

DR. MAXWELL SHIMBA

Published in Manhattan, New York by Shimba Publishing, LLC.

Shimba Publishing LLC

Table of Contents

Chapter 1 1
THE TRADITIONAL VIEW OF JUSTICE 1
Chapter 02 19
WHY RESTRUCTURE THE CRIMINAL JUSTICE SYSTEM? 19
Chapter 03 50
A DIFFERENT VIEW OF JUSTICE 50
Chapter 04 92
CONCEPTUAL FRAMEWORKS OF RESTORATIVE JUSTICE 92
Chapter 05 121
PROMISING PRACTICES OF RESTORATIVE JUSTICE 121
Chapter 06 189
SHOULD THE CHURCH GET INVOLVED IN RESTORATIVE JUSTICE? 189
Chapter 07 245
THE RESTORATIVE JUSTICE MINISTRY PARADIGM 245
Chapter 08 297
HOW THE CHURCH CAN IMPACT CORRECTIONS 297
Chapter 09 333
ORGANIZATIONAL CHANGE 333
Chapter 10 367
CONCLUSION 367

INTRODUCTION

Justice stands as a foundational pillar of human civilization. From the ancient codes of Babylon to the common law of England and the constitutional frameworks of modern nations, the pursuit of justice has been a central project of society. It is the mechanism by which we seek to maintain order, protect the innocent, and respond when that order is broken. At its core, justice addresses a fundamental question: what is the proper response to wrongdoing? For centuries, the dominant answer in Western societies has been retribution. This approach, encapsulated in the ancient principle of *lex talionis*—"an eye for an eye, a tooth for a tooth"—posits that justice is achieved when an offender receives punishment proportional to the harm they have caused. The focus is retrospective: a crime has been committed, a law has been broken, and the state, acting on behalf of society, must exact a penalty. This system, which we will refer to as the traditional or retributive justice model, is deeply ingrained in our legal structures and, perhaps more profoundly, in our collective psyche.

However, despite its long history and intuitive appeal, there has been a growing chorus of dissatisfaction with this model. It is a dissatisfaction born not of a desire for less justice, but for *more*—a justice that is more effective, more humane, and more complete. This book explores an alternative paradigm that has emerged from this discontent: **restorative justice**. It is a paradigm that shifts the focus from punishment to healing, from abstraction to relationship, and from retribution to restoration. This introduction will lay the groundwork for that exploration by examining the traditional model, the reasons for its perceived failure, and the contours of the restorative alternative, grounding this analysis in the disciplines of psychology, philosophy, and theology, and pointing towards a more comprehensive and biblical vision of justice.

The Retributive Paradigm: A Philosophical and Theological Examination

Retributive justice, in its purest form, is a system that seeks to "repair" justice through the imposition of punishment. Philosophically, it is rooted in the concept of *desert*—the belief that wrongdoers *deserve* to suffer in proportion to the suffering they have inflicted. This is often justified by the principle of *lex talionis*, which was not, as is commonly misunderstood, a license for bloodlust, but rather a mechanism for *limiting* revenge. In a world without a central authority, cycles of vengeance could spiral out of control. The "eye for an eye" law was a revolutionary constraint, insisting that the punishment must fit the crime and go no further. It established proportionality and, in a sense, equality before the law, at least in theory.

From a theological perspective, this principle finds its echo in the Mosaic Law, given to the nation of Israel. Passages like Exodus 21:23-25 ("life for life, eye for eye, tooth for tooth") were part of a covenantal legal system designed to govern a theocratic community. It served a crucial purpose: it established that wrongdoing had consequences and that God's standard of holiness required accountability. As the Apostle Paul explains in Galatians 3:24, the law served as a "schoolmaster" or "tutor" to bring us to Christ. Its purpose was not to impart righteousness, but to reveal our inability to achieve it, thereby highlighting our desperate need for a savior. The law demonstrated God's justice, but it could not, in itself, restore the broken relationship between humanity and God.

This is the fundamental limitation of a purely retributive system, whether divine or secular. Its advantages are clear and often cited: it provides a societal catharsis, a sense that order has been restored and the offender has "paid their debt." It serves as a formal deterrent, signaling to the broader community that certain actions carry severe consequences. It is, in principle, a system of equality, where the punishment is ostensibly the same for the same crime, irrespective of the individuals involved.

Yet, its disadvantages are equally profound. From a **psychological** standpoint, retribution focuses on the offender's past actions but ignores the complex web of factors—trauma, poverty, addiction, cognitive impairments, and social learning—that may have contributed to the behavior. It treats the symptom (the crime) while neglecting the underlying disease. It is akin to treating a patient with a raging fever by constantly applying ice packs, never investigating or curing the infection causing it. The offender, processed through this system, often emerges more embittered, more traumatized, and less capable of pro-social behavior. Incarceration, the primary tool of retribution, is a psychologically damaging environment that can exacerbate mental health issues, sever family bonds, and reinforce criminal identities, creating a cycle of recidivism. The "debt" is never truly paid; the offender is simply marked, isolated, and returned to society—often to the same conditions that fostered the crime in the first place—with few skills and fewer prospects.

Philosophically, a purely retributive system is incomplete. It answers the question of *what* should be done (punish the offender) but fails to ask the more important questions of *why* the harm occurred and *how* it can be truly repaired. It defines crime as an act against the state, an abstract entity, thereby sidelining the real people most impacted: the victim and the community. This creates a profound disconnect. The victim is reduced to a witness, a tool for the state's case, their emotional and psychological needs often ignored. The community is rendered a passive audience, their fear and anger left unaddressed, their potential to be part of the solution untapped.

The Emergence of a New Paradigm: Restorative Justice

It is from this dissatisfaction that restorative justice has emerged, not as a soft alternative, but as a more rigorous and holistic framework. Restorative justice begins with a different set of foundational premises. It defines crime not primarily as a violation of the law, but as a violation of people and relationships. As the principles in this book outline, crime creates an injury—to the victim, to the community, and even to the offender themselves, who is alienated from their own humanity and from the social bonds that give life meaning. The central goal of justice, therefore, is not to inflict more injury (punishment) but to repair the injury that has been done. This is the essence of *restoration*.

This shift from retribution to restoration has deep roots, not as a modern invention, but as a rediscovery of ancient wisdom. Long before the modern nation-state monopolized the administration of justice, communities around the world practiced restorative approaches. The document highlights a powerful example from Tanzania, where the Nyamwezi people, under the leadership of King Mirambo in the 19th century, practiced a form of restorative justice for millennia. When conflict arose, the community would gather—not in an imposing courthouse, but around the fireplace, a place of warmth, story, and communal life. Elders and chiefs would guide a process where the complainant and the accused could speak, be heard, and be questioned by the community. The goal was not to determine who could present the most convincing legal argument, but to uncover the *truth*—the full story of what happened, why it happened, and the harm it caused. This pursuit of truth was a communal endeavor aimed at understanding, healing, and preventing future harm. Reconciliation was sealed not with a verdict of guilt, but with a shared meal, a powerful symbol of restored fellowship. This practice, and countless others like it in African, Asian, and Indigenous cultures worldwide, demonstrates that restorative justice is not an untested theory but a time-honored practice of social cohesion. It is a testament to the human capacity for healing and the wisdom of community-based conflict resolution.

This approach resonates deeply with modern psychological understanding. Restorative practices like victim-offender mediation directly address the trauma of crime. For victims, having a voice, receiving answers to their questions, and hearing an offender acknowledge the harm can be profoundly therapeutic. It validates their experience, reduces feelings of powerlessness, and can mitigate symptoms of post-traumatic stress. For offenders, confronting the human impact of their actions is a powerful catalyst for change. It moves them from abstract remorse ("I broke the law") to genuine empathy ("I hurt this person"). This process, which the book refers to as "godly sorrow," is psychologically distinct from the shame of being caught. It is a recognition of the harm caused to another human being, which can motivate genuine accountability, reparative action, and a fundamental shift in self-perception. It transforms the offender from a passive recipient of punishment to an active participant in making things right.

A Theological and Philosophical Foundation for Restoration

This restorative vision finds its ultimate and most profound foundation in the Christian faith. The biblical narrative is, from beginning to end, a story of restoration. It begins with creation in perfect harmony—God, humanity, and creation in a state of *shalom*, a Hebrew word for peace that signifies wholeness, flourishing, and right relationship. The fall introduced sin, which is fundamentally a rupture in these relationships. The rest of Scripture is the account of God's relentless mission to restore that *shalom*—to reconcile humanity to Himself and to one another.

This is the heart of the Gospel. 2 Corinthians 5:18-19 declares, "All this is from God, who reconciled us to himself through Christ and gave us the ministry of reconciliation: that God was reconciling the world to himself in Christ, not counting people's sins against them." This is the ultimate paradigm of restorative justice. Humanity, the offender, stood guilty and alienated from a holy God. The victim was God's own righteous character and the created order. The just requirement was death—the wage of sin. But God did not merely exact retribution. Instead, in Christ, He absorbed the cost of the harm Himself. He satisfied the demands of justice on the cross, not to condemn the world, but to save it. This act is the ultimate model: accountability was fully met, but the goal was not punishment for its own sake; it was reconciliation, healing, and the restoration of the relationship. God, the primary "victim," initiated the process and made it possible for the offender to be restored. This is the "ministry of reconciliation" that has been entrusted to every believer. As this book will explore, the Church is not merely an observer of the criminal justice system; it is God's chosen instrument to bring this restorative paradigm to bear on the brokenness of crime, offering the same grace, accountability, and path to healing that we have received in Christ.

Philosophically, this aligns with a teleological view of justice—one concerned with the ultimate purpose or end goal.

Retributive justice is deontological, focused on the duty to punish the past wrong. Restorative justice is teleological, focused on the future good—healing the victim, reintegrating the offender, and rebuilding a healthy community. It asks not just "What rule was broken?" but "What good can we achieve now?" This vision is echoed in the words of the prophet Micah, who summarizes what God requires: "to act justly and to love mercy and to walk humbly with your God" (Micah 6:8). Biblical justice is inextricably linked with mercy and humility. It is not a cold, mechanical process of doling out punishment, but a passionate, creative pursuit of setting things right.

The Path Forward: From Retribution to Restoration

The growing interest in restorative justice, recognized even by the United States Department of Justice, reflects a collective yearning for a justice system that works. It is a response to a system that has left citizens feeling disconnected, victims dissatisfied, offenders embittered, and its own professionals frustrated. The "tall fences, razor-wire, and iron bars" have proven to be mere symptom-treaters, failing to address the root causes of criminal behavior and often compounding the problem. As the statistics show, with millions victimized each year and an incarceration rate that dwarfs the rest of the world, the old paradigm is demonstrably failing.

This book is an exploration of a different path. It is a guide to understanding the principles and practices of restorative justice through a biblical lens. It is a call to the Church to reclaim its God-given mandate to be a community of reconciliation—ministering to victims, walking with offenders, supporting families, and partnering with justice professionals. It moves beyond the simple dichotomy of punishment versus leniency to offer a vision of a justice that is both just and merciful, a justice that holds offenders accountable while creating a pathway for them to become restorers, a justice that heals the harm and rebuilds the community. By integrating insights from psychology, philosophy, theology, and real-world practice, this book aims to equip the reader with a comprehensive understanding of this transformative paradigm, answering the tough questions and providing a hopeful vision for a future where justice truly means restoration.

CHAPTER 1

THE TRADITIONAL VIEW OF JUSTICE

Before we can fully appreciate the beauty and transformative power of restorative justice, we must first understand the system it seeks to reform. The traditional view of justice is not merely a set of laws and procedures; it is a deeply ingrained worldview that shapes how we think about crime, punishment, and human nature itself. In this chapter, we will explore this traditional paradigm together, examining its foundations, its justifications, its consequences, and ultimately, its profound inadequacy in addressing the full scope of harm caused by crime. My hope is that by the end of this chapter, you will see not only what is wrong with the old way of thinking but also why a new vision is so desperately needed.

Let us begin with a simple but foundational question: what is the traditional view of justice? At its most basic level, it rests upon a premise that feels almost self-evident to most of us. When someone does wrong, they should be punished. This concept, which scholars call retributive justice, holds that the primary purpose of our justice system is to ensure that offenders receive what they deserve for their actions. The punishment must fit the crime. This principle resonates with something deep within us, with our innate sense that the moral order of the universe demands balance.

Think about how this works in practice. When a crime occurs, our system defines it first and foremost as an offense against the state, against the laws that govern our society. The offender has broken a rule, and the state's responsibility is to enforce that rule through the application of consequences. This may take the form of fines, community service, probation, or imprisonment, depending on how serious the offense was. The state prosecutes the case, the court determines guilt or innocence, and if guilt is found, the state administers the punishment.

Now consider where the victim fits into this picture. In the traditional model, the victim plays a surprisingly minor role. They are essential as a witness, of course, providing testimony that helps secure a conviction. But their personal needs—their emotional pain, their psychological trauma, their spiritual questions, their desire for answers—these are largely irrelevant to the legal proceedings. The state prosecutes the case on behalf of society, and the victim watches from the sidelines, hoping that the outcome will bring some measure of satisfaction. The community, too, is kept at arm's length. Ordinary citizens may serve on juries from time to time, and public opinion may influence sentencing policies through the political process, but for the most part, the community is a spectator, not a participant.

What drives this system? If we are honest with ourselves, we must acknowledge that at its core, it is fueled by a need for revenge. This may sound harsh, but it is the truth. When we are harmed, our natural human impulse is to strike back, to make the offender feel some measure of the pain they have caused us. The traditional justice system channels this impulse into formal structures, replacing personal vengeance with state-administered punishment. Incarceration serves two purposes in this model, and both flow from the same retributive source. First, it punishes the offender by depriving them of their liberty, making them suffer a consequence deemed proportional to their crime. Second, it protects society by removing the offender from our midst, at least for a time.

Yet this focus on punishment raises troubling questions that the traditional model struggles to answer. When an offender's sentence is complete, what have we actually accomplished? Have we made them better people? Have we addressed the underlying issues that led them to commit crimes in the first place? Have we healed the wounds suffered by victims? Have we made our communities safer in any lasting way? The traditional model offers no mechanism for answering these questions because it was never designed to ask them. Its goal is punishment, period. Once the punishment has been inflicted, the system's work is done.

To understand where this way of thinking comes from, we need to look back at the ancient roots of retributive justice. The philosophical foundation of the traditional view finds its most famous expression in the Latin term *lex talionis*, which means the law of retaliation. You probably know it better by its biblical phrasing: "an eye for an eye, a tooth for a tooth."

Now, this principle is often misunderstood in our modern context. People tend to hear "an eye for an eye" as a cry for vengeance, as permission to hurt others as they have hurt us. But historically, the opposite is true. The law of retaliation was actually a revolutionary force for *limiting* violence and revenge.

Consider the world in which *lex talionis* first appeared. This principle did not originate with the Israelites. We find it in the Code of Hammurabi, a Babylonian legal code dating to approximately 1750 BC, and it was present in early Roman law as well. In the ancient world, where centralized authority was weak and powerful families could wage bloody feuds against each other for generations, something was desperately needed to stop the cycle of escalating violence. Think about what happened when there was no principle of proportionality. If a man put out another's eye, the injured party's family might retaliate by killing not only the offender but his brothers, his sons, his cousins. And then the offender's family would retaliate against them, and on it would go, generation after generation, until entire families were destroyed.

Lex talionis stepped into this chaos and said: stop. The punishment must match the crime and go no further. One eye for one eye, not a life for an eye. The response must be proportionate, not excessive. This was genuine progress in the development of human civilization. It established that justice requires measured responses, not unlimited vengeance. It introduced the concept that individuals deserve to be treated according to what they have done, but also that they should not suffer beyond what they have inflicted.

When we turn to the Scriptures, we find this principle embedded in the Mosaic Law that God gave to Israel. Passages such as Exodus 21:23-25, Leviticus 24:19-20, and Deuteronomy 19:21 articulate this teaching as part of God's covenant with His people. Here, it served multiple purposes. It established that God's justice is not arbitrary but is grounded in righteousness and order. It taught the people that actions have consequences and that the community must uphold standards of behavior.

But there is something deeper here, something that the Apostle Paul helps us understand in his letter to the Galatians. In Galatians 3:24, Paul writes something remarkable: "Therefore the law was our tutor to bring us to Christ, that we might be justified by faith." The Greek word he uses for tutor is *paidagogos*. In the ancient world, a *paidagogos* was a slave assigned to accompany a child to school, to instruct them, and to discipline them when necessary. The tutor's job was not to be the final teacher but to prepare the child for the real teacher who would come later.

Paul says the Law functioned in exactly this way. By setting a standard of perfect justice that no human being could fully satisfy, the Law exposed our sin and our inability to save ourselves. It showed us that we could never be good enough on our own. It was never intended to be the final word on God's relationship with humanity. Instead, it pointed beyond itself to the One who would fulfill the Law and provide a different kind of justice—a justice that could not only punish but also forgive and restore.

This is a crucial insight for us as we think about criminal justice. The principle of "an eye for an eye" was given to a people without Christ to limit their revenges and establish order in a fallen world. But with the coming of Christ, a higher standard emerges. The law of retaliation begins to teach us something important: revenge was never part of God's ultimate justice, and punishment alone does not yield righteousness. Jesus came not to abolish the Law but to fulfill it, and in doing so, He provided a higher standard for those needing restoration.

Now, let us consider something very personal and human: how we respond when we or our loved ones are harmed by violent crime. The natural response, the one that rises up from somewhere deep within us, is a powerful desire for revenge. When a person or a community has been violated, the emotional impact is overwhelming. Fear floods in. Anger surges up. Grief overwhelms us. Helplessness makes us feel small and powerless.

In the midst of this emotional turmoil, the desire for revenge arises almost instinctively. We want the offender to suffer as we have suffered. We want them to understand the pain they have caused. We want justice to be done, and in that moment, justice feels like making them pay.

Now, here is something important for us to understand. This response is not wrong in itself. It reflects something God has placed within us—a sense that evil should not go unpunished, that the innocent deserve protection, that the moral order of the universe actually matters. The Psalms are filled with cries for God to arise and judge the wicked. The impulse for justice is woven into our very fabric as human beings created in the image of a just God.

But the Scriptures also warn us repeatedly about the dangers of taking vengeance into our own hands. In Deuteronomy 32:35, God declares, "Vengeance is Mine, and recompense." This is not merely God claiming a divine prerogative, as if He is hoarding the right to punish for Himself. It is a profound statement about the nature of true justice. Human vengeance is partial, passionate, and prone to excess. It is blind to the full picture of what has happened and why. It is often driven by the very sin it seeks to punish—anger, hatred, the desire to hurt. Only God, who knows every human heart perfectly and sees the end from the beginning, can administer perfect justice.

The danger of personal and collective revenge is that it perpetuates cycles of violence. When we respond to harm by inflicting harm, we simply continue the chain of injury. The offender who is treated with cruelty and degradation during incarceration is far more likely to emerge from prison more bitter, more angry, and more dangerous than when they entered. The victim who fixates on revenge often finds that satisfaction remains elusive, because punishment alone cannot heal the deeper wounds of trauma.

Modern justice systems have tried to address these dangers by channeling the desire for revenge into structured legal processes. The state takes over the role of avenger, administering punishment according to established laws and procedures rather than leaving it to individuals and families. But we must honestly ask ourselves whether we have really moved beyond the ancient blood feud or simply given it a bureaucratic face. When the primary goal of our system is punishment, when we measure justice by the severity of sentences, when politicians compete to prove who is toughest on crime, we must wonder whether we have truly transcended the impulse for retaliation.

This brings us to a troubling observation about our own nation. In the United States, when heinous crimes occur, the public outcry for punishment can be overwhelming. We have all seen it happen. A terrible crime captures the nation's attention. Politicians rush to cameras to demonstrate their toughness by proposing harsher sentences, new laws, expanded prison construction. The offender becomes a symbol of pure evil, and punishment becomes a public ritual of condemnation.

I understand this response. I have felt it myself. In the face of terrible evil, we want to affirm that such actions are unacceptable. We want victims to know that their suffering matters. We want society to be protected. The desire for retribution flows from legitimate concerns for justice and safety.

But we must also recognize that this cry for punishment, however understandable, often fails to address the deeper issues. The complex factors that contribute to criminal behavior—poverty, trauma, addiction, mental illness, lack of education, social isolation—are largely ignored when the focus narrows to punishment alone. The offender who emerges from prison after decades of incarceration is often the same person who entered, carrying the same traumas, the same addictions, the same lack of skills, the same patterns of thinking. They are just older now, and more alienated from society than ever before.

This is not a call for leniency. Please do not misunderstand me. It is a call for effectiveness. A justice system that simply warehouses human beings and returns them to society unchanged is not truly just, because it fails to protect society in the long run and fails to offer offenders any genuine path to transformation.

When public outrage drives justice policy, the consequences can be severe and far-reaching. Let me describe some of the effects we have seen in recent decades.

First, we have witnessed the steady march toward harsher punishments and longer sentences. Legislators, responding to public demands for action, have passed law after law increasing penalties for various offenses. While this may provide temporary satisfaction to an angry populace, it has not addressed the root causes of crime. Instead, it has overcrowded our prisons and strained our resources to breaking points.

Second, many states have enacted what are called "three strikes" laws. These laws mandate lengthy sentences—often life imprisonment—for individuals convicted of a third felony. Proponents argue that such laws incapacitate dangerous criminals. But critics note, correctly, that they can lead to disproportionately severe sentences for relatively minor offenses. A person whose three strikes include non-violent crimes may spend the rest of their life in prison at enormous public expense, even though they pose little danger to anyone.

Third, some states have abolished parole entirely and implemented "truth in sentencing" reforms requiring offenders to serve a substantial portion of their sentences before release. These measures reflect a public demand for certainty in punishment. But they also eliminate incentives for good behavior and participation in rehabilitation programs. If there is no possibility of early release, why bother with education or treatment?

The cumulative effect of these policies has been a dramatic expansion of our prison population without corresponding reductions in recidivism. We have built more prisons, filled them with more people, kept them there longer, and wondered why crime persists. The answer is actually quite simple: punishment alone, unaccompanied by rehabilitation and support, does not transform lives.

Nowhere are these dynamics more evident than in my own state of Texas. For decades, Texas has pursued what is called a "tough on crime" approach that prioritizes punishment over rehabilitation and prevention. The philosophy behind this movement is captured in a popular saying you have probably heard: "If you can't do the time, don't do the crime."

The results of this approach have been dramatic and, I would argue, deeply troubling. The prison population in Texas has grown by over 500 percent in less than a quarter century. Today, approximately 238,000 individuals are incarcerated in the Texas Department of Criminal Justice. Let that number sink in for a moment. That is more people than live in many entire cities across our nation.

Yet despite this massive prison population, relatively few incarcerated individuals receive the help they need to successfully reintegrate into society after their release. According to some estimates, less than 2,000 of those 238,000 individuals receive meaningful treatment for mental health or substance abuse issues. Think about what that means. Mental health problems and addiction are precisely the kinds of issues that drive criminal behavior and contribute to recidivism when left unaddressed. But we are not addressing them.

The vast majority of Texas prisoners simply serve their sentences and, if they are granted parole, return to their communities with the same needs, the same issues, the same struggles they had before incarceration. They have been punished, yes. But they have not been helped. They have served time, but they have not been changed. The revolving door continues to turn, bringing them back into the system again and again.

This approach treats the offender as a problem to be managed rather than a person to be transformed. It reflects a worldview that sees crime as nothing more than a choice and punishment as the only appropriate response. It fails to grapple with the complex realities that shape human behavior—addiction, trauma, mental illness, poverty, lack of education, the absence of healthy relationships and community support.

The cycle is predictable and heartbreaking. A person enters prison with certain needs. Those needs go unaddressed during their incarceration. The person is released, often to the same environment and circumstances that contributed to their original offense. Without support and resources, they struggle to find housing, to find employment, to rebuild relationships. Eventually, they may reoffend, and the cycle begins again.

This is not justice. It is not even effective punishment, if effectiveness is measured by public safety. It is merely a costly and destructive way of managing social problems without ever solving them.

To truly understand the scope of what has happened in our country, we need to look beyond our borders. The United States has the highest incarceration rate of any nation in the world. Approximately 639 people out of every 100,000 are behind bars in America. The only countries that even come close to this staggering figure are Russia, with about 418 per 100,000, and South Africa, with about 341 per 100,000.

These numbers are not merely abstract statistics. They represent over two million human beings—fathers and mothers, sons and daughters, human beings created in the image of God. They represent families separated, children growing up without parents, communities devastated by the constant removal of their members. They represent enormous resources—over one hundred billion dollars annually—diverted from education, healthcare, infrastructure, and other social needs.

The factors contributing to these high rates are complex. They include actual crime rates, certainly. But they also include policy choices. Mandatory minimum sentences, three-strikes laws, the war on drugs, and other tough-on-crime initiatives have dramatically increased both the number of people entering prisons and the length of time they stay there. Socioeconomic factors such as poverty, unemployment, and lack of access to education contribute to both crime and incarceration. Racial disparities in policing and sentencing mean that communities of color bear a disproportionate burden of this system.

But perhaps most troubling is the cultural attitude that underlies these policies. When we view incarceration as the primary response to crime, when we measure justice by the severity of punishment, when we define offenders primarily by their worst actions, we reveal something important about our values.

The Norwegian criminologist Nils Christie offered a penetrating critique of American incarceration that should give every

Christian pause. He stated simply that it is "incomprehensible that a nation so religious could misuse incarceration to this extent."

Think about that statement for a moment. Here is a secular scholar, looking at the United States from the outside. He sees a nation where the vast majority of citizens profess belief in God. He sees churches dotting every landscape, religious language permeating public discourse, politicians routinely invoking divine blessing. And he finds our incarceration practices incomprehensible given our religious profession. How can a nation that sings "Amazing Grace" and celebrates redemption be the world's leader in locking people away and throwing away the key?

Christie's alternative vision is striking. He suggests that prisons should function more like hospitals. Think about what a hospital does. It does not punish the sick for being sick. It treats them. It addresses their underlying condition, provides care, and works toward healing. The patient is not condemned for having cancer; they are helped to overcome it.

Christie applies this metaphor to criminal justice. Offenders, he argues, are often "sick" in a sense. They are struggling with issues that led to their criminal behavior—addiction, trauma, mental illness, social dysfunction, spiritual emptiness. They need help, not merely punishment. A prison that functioned like a hospital would address the emotional and spiritual needs of offenders, just as a hospital cares for the physical needs of patients.

This vision aligns remarkably with the ministry of Jesus Christ. Throughout the Gospels, we see Jesus consistently reaching out to the sick, the broken, the outcast. He did not come to condemn the world but to save it. He described His own mission in terms that should shape our understanding of justice: "It is not the healthy who need a doctor, but the sick. I have not come to call the righteous, but sinners."

If we take Christ's example seriously, we must ask ourselves whether our justice system reflects His compassion or contradicts it. Do we see offenders as human beings made in the image of God, capable of change, deserving of dignity? Or do we reduce them to their crimes and consign them to warehouses of punishment?

Given the massive scale of incarceration in America, we must ask another honest question: why has all this punishment not satisfied our thirst for revenge? Why has our hatred, our anger, our intolerance for offenders grown rather than diminished?

The answer lies in the nature of revenge itself. Revenge promises satisfaction but delivers only more hunger. It is a fire that consumes everything but never satisfies the one who feeds it. When we focus on making offenders suffer, we remain fixated on them, allowing them to occupy space in our hearts and minds that should be devoted to healing and hope. Our anger, rather than being discharged through punishment, is often amplified by it.

This dynamic has profound psychological and spiritual consequences. When we dehumanize offenders—reducing them to labels like "criminal," "offender," "inmate"—we lose sight of their humanity and, in doing so, we lose sight of our own. We become people defined by anger rather than love, by hatred rather than grace. The very emotions we seek to satisfy through punishment end up consuming us.

Those who defend retributive justice offer several justifications, and we should consider them honestly.

The first is deterrence. The idea is that punishing offenders discourages future crime, both by the individual who was punished and by others who might consider similar actions. This justification has intuitive appeal. But research suggests its effects are limited. Certainty of punishment matters far more than severity, and our system is far from certain. Most crimes never result in arrest, let alone conviction and punishment. The offender sitting on death row is statistically irrelevant to the vast majority of potential offenders.

The second justification is just desserts. This is the belief that offenders simply deserve to suffer for their crimes, regardless of any practical benefits. This appeals to our moral intuitions, but it offers no guidance about what constitutes appropriate punishment or how to measure proportionality. How much suffering is enough? Who decides?

The third is restitution. The idea is that punishment should include compensation to victims or the community. This is a valuable principle. But in practice, restitution is often an afterthought. Fines go to the state, not to victims. The victim's actual losses remain unaddressed.

The fourth is protection. Incarceration removes dangerous individuals from society, preventing them from committing further crimes at least for a time. This justification is valid but limited. Over 95 percent of incarcerated individuals will eventually be released. If they emerge from prison more damaged than when they entered, society's protection proves temporary indeed.

Against these justifications stand powerful criticisms that we cannot ignore. Retribution has proven ineffective at reducing crime, as our high recidivism rates demonstrate. It often violates human dignity, treating persons made in God's image as objects for punishment rather than subjects of grace. It perpetuates racial disparities that undermine any claim to equal justice. It raises profound moral objections from those who believe that intentionally inflicting harm is wrong, even in response to wrongdoing.

Let me ask you a question. Do we punish individuals for being sick with cancer? Do we expect them to heal without any treatment? Of course not. We send them to doctors. We send them to hospitals. We surround them with care and expertise. Does every cancer patient recover? No. But we do not abandon them to suffer alone.

Shouldn't our approach to justice be similar in nature to how we care for the physically ill? I am not saying crime and illness are identical. Crime involves moral agency in ways that cancer does not. But the analogy contains truth. Punishment alone cannot heal the brokenness that produces criminal behavior. Treatment, support, and transformation are required.

I understand that Americans often love the feeling associated with revenge and retribution. It provides a partial satisfaction of our emotional needs. When we have been wronged, seeing the wrongdoer suffer can feel good, at least for a moment.

But partial satisfaction is not true satisfaction. The temporary emotional release that comes from seeing an offender punished does not heal the deeper wounds. It does not restore what was lost. It does not address the fear, the grief, the shattered sense of safety that crime leaves in its wake. It does not answer the questions that haunt victims and their families. It does not rebuild the trust that was broken.

This is why we need a different vision. Not a vision that ignores accountability or minimizes harm. Quite the opposite. We need a vision that takes harm more seriously than the current system does, because it seeks not merely to punish but to repair. It recognizes that true justice must address the needs of all affected parties, not merely satisfy the state's demand for punishment.

In this chapter, we have examined the traditional view of justice together. We have seen its ancient roots in the law of retaliation, its alignment with natural human emotions, the justifications offered for it, and the consequences it has produced when implemented on a massive scale.

The traditional view of justice, for all its historical importance and intuitive appeal, ultimately falls short. It answers the question of guilt but ignores the question of healing. It satisfies the demand for punishment but neglects the need for restoration. It processes offenders through the system but returns them unchanged to the communities they harmed.

A different vision is possible. It is a vision that flows from the heart of a God who reconciles the world to Himself, not counting our trespasses against us. It is a vision that takes seriously both the reality of harm and the possibility of healing. It is a vision that holds offenders accountable while offering them a path to transformation, that supports victims while giving them voice, that involves communities in the hard work of restoration.

In the chapters that follow, we will explore that vision together. We will see what restorative justice looks like in practice, how it differs from the traditional model, and how the Church can embody this ministry of reconciliation in a broken world.

CHAPTER 02

WHY RESTRUCTURE THE CRIMINAL JUSTICE SYSTEM?

In the previous chapter, we examined the traditional view of justice—its ancient roots, its psychological appeal, its philosophical justifications, and its troubling consequences. We saw how a system designed to punish has grown into a massive enterprise that now incarcerates more of its citizens than any other nation on earth. We explored how the understandable desire for revenge, when channeled through institutional structures, has produced outcomes that leave victims unsatisfied, offenders unchanged, and communities fractured.

Now we must ask a difficult but necessary question: why should we restructure this system? If the traditional approach has been with us for millennia, if it feels natural to our sense of moral order, if it provides at least some measure of satisfaction when wrongdoers are punished—why change it?

The answer, as we shall see, is that the current system is failing on its own terms. It is not achieving what it claims to achieve. It is not making us safer. It is not providing justice for victims. It is not holding offenders accountable in any meaningful way. It is not building stronger communities. And it is doing all of this at a cost that is simply unsustainable.

Let us begin with something we can all understand: money.

The Soaring Cost of Justice

One of the most hotly debated subjects of the twenty-first century has been the burgeoning cost of justice and its apparent impotence in preventing crime. These two issues are intimately connected. We are spending more and more on a system that seems to deliver less and less in return.

Consider the numbers. The traditional approach of punishing offenders through incarceration has proven to be incredibly expensive. Depending on which state you look at, the cost of keeping a single inmate in prison for one year ranges from approximately $31,000 to over $69,000. That is per person, per year. Multiply that by the over two million individuals currently incarcerated in the United States, and you begin to grasp the scale of the expenditure.

And those costs have been rising rapidly. In 1997, total corrections expenditures in the United States stood at about $44 billion. By 2006, that figure had more than doubled, exceeding $100 billion. As the prison population grows, so does the price of carrying out justice. We are building more prisons, hiring more staff, feeding more inmates, providing more healthcare, managing more lawsuits. The financial burden on taxpayers is enormous and growing.

Now, if all this spending were actually making us safer, perhaps we could justify it. If crime rates were plummeting, if victims felt truly served, if offenders were emerging from prison transformed and ready to contribute positively to society—then maybe the cost would be worth bearing.

But that is not what is happening. The high rate of recidivism—the term scholars use for re-offending—tells a different story. Study after study has shown that a significant percentage of released inmates will be arrested again within three years. Many will return to prison. The system is not rehabilitating; it is simply cycling people through, again and again, at enormous expense, with little to show for it.

This is why evaluations of the criminal justice system have not been favorable. When researchers look objectively at what the system accomplishes, they find a troubling picture. The focus on punishment rather than addressing underlying causes means that the same problems that led to crime in the first place—addiction, trauma, mental illness, poverty, lack of education and employment—remain untouched. Offenders are punished and released, still carrying all the burdens that contributed to their criminal behavior, and often with new burdens added by the experience of incarceration itself.

The system has also been criticized for its disproportionate impact on marginalized communities. We saw some of this in the previous chapter when we discussed racial disparities in incarceration rates. But it goes deeper than numbers. The same behaviors that might lead to treatment and diversion for affluent white offenders often lead to arrest and imprisonment for poor minorities. The system, for all its claims of equal justice, operates in ways that reflect and reinforce existing social inequalities.

As a result of these failures, there has been increasing interest in alternative approaches to justice. Restorative justice, community justice, and other reform movements have gained traction precisely because the old ways are not working. These approaches focus on prevention, rehabilitation, and addressing the root causes of criminal behavior. They are generally more cost-effective than incarceration and, more importantly, they have the potential to actually reduce crime rates over time rather than simply managing them.

The Public's Fear and Frustration

But the problems with the current system are not only about money and effectiveness. They are also about how the system makes people feel—and I am not just talking about offenders.

There is a sweeping judgment, often applied toward both offenders and criminal justice personnel, that tends to globalize the public's fear and anxiety. Let me explain what I mean by this. When crime occurs, the fear and anxiety it generates are often generalized. People begin to see all offenders as threats, all young men in certain neighborhoods as potential criminals, all strangers as dangers. At the same time, those feelings can also be directed at the people who work in the justice system. Police officers, prosecutors, judges, correctional officers—they can become symbols of a system that seems either too harsh or too lenient, too aggressive or too passive, but in any case, not quite right.

This creates a cycle of fear and mistrust that further harms the effectiveness of the justice system. When the public does not trust the system, they are less likely to cooperate with it. They may not report crimes. They may not serve as witnesses. They may not serve on juries willingly. They may not support the funding needed for effective programs. The system and the community become locked in a relationship of suspicion rather than partnership.

How do we solve this? How do we address the public's response to a lack of familiarity with the justice process?

The frustration and anger that many people feel toward the justice system are understandable. For most citizens, the system is opaque, bureaucratic, and deeply impersonal. It is difficult to understand how decisions are made, who makes them, and on what basis. This lack of transparency breeds suspicion. When people cannot see how justice works, they naturally wonder whether it works at all.

Consider the perceived lack of transparency. Many people feel that the legal system is shrouded in mystery. Decisions seem to be made behind closed doors. Information is difficult to obtain. When high-profile cases produce outcomes that seem unfair or unjust, the suspicion deepens. People wonder what really happened, what evidence was considered, what arguments were made. Without access to that information, they fill the gaps with their own assumptions, and those assumptions are often negative.

Then there is the perceived lack of accountability. Many people feel that judges, lawyers, and other legal professionals are too insulated from public opinion. They seem to operate by their own rules, answerable to no one. When judges appear more concerned with protecting their own interests or the interests of the system than with promoting justice, public trust erodes further.

And perhaps most damaging of all, there is a widespread sense that the justice system prioritizes the interests of the wealthy and powerful over those of ordinary people. This perception is not entirely unfounded. Those who can afford high-quality legal representation often fare better than those who cannot. The system, for all its rhetoric about equality before the law, seems to have one set of rules for the rich and another for the poor. This creates deep resentment and a feeling that justice is not really for everyone—it is for those who can pay.

To address these frustrations, the justice system must become more transparent, more accountable, and more responsive to the public it serves. This means greater access to information. It means greater public participation in legal processes where appropriate. It means a greater emphasis on fairness and impartiality in the administration of justice. By building trust and confidence, we can create a society that is more just and equitable for all.

When Courts Were Connected to Community

There was a time, not so long ago in historical terms, when the courts were closely connected to the communities in which they operated. This was not by accident but by necessity. In earlier times, the justice system was less formalized and less centralized. Communities were responsible for maintaining order and resolving disputes within their own boundaries.

In many traditional societies, the community played a central role in resolving conflicts and ensuring justice. Disputes were often settled through mediation or arbitration, with community leaders or elders serving as neutral mediators. This approach was rooted in a sense of communal responsibility. Everyone understood that all members of the community had a stake in maintaining peace and resolving conflicts. When two people were in dispute, it affected everyone. When a crime was committed, the entire community felt the impact.

This is the note you saw earlier: community affairs, including the problems of crime, were a concern for the entire community. They assumed responsibility for all matters and thus maintained a close connection to the courts. Justice was not something that happened in a distant building, administered by distant officials using language ordinary people could not understand. It happened where people lived, with people they knew, in ways they could see and participate in.

But as legal systems became more formalized and centralized, the role of the community in justice became more limited. Courts moved away from the people they served. The legal process became more bureaucratic and impersonal. This was particularly true in urban areas, where the sheer scale of the justice system made it difficult for individual communities to have any meaningful impact on the process.

Think about what this means for ordinary citizens. The justice system that once felt like their system, something they participated in and understood, became something foreign. It became something done to them rather than by them or for them. Is it any wonder that people feel disconnected?

In recent years, there has been a growing movement toward restorative justice, which emphasizes the importance of community involvement in the justice process. Restorative justice programs often involve mediation or dialogue between victim and offender, with the goal of repairing harm and addressing underlying issues that may have contributed to the crime. Through these programs, communities can play a more active role in promoting justice and healing. They can support victims, hold offenders accountable, and work to prevent future harm. This approach recognizes what traditional societies knew all along: community connections and relationships are essential to a just and peaceful society.

Societal Change and Antidotal Laws

The modern justice service delivery process has been shaped by two powerful forces: societal change and the passing of antidotal laws.

Societal change refers to shifts in the attitudes, values, and beliefs of people in a society. As societies change, so do their expectations of the justice system. For example, changes in societal attitudes toward certain crimes or offenders may lead to changes in how those crimes are punished or how offenders are treated. When public opinion shifts on issues like drug use or domestic violence or sexual assault, the justice system eventually shifts with it—sometimes slowly, sometimes more quickly.

Public opinion can also influence the development of new laws or policies that address emerging social issues. Think about the legalization of marijuana in many states. This did not happen because politicians suddenly had a change of heart. It happened because societal attitudes toward marijuana use changed dramatically over several decades. The same could be said for the recognition of same-sex marriage or the increased attention to sexual harassment in the workplace. Laws often follow culture rather than leading it.

Antidotal laws are a different matter. These are laws passed by legislatures in reaction to some high-profile crime or perceived problem in society. They are often passed quickly, with little debate, in an effort to show that the government is taking action. The message is: we see that you are frightened and angry, and we are doing something about it.

Examples of antidotal laws are not hard to find. Mandatory minimum sentencing laws were often passed in response to particular crimes that outraged the public. Three-strikes laws emerged from high-profile cases involving repeat offenders. Sex offender registration laws followed horrific crimes against children. In each case, the impulse was understandable. When something terrible happens, we want to prevent it from happening again. We want to feel that something is being done.

But here is the problem. While these laws may be well-intentioned, they often have unintended consequences. Mandatory minimum sentencing laws can result in disproportionately harsh sentences for minor offenses. Three-strikes laws can lead to life sentences for relatively minor crimes. Sex offender registration laws can make it extremely difficult for individuals to reintegrate into society, even after they have served their sentences and even when they pose no ongoing threat.

The challenge is to respond to legitimate public concerns without creating new problems in the process. This requires careful consideration of the potential consequences of new laws or policies. It requires asking not only whether a law will make people feel better, but whether it will actually make them safer. It requires looking at the evidence rather than just reacting to emotion.

Factors That Have Affected the Judicial System

Several factors have historically affected the court's judicial system, and understanding them helps us see why the system operates as it does today.

The first factor is the shift of control from the community. In many traditional societies, the community played a significant role in the administration of justice. Disputes were resolved through mediation, arbitration, or other means of conflict resolution that involved community members. But with the rise of centralized states, the administration of justice shifted from the community to the state. This led to the creation of formal legal systems that operate independently of the communities they serve.

The second factor is specialization. As legal systems became more complex, the need for specialized courts and judges arose. We now have separate courts for civil, criminal, family, juvenile, bankruptcy, and administrative matters. This specialization has allowed for greater expertise and efficiency in the administration of justice. But it has also made the system more difficult for ordinary people to navigate. The average person cannot be expected to understand the differences between various courts and their procedures.

The third factor is court unification. In some countries, courts were historically organized into separate jurisdictions based on geography or subject matter. Over time, many jurisdictions have been unified into a single court system. This has led to greater consistency in the interpretation and application of the law. But it has also contributed to the centralization and bureaucratization of justice, making courts feel even more distant from the communities they serve.

The fourth factor is the severance of the link between courts and community politics. In some societies, courts were closely linked to community politics, and judges were appointed or elected based on political considerations. This practice led to perceptions of judicial bias and undermined the independence of the judiciary. As a result, many countries have taken steps to separate the judiciary from politics, establishing judicial selection commissions or independent judicial councils. While this has strengthened judicial independence, it has also further separated courts from community input and accountability.

Each of these factors represents a trade-off. Greater specialization and centralization have brought benefits in terms of consistency and expertise. But they have also made the justice system less accessible, less understandable, and less connected to the communities it exists to serve.

How the System Isolates the Public

The current criminal justice system's process tends to isolate the public and create a cycle of fear and anxiety. Let me explain what I mean by this.

First, the system isolates individuals who are accused or convicted of crime. Pre-trial detention, imprisonment, and other forms of punishment physically separate individuals from their families, communities, and support networks. This isolation is often justified as necessary for public safety or to ensure that defendants appear for trial. But it has profound consequences. People held in jail before trial may lose their jobs, their housing, and their relationships—all before they have been convicted of anything. People sentenced to prison are removed from their communities for years or decades, severed from the very connections that might help them reintegrate successfully upon release.

Second, the system creates fear among the public, particularly among those who are vulnerable or marginalized. This fear arises from concerns about crime rates, certainly. But it also arises from concerns about the justice system itself. Police brutality, racial profiling, wrongful convictions, excessive punishment—these realities create fear of the system as much as fear of crime. People wonder whether they can trust the police to protect them. They wonder whether the courts will treat them fairly. They wonder whether they might themselves become victims of the system.

Third, the system creates anxiety among individuals who are involved in it. Victims, witnesses, defendants—all experience the stress of going to court, testifying, waiting for verdicts. The process can be traumatic, and its effects can last long after the legal proceedings are complete.

Now, I should acknowledge that the criminal justice system can also have positive impacts on society. It can deter crime, at least to some extent. It can protect victims' rights. It can promote justice and accountability. But these positives do not cancel out the negatives. The system is not perfect, and there is ongoing debate about how it can be reformed to better serve all members of society.

Let me be more specific about the features of the current system that create isolation.

Pre-trial detention is a major factor. Individuals who are accused of a crime and cannot post bail may be held in jail for extended periods before their trial. This isolates them from family, friends, and community support networks. It separates them from their employment and other responsibilities. And all of this happens before they have been found guilty of anything.

Prison sentences create long-term isolation. Individuals convicted of crimes may spend years or decades separated from their families and communities. This has devastating effects on mental health and well-being. It also makes reintegration upon release much more difficult. The longer a person is isolated, the harder it is to reconnect.

Solitary confinement represents isolation taken to its extreme. Some prisons use solitary confinement as punishment or to manage difficult inmates. But prolonged periods of isolation can cause severe psychological harm—depression, anxiety, paranoia, hallucinations. It exacerbates feelings of despair and can leave lasting damage even after the isolation ends.

Geographic isolation is another factor. Prisons are often located in remote areas, far from the communities where inmates lived. This makes it difficult for family members to visit and provide support. The cost and time required for travel may be prohibitive for families with limited resources. The result is that inmates become even more cut off from the relationships that might help them maintain hope and prepare for reentry.

Additional Features That Create Isolation

Beyond these obvious factors, there are more subtle features of the justice system that contribute to isolation.

Consider data privacy and access to information. Every state has laws prohibiting the release of private information about offenders. The sensibility of these laws cannot be argued—privacy matters, and offenders retain certain rights even after conviction. But these laws also have the effect of isolating the public from information about what is happening in the justice system. When people cannot access information about offenders, about cases, about outcomes, they are left with a fear of the unknown. They do not know who has been released, who is living in their neighborhood, what risks may exist. This uncertainty breeds fear.

Then there is the sterilization of information. Public agencies are given access to private data that is vital for developing public policy. But when this information is shared with the public, it is often sterilized—cleaned of identifying details, aggregated, anonymized. While this protects privacy, it also makes it difficult for ordinary citizens to understand what is really happening. It usually takes persistent inquiries and thorough analysis to determine what policy implications might be drawn from the data. Most people do not have the time, resources, or expertise for this.

Consider the physical structures of courthouses. The architectural design of most courthouses is imposing and intimidating. They are built to impress, with marble tile and mahogany paneling, high ceilings and grand entrances. Judges sit elevated above everyone else, wearing robes that set them apart. When the judge enters, everyone must stand. The surroundings may include bulletproof glass, metal detectors, bailiffs maintaining order. Even the use of the gavel—that small hammer striking wood—is a signal of authority and distance.

In this setting, ordinary people feel small. They feel like outsiders in a place where they do not belong. There is no formal or informal welcome. No one asks for their input or suggests that their perspective matters. They are there to observe, not to participate.

And then there is the issue of emotions. The orderly environment of the justice process is intolerant of emotional expression. When people succumb to raw emotions—when they cry, when they shout, when they show anger or grief—attempts are made to control or even remove these expressions from the proceedings. But think about this. Crime is a form of interpersonal conflict. It is by its very nature emotionally charged. Those emotions are not extraneous to the conflict; they are central to it. They are precisely what we need to understand while evaluating what happened and what should be done.

By suppressing emotions, the system loses vital information. It also loses the opportunity for restoration. The goal of "speedy processing" eliminates the time and space needed for healing. The system prioritizes efficiency over effectiveness, moving cases through the pipeline as quickly as possible rather than taking the time to address the underlying harm.

Professionalism presents another barrier. The entire justice system, with its carefully scripted procedures, court rules, laws, policies, and practices, requires extensive education and experience to understand. As justice system personnel gain more education and expertise, they develop specialized jargon and procedures that function like a foreign language to outsiders. A type of dress and conduct becomes established in each courtroom, with unwritten rules about appropriate protocol that cannot be known unless you are an accepted member of what we might call the "justice club."

As friendships and social cliques develop among those who work in the system, a closed system emerges that shuns public influence. Public input tends to interfere with the tidy set of procedures that insiders have developed. So outsiders quickly discover that they should not speak unless spoken to. Their participation is not welcome.

Finally, consider the convenience of public service. American society, I would argue, does not know how to handle its interpersonal conflicts. We are handicapped by what might be called a "911 mentality." Whenever problems arise between members of the community, the natural reaction is to dial 911 without first trying to resolve the conflict. In each instance, the conflict is referred to those in authority rather than resolved directly by the parties involved.

These conflicts are then resolved by professional experts—police, child protective services, housing authorities, animal control officers, environmental protection agencies, probation and parole officers. The experts take over, and the parties lose ownership of their own conflicts. We have outsourced the most basic human skill of conflict resolution to professionals, and in doing so, we have lost the ability to do it ourselves.

Christie's Insight: Conflict as Personal Property

This brings us to the work of Nils Christie, the Norwegian criminologist we encountered in the previous chapter. Christie offered a powerful way of understanding what has happened to conflict in modern societies.

Christie argued that interpersonal conflict can be seen as personal property. In modern societies, conflict is often treated as a matter to be dealt with by the state, with the state taking on the role of neutral third party in resolving disputes. But Christie believed that this approach overlooks something crucial: conflicts are deeply personal and emotional, and individuals have a strong sense of ownership over them.

Think about it this way. When you have been wronged, the conflict belongs to you. It is your pain, your anger, your sense of violation. The story of what happened is your story. The resolution of the conflict affects your life in profound ways. Yet the modern justice system takes this property away from you. It becomes the state's case—The People versus the defendant, or The State versus the offender. You become a witness, not a party. Your voice becomes evidence, not the voice of one seeking resolution.

According to Christie, conflicts can be seen as personal property in several ways. First, conflicts are based on personal values, beliefs, and experiences. They are deeply connected to an individual's sense of identity. When someone harms you, they have harmed not just your body or your property but your sense of who you are in the world.

Second, conflicts can be seen as a form of social currency. Individuals may use conflicts to gain status, power, or resources within their social networks. The way a conflict is resolved can affect one's standing in the community for years to come.

Third, conflicts can be seen as a form of social exchange. People use conflicts to negotiate and establish relationships with others. The resolution of a conflict can strengthen or weaken bonds between individuals and groups.

By viewing conflicts as personal property, Christie argued that individuals should be given greater control over their resolution. He advocated for alternative forms of conflict resolution—mediation, restorative justice, community conferencing—that prioritize the needs and perspectives of those involved. His work has contributed to a broader shift in criminology toward a more humanistic and restorative approach to justice, one that prioritizes the needs and experiences of individuals over the needs of the state.

This is where Christie's provocative phrase comes in. He described justice representatives as "professional thieves" who are trained at stealing our conflicts. Now, before you react to that phrase, understand the context. Christie was not saying that police officers, prosecutors, and judges are corrupt or malicious. He was saying that they operate within a system that is structured in a way that prioritizes the needs of the state over the needs of individuals. The system takes away individuals' control over their own conflicts and imposes solutions that may not serve their best interests.

By recognizing the personal and emotional nature of conflicts, and by involving individuals more directly in the resolution process, Christie believed we could create a more just and humanistic approach to conflict resolution. His work was critical of certain aspects of the criminal justice system, but it was ultimately aimed at creating something better.

What Happens When the Experts Take Over

When justice representatives take over our conflicts, the effect on victims and communities can be paralyzing. They are disempowered, deprived of agency and control over matters that deeply affect their lives.

Consider what happens. First, there is loss of control. When the state takes over the resolution of a conflict, victims and communities lose control over the process and the outcome.

The criminal justice system operates according to legal procedures and rules that may not take into account the specific needs and perspectives of those involved. Victims may feel that their voices are not being heard, that their experiences are not being valued. This leads to frustration and a sense of disempowerment.

Second, there is lack of participation. Victims and communities may be excluded from the resolution process altogether. In a criminal trial, victims may be required to testify as witnesses, but they have no say in the ultimate outcome. They cannot decide whether to accept a plea bargain. They cannot influence the sentence. They cannot determine what would constitute justice in their particular case. For victims who have experienced trauma, this exclusion can be deeply re-traumatizing.

Third, there is the impersonal nature of the system. The criminal justice system is bureaucratic and impersonal. Justice representatives can seem distant and unapproachable. The legal language and procedures are confusing and intimidating. Victims and communities feel like outsiders in a process that is supposedly about them.

The result is a sense of frustration, disillusionment, and mistrust toward the criminal justice system. Victims may be discouraged from seeking justice in the future. Communities may become disengaged from efforts to address crime. The very people the system is supposed to serve become its critics and opponents.

Over time, as we continue to avoid and relinquish our conflicts to experts, we lose our autonomy and our ability to influence outcomes. This happens for several reasons.

First, the criminal justice system is genuinely complex and difficult to navigate. People who are unfamiliar with the legal system, who lack resources and support, naturally turn to lawyers, police, and other experts for help. In doing so, they relinquish some of their own agency.

Second, the system is designed to prioritize the needs of the state over the needs of individuals and communities. The outcomes it produces may not align with what those involved actually want or need. But because the system has taken over, there is little they can do about it.

Third, and perhaps most troubling, our willingness to seek solutions from professionals has diminished our sense of community responsibility. When individuals and communities turn to experts to solve their problems, they feel less personal stake in the outcome. They become less likely to take responsibility for resolving conflicts themselves.

This is particularly true in the criminal justice context. People may feel that addressing crime and justice is not their responsibility—it is the responsibility of police, prosecutors, and other professionals. This leads to detachment and disengagement from the very issues that affect their communities most deeply.

The note in your materials makes an important point: we also breed a generation of people who do not know how to resolve conflict. When every disagreement, every dispute, every problem is referred to authorities, we never develop the skills to handle these things ourselves. We become dependent on experts for something that should be a basic human competency.

The Paralyzing Effect of Crime on Victims and Communities

Crime has a paralyzing effect on both victims and communities. Victims may feel helpless, violated, and afraid. Communities may feel threatened, anxious, and mistrustful of one another. These emotions have powerful impacts and can make it difficult to move forward and address the underlying issues that contribute to crime.

When people experience anger and fear as a result of crime, their natural response is often to take measures to protect themselves. Some people move to what they perceive as safer neighborhoods. Others build taller fences, install additional locks, add alarm systems, put up floodlights, or even install burglar bars on their windows. Yet others may purchase firearms or other devices for protection.

These responses are understandable. When we feel threatened, we want to protect ourselves and our loved ones. But isolation may not be the best or most effective response. While it is natural to want to protect ourselves, isolation can contribute to a sense of disconnection and mistrust within communities. It can make it more difficult to address the root causes of crime because we are not working together.

Instead of isolating ourselves, it may be more effective to find ways to build stronger, more connected communities that can work together to address underlying issues. This might involve building relationships with neighbors, getting involved in community groups and organizations, and supporting policies and programs that promote safety, justice, and equity for all.

It is also important to seek support if you or someone you know has been affected by crime. This might mean reaching out to friends, family members, or community organizations. It might mean seeking professional help from a therapist or counselor. The trauma of victimization is real, and it deserves to be taken seriously.

In our pursuit of isolation, however, we have often abandoned our collective responsibility for the safety and welfare of our neighbors. When we focus solely on protecting ourselves and our immediate families, we become less invested in the well-being of those around us. We may not even know the names of our neighbors. And if we do not know them, we ask ourselves: why should we take responsibility for their safety and welfare?

This is a fair question, but it points to a deeper problem. When we look out only for ourselves, we lose the benefits of community. We lose social support. We lose shared resources. We lose a sense of belonging. We also lose the informal social controls that help prevent crime—neighbors watching out for each other, reporting suspicious activity, looking after each other's property.

This isolation is producing a new generation of individuals who lack social bonding skills. They do not know how to form connections, how to build trust, how to work together with others toward common goals. And that has consequences not only for crime prevention but for the overall health and functioning of our society.

The Importance of Social Bonding

Interpersonal relationships are promoted and strengthened through social bonding between neighbors. When we form social connections with those around us, we build a sense of community and shared responsibility for the well-being of our neighborhoods.

Social bonding can take many forms. It might be casual interactions—waving to a neighbor, stopping to chat, sharing a meal. It might be more formal—joining community groups, participating in neighborhood organizations, attending community events. The key is getting to know those around us and working together toward common goals.

Through social bonding, we build trust, foster empathy and understanding, and create a sense of belonging and connectedness. These are not just warm feelings; they have real impacts on crime and justice. When we have strong relationships with our neighbors, we are more likely to report suspicious activity. We are more willing to work with law enforcement and community organizations to address crime and promote safety.

The activities that promote social bonding are many and varied. Block parties bring neighbors together for food and conversation. Potluck dinners allow people to share their culinary traditions and learn about each other. Neighborhood picnics create opportunities for families to connect. Community clean-up events give people a shared purpose and a chance to work side by side.

Yard sales and flea markets create casual interactions and opportunities for conversation. Walking groups and fitness classes promote health while building relationships. Book clubs and discussion groups bring people together around shared interests. Movie nights and outdoor screenings create community gathering spaces.

Volunteer projects and service activities allow neighbors to work together for the common good. Sports leagues and recreational activities build teamwork and camaraderie. Neighborhood gardens and community farming projects create shared resources and ongoing interactions. Holiday celebrations and cultural events honor traditions and bring diverse people together.

Block-wide garage sales, dog-walking groups, outdoor games and competitions—the list goes on. The specific activity matters less than the fact of coming together, getting to know each other, building relationships.

These activities produce familiarity and trust. When we spend time together, share experiences, and engage in common activities, we develop a greater sense of familiarity and understanding of one another. This leads to increased trust, empathy, and mutual support. It fosters a stronger sense of community and shared responsibility.

Through social bonding, individuals are more likely to see each other as partners in promoting safety and preventing crime, rather than as strangers or potential threats. This builds what scholars call collective efficacy—the belief that together, community members can effectively address the challenges of crime and justice.

What Isolation Produces

Isolation produces several negative outcomes. Let me name three.

First, distrust. When people are isolated from one another, they become less familiar and less likely to rely on each other for support. Without regular interaction, trust does not develop. Without trust, suspicion fills the void.

Second, unfamiliarity. Isolation means people do not know each other. They do not know their neighbors' names, their faces, their habits. This unfamiliarity makes it difficult to distinguish between normal activity and suspicious activity. It makes everyone seem like a potential threat.

Third, a cycle of crime. Isolation creates a fertile environment for criminal activity. When individuals and communities are isolated, they become more vulnerable. There is less social control, less willingness to report crime, less access to resources and support that can help prevent crime.

Beyond these, isolation produces indifference—a lack of concern for others. It produces lack of empathy—an inability to understand or share the feelings of others. It may even produce hostile or negative attitudes toward people who are different or unknown.

Once a cycle of isolation develops, it creates a fertile environment for crime. If no one in the neighborhood is concerned about the safety and welfare of others, then the drug dealer is free to deal drugs on the corner. The thief can easily kick in a back door without worry of being seen or heard.

Criminals are more likely to target isolated individuals or homes because there is less risk.

When there is no sense of collective responsibility or shared concern for the community as a whole, there is less willingness to report crime or work together to prevent it. This creates a cycle of isolation and vulnerability. Individuals and communities become increasingly isolated and increasingly vulnerable to crime.

Isolation also creates a condition of anonymity for offenders. When people are unknown to the community, they are free from the informal constraints that would otherwise discourage criminal behavior. In a connected community, a person might be reluctant to engage in illegal activity for fear of being caught or shunned. In an isolated community, there is less informal social control. The offender may feel free to engage in criminal activity without fear of being identified or ostracized.

The freedom resulting from anonymity is void of accountability. Without accountability, offenders are encouraged to continue anti-social activities and criminal behavior. They face no consequences for their actions. The combination of anonymity and lack of accountability creates a dangerous environment where crime is more likely to occur and persist.

By promoting social bonding and connectedness, we can create a stronger sense of shared responsibility. We can encourage more informal social control. We can prevent crime and promote community safety and well-being.

Justice System Personnel and Isolation

It is also common for justice system personnel—police officers, prosecutors, judges, correctional officers—to become isolated from the communities they serve. This is especially true when there is a perception of blame or criticism. When the public blames them for crime and recidivism, these professionals may withdraw into themselves and their institutions.

This isolation makes it difficult for justice system personnel to understand and respond effectively to the needs and concerns of the community. When they feel isolated or defensive, they may be less likely to engage in community outreach and collaboration. This contributes to a breakdown in communication and trust between the justice system and the community, making it harder to prevent and address crime.

It is important for justice system personnel to recognize the importance of maintaining positive relationships with the communities they serve. They need to take proactive steps to engage with community members and address their concerns. This might mean participating in community events, listening to community feedback, and working collaboratively with community organizations and leaders to develop effective strategies.

By building trust and rapport with the community, justice system personnel can help create a safer and more cohesive society. They are not enemies of the community; they are members of it. But they must act like it.

The justice system also protects itself from scrutiny and criticism in various ways. It limits access to information. It controls the nature of released information. It restricts public access to court records. It seals court proceedings. It limits public statements about ongoing investigations or prosecutions.

The system may also use its authority to shield its personnel from public scrutiny. Police departments invoke qualified immunity to protect officers from civil lawsuits. Prosecutors decline to prosecute cases where there is risk of negative publicity. While there may be legitimate reasons for some of these practices, they can also undermine transparency and accountability.

When the public encounters obstacles while seeking information from the justice system, the reaction is often frustration and anger. Trust erodes. A wall of separation grows. A spiraling effect of mistrust develops. The public perceives that the system is not being transparent or forthcoming, which fuels suspicions and conspiracy theories. This damages the relationship further and undermines the legitimacy of the justice system.

The justice system must recognize the value of transparency and accountability. It must work toward making information as accessible as possible while still protecting legitimate rights and privacy. Building trust and maintaining open lines of communication can bridge the gap between the system and the public.

Four Questions to Understand Isolation

One way to understand the effects of isolation is to examine how the criminal justice system might answer four simple questions.

First, is the current justice process easy for the public to understand, or is it filled with expert and legal jargon that is largely incomprehensible? If ordinary people cannot understand what is happening in their own justice system, they cannot meaningfully participate in it. They cannot evaluate whether justice is being done. They cannot hold the system accountable.

Second, is the system accessible to the public, or do they encounter roadblocks to participation? Can people find information about cases? Can they attend proceedings? Can they make their voices heard? Or are there barriers—physical, financial, bureaucratic—that keep them out?

Third, is the outcome entirely determined by system personnel, or does the community truly have a voice and influence in the justice process? Do the people most affected by crime have any say in what happens? Or are they passive recipients of decisions made by others?

Fourth, is the justice system respectful of gender, socioeconomic, and cultural differences in the way it operates, or is it inflexible? Does it treat all people with dignity and respect, regardless of who they are? Or does it impose one standard on everyone, ignoring the different needs and circumstances of different groups?

These questions get to the heart of what is wrong with the current system. It is incomprehensible to ordinary people. It is inaccessible. It excludes community voice. It is inflexible and often disrespectful of difference. These are not minor problems. They are fundamental flaws that undermine the legitimacy and effectiveness of the entire enterprise.

As we have seen throughout this chapter, the case for restructuring the criminal justice system is overwhelming. The system costs too much and accomplishes too little. It isolates the public and creates fear rather than safety. It steals conflicts from those to whom they belong and processes them in ways that leave everyone unsatisfied. It has abandoned community responsibility and produced a generation that does not know how to resolve its own disputes.

The question is not whether we should restructure, but how. And that is where restorative justice enters the picture. Unlike the current system, restorative justice seeks to involve all parties—victims, offenders, and community members—in the process of addressing harm and finding resolution. It prioritizes healing over punishment, participation over exclusion, and community over bureaucracy.

In the chapters that follow, we will explore what restorative justice looks like in practice. We will see how it addresses the failures we have identified in this chapter. And we will consider how the Church, as the body of Christ, can lead the way in this ministry of reconciliation.

CHAPTER 03

A DIFFERENT VIEW OF JUSTICE

In the first two chapters, we walked through the landscape of traditional justice. We examined its ancient roots in the law of retaliation, its psychological appeal to our desire for revenge, its philosophical justifications, and its troubling consequences. We saw how a system designed to punish has grown into a massive enterprise that costs billions, isolates communities, steals conflicts from those to whom they belong, and returns offenders to society unchanged and often worse than when they entered.

We also explored why restructuring this system is not merely desirable but necessary. The current approach is failing on its own terms. It is not making us safer. It is not satisfying victims. It is not rehabilitating offenders. It is not building stronger communities. And it is doing all of this at a cost that is simply unsustainable.

Now we turn to something different. We turn to a vision of justice that has been practiced in various forms for millennia, that is rooted in ancient wisdom and confirmed by modern research, that aligns with the deepest teachings of Scripture and the example of Jesus Christ. We turn to restorative justice.

In this chapter, we will explore what restorative justice is, how it differs from the traditional model, and why it offers hope for a better way. We will consider the questions it raises and the answers it provides. We will examine its principles and practices, its strengths and limitations. And we will see how this different view of justice points toward healing, reconciliation, and restoration for victims, offenders, and communities alike.

Why Restorative Justice Has Become a Widely Debated Subject

Let us begin with an observation. The philosophy known as restorative justice has become one of the most widely debated subjects of the twenty-first century. This is not accidental. It reflects a growing recognition that something is deeply wrong with our current approach to justice and a growing hunger for alternatives.

Restorative justice is based on a simple but profound principle: rather than solely punishing the offender, justice should focus on repairing the harm caused by crime. It aims to bring together the victim, the offender, and the community to address that harm and to promote healing and reconciliation. This approach represents a fundamental shift in how we think about crime and justice.

Think about what this means. In the traditional model, the central question is: what law was broken, and what punishment does the offender deserve? In restorative justice, the central questions are different: who has been harmed, what do they need, and whose obligations are these? The focus shifts from the abstract violation of law to the concrete reality of harm done to real people.

This approach has gained increasing attention and interest in recent years, and not just in academic circles. Around the world, criminal justice systems have begun incorporating restorative justice processes in cases ranging from minor offenses to serious crimes. Schools have adopted restorative practices to address conflict and discipline. Workplaces have used restorative approaches to repair relationships after incidents of harassment or misconduct. Communities have turned to restorative justice to address historical harms and build bridges across divisions.

At the same time, there has been significant debate about restorative justice. Critics raise important questions. Is it appropriate for serious or violent crimes? Does it provide adequate protection for victims? Is it truly an alternative to punitive justice, or merely a supplement? These are legitimate concerns that deserve careful consideration.

The debate itself is healthy. It reflects the fact that people care deeply about justice and want to get it right. As we explore restorative justice in this chapter, we will engage with these questions honestly. We will consider both the promise and the limitations of this approach. And we will see that while restorative justice is not a panacea, it offers something that the traditional model cannot: a path toward genuine healing.

Questions We Must Ask Ourselves

Before we go further, I want to invite you to do something important. I want to invite you to examine your own view of justice. The questions that follow are not rhetorical. They are worth sitting with, thinking about, and answering honestly.

How do I view justice? This is the foundational question. When you hear the word "justice," what comes to mind? Is it punishment? Is it fairness? Is it healing? Is it something else? Your answer reveals a great deal about how you think about crime and the proper response to it.

Do I believe in rehabilitation and restoration of the offender? This question gets to the heart of how you view human nature. Do you believe people can change? Do you believe that even those who have committed serious wrongs can be transformed? Or do you see offenders as fixed in their identity, defined forever by their worst actions?

Do I support retributive efforts to administer justice? This is not a trick question. Retribution has its place. There is such a thing as just punishment. The question is whether retribution should be the primary goal of justice or merely one element among others.

What should be the goal of our criminal justice system? Is it to punish wrongdoers? To protect society? To rehabilitate offenders? To satisfy victims? To restore community? To deter future crime? All of these are legitimate aims, but they cannot all be primary. We must decide what matters most.

Is the current punitive justice system effective? Look at the evidence we have reviewed in previous chapters. Look at the costs, the recidivism rates, the impact on communities, the dissatisfaction of victims. Ask yourself honestly whether the system is achieving what it claims to achieve.

These are just the beginning. There are more questions to consider.

What role should the victim play in the justice process? In the traditional model, victims are witnesses, not participants. Their needs are secondary to the state's interest in prosecution. Is this how it should be? Or should victims have a more central role?

How should the community be involved in the justice process? In traditional societies, communities played a central role in resolving conflicts and restoring harmony. In our system, communities are largely excluded. Which approach is better?

Should restorative justice be the primary approach to justice, or should it be combined with other approaches? This is not an either-or question. Most restorative justice advocates see their approach as complementing rather than completely replacing traditional systems. The question is about balance and priority.

How should we balance the needs of the victim, offender, and community in the justice process? These needs can conflict. A victim may want something different from what an offender is willing to provide. The community may have its own interests. How do we navigate these tensions?

How should we address systemic injustices and inequalities in the criminal justice system? The system does not treat all people equally. Racial disparities, economic biases, and other forms of inequality are well-documented. How should a just response to crime account for these realities?

Should punishment always be the primary goal of the justice system, or should rehabilitation and prevention also be prioritized? This is not an abstract question. It has concrete implications for how we allocate resources, how we design programs, and how we measure success.

How should we address the root causes of crime, such as poverty, addiction, and mental illness? If we simply punish people for behaviors driven by underlying problems, we are treating symptoms rather than causes. What would it look like to address those causes directly?

Should the justice system be focused on individual accountability, or should it also consider broader social and economic factors? This is a difficult question. Individuals are responsible for their choices. But those choices are shaped by circumstances beyond their control. How do we hold people accountable while also acknowledging the role of social context?

How can we ensure that the justice system is fair, impartial, and equitable for all individuals, regardless of their background or circumstances? This is the ultimate question. If justice is not fair, it is not justice.

I raise these questions not to overwhelm you but to invite you into a process of reflection. The answers are not simple. They require careful thought, honest self-examination, and willingness to consider perspectives different from your own.

One thing I will say directly: if you feel that offenders and ex-offenders are a "lost cause," you will not be able to minister effectively to them. The belief that people cannot change becomes a self-fulfilling prophecy. Those who are treated as hopeless tend to become hopeless. Those who are offered genuine pathways to transformation are more likely to find them.

How Restorative Justice Brings Resolution, Healing, and Reconciliation

Now let us turn to restorative justice itself. What makes it different? Why does it offer something that the traditional model cannot provide?

Restorative justice aims to repair the harm caused by crime by involving all parties affected by that harm—the victim, the offender, and the community—in a process of dialogue and reconciliation. It prioritizes the needs of the victim and seeks to address the underlying causes of the offender's behavior, with the goal of promoting healing and preventing future harm.

This is fundamentally different from the traditional approach. In the traditional model, crime is defined as a violation of the law. The state prosecutes the offender, and if guilt is found, punishment is imposed. The process is adversarial, with the state and the offender as opposing parties. The victim is largely a witness. The community is largely absent.

Restorative justice views crime differently. It sees crime not just as breaking the law but as causing harm to people, relationships, and the community. A just response, therefore, must address those harms as well as the wrongdoing. It must seek not only to punish but to repair.

This means that restorative justice recognizes that crime causes harm not only to the victim but also to the offender, the community, and the relationships between them. The offender is harmed because they are alienated from their own humanity and from the community. The community is harmed because its sense of safety and trust is damaged. The relationships between all parties are harmed because trust is broken and fear takes its place.

Therefore, a just response to crime must do more than address the wrongdoing. It must seek to repair the harm and restore the relationships. This requires the active participation of all parties affected by the crime. They must have the opportunity to communicate, to understand each other's perspectives, and to work together to find ways to repair the harm done.

This is why restorative justice is not simply a different set of programs but a different paradigm altogether. It asks different questions, pursues different goals, and measures success by different standards.

To Whom Does Crime Cause Injury?

In the traditional model, crime is understood primarily as an offense against the state. The state brings charges. The state prosecutes the case. The state imposes punishment. The victim is present but peripheral.

Restorative justice offers a different understanding. It suggests that crime is an injury not only to the immediate victim but also to the wider community. Crime violates the relationships and trust that exist within a community. It damages the fabric of social life.

Think about what happens when a crime occurs in a neighborhood. Even those who were not directly victimized feel its effects. Fear increases. Trust decreases. People become more suspicious of each other. They may withdraw from community life. The harm radiates outward from the victim to affect everyone.

Restorative justice recognizes this ripple effect. It seeks to address the harm caused by the crime by involving all parties in a process of healing and repair. This includes the victim, certainly. But it also includes the community, which has been harmed in its own way. And it includes the offender, who is part of the community and whose actions have damaged the relationships that sustain it.

This is why effective restorative justice includes four key components. First, inclusion of all parties. No one who has been affected by the crime should be excluded from the process of addressing it. Second, encountering the other side. Victims and offenders need the opportunity to meet, to speak, to listen, to understand. Third, making amends for the harm. The offender must take concrete steps to repair what has been damaged. Fourth, reintegration of the parties into their communities. The goal is not permanent separation but restored belonging.

In this understanding, crime is an injury to the victim, the community, and the offender. All have been harmed. All need healing. All must be part of the solution.

Repentance and Restoration

One of the most important aspects of restorative justice is the role it gives to repentance. In a restorative paradigm, the offender at some point recognizes the hurt they have caused and experiences remorse for their actions. This remorse, when genuine, leads to repentance.

Someone has said that an offender can recognize the hurt they have caused and experience remorse without repenting, but an offender who repents has certainly recognized the hurt they have inflicted and experienced true remorse. This distinction is crucial.

Remorse is feeling sorry for what one has done. Repentance is turning away from that behavior and committing to change. Remorse can be shallow and temporary. Repentance involves a fundamental reorientation of one's life.

In restorative justice, the focus is not just on punishing the offender but on repairing the harm caused by the crime. This requires the offender to take responsibility for their actions, to express genuine remorse for the harm caused, and to take steps to make amends. The goal is to restore relationships and heal the harm, not simply to inflict suffering.

This is why repentance is so important. Without it, any attempt at repair is hollow. The offender may go through the motions of making amends without any real change of heart. But with genuine repentance, the offender becomes an active participant in the work of restoration. They are not merely complying with requirements; they are seeking to make things right.

Addressing Both Short-Term and Long-Term Damages

For an offender to move toward complete restoration, they must deal with both the short-term and long-term damages caused by their actions. This is not a simple process. It requires sustained effort and genuine commitment.

In the short term, the offender must address the immediate consequences of their crime. This may involve making financial restitution to the victim, repairing or replacing damaged property, or performing community service that directly benefits those who were harmed. These actions demonstrate accountability and begin the process of repair.

But short-term measures are not enough. The offender must also address the long-term damages. This means repairing relationships with the victim and the community, which may take months or years. It means addressing any underlying issues that contributed to the offending behavior—addiction, mental health problems, lack of education or employment skills, damaged relationships, spiritual emptiness. It means taking steps to ensure that similar harm does not occur in the future.

The goal is not only to hold the offender accountable for what they have done but to help them become a responsible and productive member of society. This requires addressing the root causes of their behavior, not just the symptoms. It requires patience, support, and genuine commitment to transformation.

Why the Victim Cannot Be the State

In the traditional criminal justice system, the state or the system assumes the position of victim. The case is styled as "The People versus the Defendant" or "The State versus the Offender." The state prosecutes on behalf of society. The victim becomes a witness, not a party.

Restorative justice recognizes that this is fundamentally wrong. The victim cannot be the state or the system because the state and the system are not capable of experiencing harm in the way that individuals and communities do. The state may be affected by crime in the abstract, but it does not feel pain, fear, grief, or violation. The victim does.

In restorative justice, the victim is typically the individual or community who has directly suffered harm as a result of the crime. This harm may be physical, emotional, or financial. It may involve loss of trust or sense of safety. The victim's experience is unique and cannot be reduced to an abstract violation of law.

This does not mean that the state has no role. The state has a responsibility to uphold the law and to provide a fair and just process for addressing crime and wrongdoing. In a restorative justice process, the state may facilitate the process and ensure that it is conducted fairly. But the primary focus is on repairing the harm caused to the victim and addressing the underlying causes of the crime.

By placing the victim at the center of the process, restorative justice seeks to create a more inclusive and collaborative approach to justice. The victim is not a bystander but a participant. Their needs, their voice, their perspective matters. This is not only more just; it is also more healing.

A Grassroots Paradigm

One of the defining features of restorative justice is that it starts at the grassroots level. It involves ordinary members of the community, victims, and offenders in the process of healing and restoration. This is fundamentally different from traditional criminal justice systems, where the process is controlled by legal professionals with little involvement from those most affected.

In traditional systems, victims and community members are largely excluded. Professionals make the decisions. Professionals control the process. Professionals determine the outcomes. Those who have been harmed and those who have caused harm are passive recipients of whatever the system delivers.

Restorative justice recognizes that this exclusion is itself a form of harm. Victims need to have a voice. They need to express their needs and desires. They need to participate in decisions that affect their lives. Offenders need to be held accountable in ways that involve them in the process of repair. Communities need to be engaged in addressing the underlying conditions that contribute to crime.

By involving ordinary people in the justice process, restorative justice builds understanding, empathy, and social bonds. It creates opportunities for healing that are simply not available in the traditional model. It also has practical benefits. When offenders are actively involved in making amends, they are more likely to take responsibility for their actions and less likely to reoffend. When communities are engaged in preventing crime, they are more effective than any outside agency could be.

There is another benefit worth noting. When offenders are restored to productive citizenship, they become taxpayers rather than tax burdens. Instead of costing society money through incarceration and supervision, they contribute to society through their labor and their participation in community life. This is not the primary goal of restorative justice, but it is a welcome byproduct.

The Purpose of Community Projects

In restorative justice, working with offenders in closely monitored community projects serves multiple purposes. Each of these purposes contributes to the overall goal of restoration.

First, it provides an opportunity for offenders to take responsibility for their actions and make amends to the community they have harmed. This is not abstract accountability. It is concrete action that benefits real people in tangible ways. When an offender cleans up a park, repairs damage they have caused, or contributes to a community project, they are doing something positive rather than simply serving time.

Second, it provides offenders with a sense of purpose and meaning. Many offenders have experienced social exclusion and disconnection. They may feel that they do not belong anywhere, that their lives have no meaning. Working on projects that benefit the community can help them develop a sense of belonging and connection. They see that they can contribute something positive, that they are not defined solely by their worst actions.

Third, it provides a supportive environment where offenders can develop skills and competencies. This includes social and emotional skills—learning to work with others, to take direction, to persist in tasks. It also includes vocational skills that can help them find employment and make a positive contribution to the community. These skills increase the likelihood of successful reintegration and reduce the risk of reoffending.

Fourth, it benefits the wider community. Community projects get done. Parks are cleaned. Facilities are repaired. Services are provided. Beyond these tangible benefits, community projects promote social cohesion and strengthen community bonds. When community members work alongside offenders who are making amends, they see that change is possible. Trust can be rebuilt.

This is what restorative justice means when it says that crime is a breakdown of society and human relationships. The response must be to mend those relationships through dialogue, community support, involvement, and inclusion. Community projects are one way of doing that.

Holding Offenders Accountable While Centering Victims

One of the criticisms sometimes leveled at restorative justice is that it is soft on offenders. This criticism misunderstands what restorative justice is about. Restorative justice holds offenders accountable, but it defines accountability differently than the traditional model.

In restorative justice, accountability means taking responsibility for one's actions and making efforts to repair the harm caused. It is not about passive suffering but active restoration. The offender is not simply punished; they are engaged in the process of making things right.

At the same time, restorative justice makes the victim central to the process. Victims are given an opportunity to share their experiences and feelings, to express how the crime has affected them. This can be deeply empowering. Instead of being a witness to someone else's proceeding, the victim becomes a participant in their own healing.

When victims are able to communicate directly with offenders, when they are able to ask questions and receive answers, when they see the offender taking genuine responsibility, the healing process can begin. This does not happen in every case, but when it does, the results can be transformative.

By making the victim central and holding offenders accountable through active restoration, restorative justice creates a more inclusive and collaborative approach to justice. The focus is on repairing harm and restoring relationships, not simply on punishment.

Creating and Restoring Equity

Restorative justice is a noun that refers, in the aggregate, to justice processes that create or restore equity, that make things right. This is a beautiful way of thinking about justice.

In the traditional model, justice is about punishment. The scales are balanced by making the offender suffer. In restorative justice, justice is about equity. The goal is to restore what has been lost, to repair what has been damaged, to make things as right as possible for all involved.

This is a more holistic and community-oriented approach. It acknowledges that crime has ripple effects that extend far beyond the immediate victim. It recognizes that crime is not just a violation of the law but a breach of relationships and trust. It seeks to address the root causes of crime by promoting dialogue, understanding, and empathy.

Restorative justice can take many forms. It may involve mediation between victim and offender. It may involve family group conferencing that brings together all those affected by the crime. It may involve community panels that develop reparative plans. It may involve circles that include victims, offenders, and community members in dialogue and decision-making.

Whatever form it takes, the aim is always the same: to create a safe and supportive environment where all parties can share their experiences and find a way forward that promotes healing and restoration. This is not about letting offenders off the hook. It is about holding them accountable in ways that actually address the harm and prevent future wrongdoing.

Restorative justice emphasizes the importance of working with prisoners and their victims in a way that promotes healing and encourages reconciliation. This is not easy work. It requires patience, skill, and genuine commitment. But when it is done well, it can transform lives.

Crime as Harm to Relationships

The restorative justice paradigm emphasizes the ways in which crime harms relationships in the context of community. This is not just a theoretical point. It has practical implications for how we respond to crime.

When a crime occurs, relationships are damaged. The relationship between victim and offender is obviously harmed—trust is broken, fear is created, anger and resentment take root. But other relationships are also affected. The victim's relationships with family and friends may suffer as they struggle with trauma. The offender's relationships with their own family may be damaged by shame and separation. Community members' relationships with each other may be strained by fear and suspicion.

Restorative justice recognizes that addressing the harm caused by crime requires addressing these damaged relationships. This cannot be done by punishment alone. Punishment may satisfy a desire for revenge, but it does nothing to repair relationships. In fact, it may damage them further.

This is why authentic restorative justice is a continuum that includes several stages. Pre-conferencing prepares all parties for the process, explaining what will happen and setting goals. The conference itself brings everyone together in a face-to-face meeting facilitated by a trained professional. Follow-up ensures that agreements are fulfilled and that all parties are satisfied with the outcome. Community involvement engages the wider community in supporting victims and offenders and in taking responsibility for preventing future harm.

Included in authentic restorative justice is a sound, comprehensive understanding of the relationships affected by crime. It focuses on the full circle of injuries, needs, and responsibilities of crime victims, offenders, community, and government. No one is left out. Everyone's needs are considered.

Cultural Expressions of Restorative Justice

Restorative justice is not a new invention. It has been practiced in various forms by cultures around the world for millennia. One example comes from Navajo Country, where restorative justice practices are based on traditional Navajo concepts of justice.

In these practices, apology and forgiveness play central roles. Offenders are expected to acknowledge the harm they have caused and to express genuine remorse. Victims are given the opportunity to hear these apologies and to extend forgiveness if they are able. The process often includes participation in culture-based cleansing ceremonies, traditional counseling, and advisement by elders and community leaders.

The goal is healing and restoration for both victim and offender, as well as the community as a whole. This is not about punishment but about restoring balance and harmony. It recognizes that when one person is harmed, everyone is affected. When one person is healed, everyone benefits.

This cultural approach aligns with the core principles of restorative justice. It emphasizes accountability, but accountability defined as taking responsibility and making amends. It centers the needs of victims and community. It seeks to repair harm and restore relationships. It recognizes that justice is not something done to people but something done with them.

Accountability as Responsibility and Repair

In restorative justice, offender accountability is defined in terms of assuming responsibility and taking action to repair harm. This is different from the traditional understanding of accountability as punishment.

When an offender is held accountable in the traditional sense, they are made to suffer. They are incarcerated, fined, or otherwise punished. The assumption is that this suffering somehow balances the scales, that the offender has "paid their debt" to society.

But what debt has actually been paid? The victim has not been compensated. The community has not been restored. The offender has not been changed. They have simply served time, after which they are released, often more damaged than when they entered.

Restorative justice offers a different understanding. Accountability means facing the harm one has caused and taking steps to repair it. This may involve financial restitution to the victim. It may involve community service that benefits those who were harmed. It may involve participating in programs that address the underlying issues that contributed to the offending behavior.

This approach focuses on the needs of the victim and the community, not just on punishing the offender. By holding the offender accountable in this way and encouraging them to make amends, restorative justice aims to promote healing, reconciliation, and a sense of closure for all parties involved.

The Community as the Prime Site of Crime Control

Central to restorative justice is the recognition of the community, rather than criminal justice agencies, as the prime site of crime control. This is a radical departure from the traditional model.

In the traditional model, crime control is the responsibility of professionals. Police catch offenders. Prosecutors charge them. Courts sentence them. Corrections supervise them. The community is largely passive, its role limited to calling 911 when something happens and perhaps serving on juries occasionally.

Restorative justice sees things differently. The community is not a passive recipient of professional services but an active participant in addressing and preventing crime. The community has a central role in repairing harm and restoring relationships. The community is involved in holding offenders accountable and promoting healing for victims.

This approach recognizes that crime is not just a violation of the law but a violation of the relationships and trust within the community. Therefore, it requires community-based solutions. Professionals may facilitate these solutions, but they cannot impose them from outside.

To accomplish this, restorative justice requires not only the willingness of the offender and the victim to meet and plan amends but also a cooperative effort by the community and law enforcement agencies. Everyone has a role to play. Everyone's contribution matters.

Elevating the Role of Victims and Community Members

Restorative justice emphasizes the importance of elevating the role of crime victims and community members through more active involvement in the justice process. It does this by providing a wide range of opportunities for dialogue, negotiation, and problem-solving.

This active involvement leads to a greater sense of community safety, social harmony, and peace for all involved. When victims are heard, when their needs are addressed, when they see offenders taking responsibility, they are more likely to feel that justice has been done. When community members are involved in addressing crime, they are more likely to feel invested in the safety and well-being of their neighborhoods.

This approach recognizes that crime harms not only the victim but also the community. Therefore, the community has a stake in the resolution and healing of the harm caused by the crime. Excluding the community from this process is itself a form of harm.

Redemptive Rather Than Retributive

Restorative justice is not retributive in nature but redemptive. This is perhaps the most important distinction between the two paradigms.

Retributive justice focuses on punishing offenders for their wrongdoing. The goal is to make them suffer in proportion to the harm they have caused. Restorative justice focuses on repairing the harm caused by crime and restoring relationships between victims, offenders, and communities.

In restorative justice, the offender is encouraged to take responsibility for their actions, make amends to the victim and the community, and work toward making positive changes in their lives. By doing so, they are able to move beyond their past mistakes and become productive members of society.

This is what makes restorative justice redemptive. It seeks to help offenders understand the impact of their actions on others, take steps to repair the harm caused, and make positive changes in their lives. Offenders are able to redeem themselves and make amends for their wrongdoing.

Rather than seeking revenge, restorative justice focuses on helping bring about healing in relationships with God and the community of man. This is not soft on crime. It is hard on the things that matter—accountability, responsibility, genuine change.

A Philosophy, Not Just Programs

It is important to understand that restorative justice is not a set of programs. It is a philosophy from which a response flows. This distinction matters.

Programs are specific interventions—victim-offender mediation, family group conferencing, community panels, and so on. These programs can be important tools for implementing restorative justice. But they are not restorative justice itself. Restorative justice is the underlying philosophy that gives these programs meaning and direction.

The philosophy emphasizes repairing harm, restoring relationships, and addressing the needs of all those impacted by crime. From this philosophy, various programs and practices can be developed and implemented. But the programs must be faithful to the philosophy. It is possible to have programs called "restorative" that do not actually reflect restorative values. This is why understanding the philosophy is essential.

Inclusive Processes and Community Justice

Restorative justice principles offer more inclusive processes that involve community justice. This is one of their great strengths.

In traditional justice systems, the focus is on punishing offenders, with little involvement from the community. This leads to alienation and disconnection. Offenders feel like outsiders. Communities feel like spectators. No one feels ownership of the process or its outcomes.

Restorative justice emphasizes the importance of involving the community in the justice process. This includes not only the victim and the offender but also family members, friends, and other community members who may have been affected by the crime or conflict. Everyone who has a stake in the outcome has a place at the table.

By involving the community, restorative justice offers more inclusive and collaborative processes that promote healing and reconciliation. The community plays an active role in addressing the underlying causes of crime and conflict and in supporting both the victim and the offender in making positive changes.

Restorative justice is also more culturally responsive than traditional approaches. It allows for greater input from diverse communities and promotes understanding and respect for different cultural perspectives. This is not a small thing in a diverse society.

Community justice includes all variants of crime prevention and justice activities that explicitly include the community in their processes. Restorative justice is one expression of this broader movement.

Mobilizing Communities as Active Partners

The primary goal of community justice is to mobilize communities to be active partners in crime control and problem-solving efforts. This is based on the recognition that crime is not just an individual problem but a community problem.

To effectively address crime and other community problems, it is necessary to involve the community in the process. This means working with community members to identify the root causes of crime and develop strategies to address them. It means creating opportunities for community members to be active partners in the justice system.

When communities are involved in this way, they develop a sense of ownership and investment in the justice system. Trust and cooperation increase. Accountability and transparency improve. The community becomes part of the solution rather than just a bystander.

Community justice also recognizes that traditional justice processes may not be effective for all types of crime and community problems. It emphasizes the importance of utilizing a variety of approaches, including restorative justice, diversion programs, and community-based alternatives to incarceration.

The goal is not simply to process cases but to create safer, healthier, and more vibrant communities.

Shifting to Community-Level Outcomes

The central focus of community justice is community-level outcomes. This shifts the emphasis from individual incidents to systemic patterns, from individual conscience to social morals, from individual good to the common good.

This is a profound shift. In the traditional model, each case is handled individually. The focus is on what happened in this particular incident and what should happen to this particular offender. Broader patterns are ignored. Systemic issues are not addressed.

Community justice recognizes that addressing crime requires looking at the bigger picture. Why is crime happening in this neighborhood? What conditions are contributing to it? What can be done to change those conditions? These are community-level questions that require community-level answers.

By engaging community members in problem-solving and decision-making, community justice seeks to address the root causes of crime—poverty, inequality, social disconnection—rather than simply punishing offenders after the fact. This is not easier than the traditional approach, but it is more effective in the long run.

Achieving community-level outcomes requires a holistic and collaborative approach. It involves working with community members, law enforcement, courts, social service providers, and other stakeholders to develop comprehensive strategies. It takes time, patience, and genuine commitment. But the results are worth it.

Restoring Community Functions

One of the goals of community justice is to facilitate the performance by private citizens of the functions that were once performed by the extended family, neighborhood, and school. This reflects a recognition that these traditional institutions have weakened and that their functions need to be restored.

In the past, families, neighborhoods, and schools played a central role in socializing young people, resolving conflicts, and maintaining order. When problems arose, they were often handled within these institutions rather than being referred to outside authorities. This created a sense of ownership and responsibility that is largely missing today.

Community justice seeks to empower community members to take on these roles again. This includes promoting community involvement in restorative justice practices, which seek to repair harm and restore relationships. It also includes partnerships with social service providers and other organizations to address underlying issues like poverty, unemployment, and inequality.

Community policing is another expression of this goal. By building trust and cooperation between law enforcement and community members, community policing aims to prevent crime rather than just respond to it. Initiatives like community patrols, citizen review boards, and police-community dialogues create opportunities for genuine partnership.

By involving private citizens in crime control and problem-solving, community justice seeks to create a more inclusive and responsive system that is better equipped to address the root causes of crime and promote community safety and well-being.

A New Way of Thinking About Police, Courts, and Corrections

Community justice initiatives offer a new way of thinking about police, courts, and corrections. These three components operate differently from the past by emphasizing problem-solving and focusing on community concerns and the victim.

The traditional criminal justice system has been criticized for being reactive and punitive. It responds to crime after it happens and focuses on punishment as the primary response. This approach has not worked well, as evidenced by high rates of recidivism and disproportionate impact on marginalized communities.

Community justice initiatives aim to be proactive and collaborative. They involve community members in every stage of the justice process. They emphasize restorative justice practices that seek to repair harm and address the needs of both victim and offender. They prioritize addressing the underlying social and economic conditions that contribute to crime.

For these initiatives to be successful, they must be grounded in strong relationships between community members, law enforcement, and other institutions. This requires building trust and engaging in open and transparent communication. It also requires adequate resources and support to ensure sustainability over the long term.

When these conditions are met, community justice initiatives offer a promising alternative to traditional models. By involving community members in problem-solving and decision-making, and by addressing the underlying causes of crime, these initiatives have the potential to create more just and equitable societies.

The Difference Between Community Justice and Restorative Justice

It is important to understand the difference between community justice and restorative justice. While they are related, they are not the same thing.

Both are more inclusive processes than the traditional criminal justice system. Both share control with the community to a greater extent. But there are significant differences in their underlying philosophies and goals.

Community justice is a model that emphasizes engaging the community in crime control and problem-solving efforts. It is based on the recognition that the criminal justice system cannot solve all of society's problems and that community members must take an active role in addressing the underlying issues that contribute to crime. The primary goal is to mobilize communities to be active partners. This approach shifts the emphasis from individual incidents to systemic patterns, from individual conscience to social morals, from individual good to the common good.

Restorative justice is a paradigm that emphasizes repairing the harm caused by crime. It views crime as more than a violation of the law—it is a harm to people, relationships, and the community. Justice must address both the harm and the wrongdoing. The primary goal is to create or restore equity, to make things right. Restorative justice makes the victim central to the process and emphasizes the importance of elevating the role of victims and community members.

Community justice efforts may or may not be restorative. They could be viewed as more of a process, while restorative justice is more of a philosophy that affects both the process and the end goal. Restorative justice includes the victim as a key focus of process and outcome, whether or not it is community-based.

In practice, these approaches can complement each other. A restorative community justice paradigm would involve both—engaging the victim and community for the purpose of repairing harm while holding the offender accountable.

A Restorative Community Justice Paradigm

A restorative community justice paradigm is a holistic approach to justice that focuses on repairing harm caused by criminal behavior while holding the offender accountable for their actions. It recognizes that crime is not just a violation of the law but also a violation of people, relationships, and the community.

This paradigm differs from traditional criminal justice in several key ways. First, it prioritizes the needs of the victim over punishment. The victim is central to the process, and their needs and desires are taken into account when determining outcomes. Victims have a voice. They are heard. They participate in healing and restoration rather than being passive recipients of whatever the system delivers.

Second, it aims to build stronger, more connected communities by involving community members in the process of justice. Community members are involved not only in responding to crime but also in preventing it. They take responsibility for their community's well-being, identify problems, and work together to find solutions. They are involved in rehabilitating offenders, helping them repair harm and reintegrate into society.

Third, it focuses on repairing the harm caused by the offender. The offender is held accountable for their actions and must take responsibility for repairing the harm. This may involve restitution, community service, therapy or counseling, or other forms of restorative justice. The goal is to address the root causes of the offender's behavior, prevent future harm, and restore the offender to their full potential.

In this paradigm, justice is seen as a process rather than an outcome. The process involves all stakeholders—victims, offenders, and community members—in a collaborative effort to repair harm and prevent future harm. The emphasis is on restoring relationships and building stronger, more connected communities. Justice cannot be achieved by punishment alone. It requires a holistic approach that addresses the needs of all involved.

A Compilation of Principles and Practices

Restorative justice is a compilation of principles and practices that come together to form an approach that involves all parties—the offender, victim, and community—to achieve justice. It is based on the principle that crime is not just a violation of the law but also a violation of people and relationships.

The key principles include accountability, repairing harm, and community involvement. Accountability means that the offender takes responsibility for their actions and works to repair the harm they have caused. This may involve restitution, community service, and steps to prevent similar harm in the future. Repairing harm involves addressing the needs of the victim and working to restore what has been lost. Community involvement means that the community is engaged in supporting both victim and offender and in holding the offender accountable.

Practices can take many forms. Victim-offender mediation brings the parties together in a facilitated dialogue. Family group conferencing involves family members and supporters in the process. Community panels bring together community members to develop reparative plans. Circles create a space for all affected parties to speak and be heard.

These processes are designed to create a safe and supportive environment for all parties and to facilitate open and honest communication. They provide an opportunity for victim and offender to work together to develop a plan for repairing harm and preventing future harm.

By bringing all parties together to work toward a common goal, restorative justice can help build stronger and more resilient communities that are better equipped to address the complex challenges of our time.

Summary of Principles and Practices

Let me summarize the many principles and practices of restorative justice.

Crime is an offense against human relationships. This is the foundational insight. Crime damages the bonds that hold communities together.

Victims and the community are central to justice processes. They are not peripheral or optional. Their participation is essential.

The first priority of justice processes is to assist victims. Their needs come first. Their healing is primary.

The second priority is to restore the community, to the degree possible. The community has been harmed and needs repair.

The offender has personal responsibility to victims and to the community for crimes committed. This responsibility cannot be delegated or avoided.

Stakeholders share responsibilities for restorative justice through partnership for action. Everyone has a role to play.

The offender will develop improved competency and understanding as a result of the restorative justice experience. This is not just about punishment but about growth.

Beyond these, restorative justice includes specific practices. Harm and needs assessment identifies what has been damaged and what is needed. A victim-centered approach ensures that victims have a voice. Offender accountability requires taking responsibility and making amends. Community involvement engages the wider community in support and prevention. Restitution and reparation require offenders to make things right. Dialogue and communication promote understanding and healing. Healing and reconciliation are the ultimate goals. Voluntary participation ensures that no one is coerced. Fairness and equity are maintained throughout. Continuity of care provides ongoing support.

These principles and practices aim to promote healing and reconciliation, encourage accountability, involve the community, and provide a more equitable and just approach to justice.

Fundamental Concepts

There are several fundamental concepts that are common among restorative justice advocates.

Repairing harm is the central focus. This includes not only tangible harm like property damage or financial loss but also intangible harm like emotional trauma and social disruption. The goal is to make things as right as possible.

Inclusivity means involving all parties affected by a crime—offender, victim, and community. Crime is not just an individual act but a violation of relationships and social bonds. All who are affected must be part of the response.

Responsibility and accountability mean holding offenders accountable by requiring them to take responsibility for the harm they have caused and to take action to repair it. At the same time, restorative justice recognizes that offenders are human beings with the potential for change and seeks to help them make amends and reintegrate into the community.

Crime is fundamentally a violation of people and interpersonal relationships. This is the foundational insight.

Violations create obligations and liabilities. Something is owed. Something must be done.

Restorative justice seeks to heal and put right the wrongs. This is its ultimate purpose.

Victims and Community Need Restoration

In traditional criminal justice systems, the focus is often solely on the offender and punishing them for their actions. The restorative justice paradigm emphasizes that the victim and the community are also harmed by crime and need restoration.

When a crime is committed, the victim is left with physical, emotional, and psychological scars. They may feel violated, vulnerable, and may struggle with feelings of anger, fear, and distrust. The harm can affect their relationships, work, and overall quality of life. Restorative justice seeks to address these harms by giving the victim a voice and an active role in the process. It creates an opportunity for the victim to express their needs, feelings, and concerns, and to have those needs heard and addressed. The process empowers the victim by giving them a sense of agency and control over what happens next, rather than leaving them feeling like a passive bystander.

The community is also affected by crime. Crime can create fear, mistrust, and division within a community. This can lead to a breakdown in social cohesion and a sense of disconnection and isolation. Restorative justice recognizes that crimes harm the social fabric of communities and seeks to repair this harm by involving the community in the justice process.

Offenders are part of the community, and their actions have an impact on the community as a whole. Punishing offenders in isolation from the community does not address the root causes of crime or promote a sense of responsibility and accountability. By involving offenders in the restorative justice process, they can come face-to-face with the harm they have caused and take responsibility for their actions.

The restorative justice paradigm recognizes that crime is not just a violation of the law but also a violation of relationships and communities. By involving the victim, the offender, and the community in the justice process, it seeks to restore these relationships and promote healing and repair.

Victims, Offenders, and Communities as Key Stakeholders

In restorative justice, victims, offenders, and the affected communities are the key stakeholders in justice. This is because the focus is on the harm that has been caused and on repairing that harm as much as possible.

The victim is central to the process. Restorative justice aims to address the harm that has been done to the victim, rather than just punishing the offender. Victims are given the opportunity to tell their story, share their feelings, and have a say in the outcome. They may receive restitution, which can include financial compensation or community service by the offender.

The offender is also a key stakeholder. Rather than being a passive recipient of punishment, the offender is an active participant in repairing the harm they have caused. They are encouraged to take responsibility for their actions, make amends to the victim and the community, and become a positive member of society.

The affected community is an important stakeholder as well. Crime does not just affect the victim and offender but also the broader community. Restorative justice seeks to involve the community in the process of repairing harm and preventing future harm. Community members participate in the justice process, share their experiences, and work together with the victim and offender to find a resolution.

Restorative justice recognizes that crime is a complex issue that requires the involvement of multiple stakeholders to achieve true justice. By involving all affected parties, it seeks to repair harm, restore relationships, and build stronger communities.

Obligations Created by Violations

When violations occur in a community, various obligations are created for different stakeholders.

For the offender, the obligation is to take responsibility for their actions and do what they can to make things right as much as possible. This includes acknowledging the harm caused, making amends to the victim or affected parties, and taking steps to prevent similar harm in the future.

For the community, there are also obligations. The community has a responsibility to the victim and the offender to ensure that justice is served in a fair and just manner. This includes providing support to the victim and ensuring that the offender is held accountable. Additionally, the community has an obligation to the general welfare of its members, which may include addressing underlying issues that contribute to crime and harm, such as poverty, inequality, and lack of access to resources.

The obligations that follow from harm inflicted by crime should be related to making things right. The community helps victims of crime and supports efforts to integrate offenders into the community. These are not optional extras but essential components of justice.

Ways Restorative Justice Heals and Makes Right

Restorative justice seeks to heal and put right the wrongs in several specific ways.

First, the needs of victims for information, validation, vindication, restitution, testimony, safety, and support are the starting points of justice. The focus is on the harm caused by the offense and how to repair it. The process aims to address the needs of the victim and create opportunities for them to receive what they need. This approach is grounded in the idea that justice should not only be about punishing the offender but also about addressing the harm done to the victim.

Second, the process of justice maximizes opportunities for the exchange of information, participation, dialogue, and mutual consent between victim and offender. Restorative justice creates opportunities for them to come together in a safe and respectful environment where they can communicate their needs and feelings. The goal is to create a dialogue that allows the victim to express the harm they have suffered and for the offender to take responsibility. This process can help both parties gain a better understanding of each other's perspectives and needs, which can lead to mutual consent and agreement on how to repair the harm.

Third, the offender's needs and competencies are addressed. Restorative justice recognizes that the offender may have needs that must be addressed to prevent future harm—addiction, mental health issues, lack of education or employment. By addressing these underlying issues, restorative justice aims to reduce the likelihood of reoffending.

Fourth, the justice process belongs to the community. The community is a key stakeholder, and its involvement can help create a sense of accountability and responsibility. The community can play a role in supporting the victim and offender as they work toward repairing the harm.

Fifth, justice is mindful of the outcomes, intended and unintended, of its responses to crime and victimization. Restorative justice recognizes that the criminal justice system can have unintended consequences—exacerbating harm, perpetuating inequality, alienating victims and offenders. The process aims to be mindful of these outcomes and work toward preventing them.

Restorative justice seeks to create a more equitable and compassionate approach to justice, one that addresses the needs of victims, provides opportunities for offenders to take responsibility, and involves the community in the process.

CHAPTER 04

CONCEPTUAL FRAMEWORKS OF RESTORATIVE JUSTICE

We have traveled a long way together in this book. In the first chapter, we examined the traditional view of justice—its ancient roots in the law of retaliation, its psychological appeal, and its troubling consequences. We saw how a system designed to punish has grown into a massive enterprise that incarcerates more of its citizens than any other nation on earth, at enormous cost and with little to show for it.

In the second chapter, we explored why this system must be restructured. We looked at the soaring costs, the public's fear and frustration, the isolation of communities, and the way the system steals conflicts from those to whom they belong. We saw how the traditional model fails victims, fails offenders, and fails communities.

In the third chapter, we began to glimpse a different view of justice. We explored restorative justice—what it is, how it differs from the traditional model, and why it offers hope for healing and reconciliation. We considered the principles and practices that make restorative justice unique, and we saw how it centers victims, holds offenders accountable through repair, and involves communities in the process of justice.

Now, in this fourth chapter, we will go deeper. We will examine the conceptual frameworks that undergird restorative justice—the ideas, theories, and models that give it shape and substance. These frameworks help us understand not only what restorative justice is but why it works and how it can be implemented in communities. They provide the intellectual foundation for the practical programs and practices we will explore in later chapters.

Let us begin with a simple but profound assertion.

The Need for Change

Without question, our method of carrying out justice in the twenty-first century must be changed. This is not a radical statement. It is a recognition of reality. The traditional method, rooted in punishment and retribution, has been with us for millennia. It has shaped our laws, our institutions, and our way of thinking about crime and justice. But it is not working.

Think about what the traditional system does. It focuses on punishing offenders for their crimes, often without considering the underlying causes of their behavior. It processes cases through courts and prisons, treating each offense as an isolated incident rather than as part of a larger pattern. It ignores the needs of victims and communities, treating them as peripheral to the main event. And it does all of this at enormous cost, both financial and social.

The evidence of failure is all around us. Despite decades of increasing incarceration, overall crime rates remain stubbornly high in many categories. The punishment-focused approach has not addressed the root causes of crime—poverty, lack of education, mental health issues, addiction, family breakdown, social isolation. In many cases, it has made these problems worse. People emerge from prison more damaged than when they entered, carrying the same issues plus new ones acquired during incarceration. They return to the same communities, the same circumstances, the same challenges. And we wonder why they so often reoffend.

The system is also failing victims. In the traditional model, victims are treated as secondary to the needs of the state and the offender. They are witnesses, not participants. Their needs for information, validation, vindication, restitution, testimony, safety, and support are largely ignored. They are left feeling powerless, frustrated, and often re-traumatized by a process that claims to serve them but actually uses them for its own purposes.

And the system is failing communities. The negative impact of incarceration on families and neighborhoods is immeasurable. Children grow up without parents. Families are torn apart. Communities lose their members and their cohesion. The social fabric is damaged in ways that cannot be easily repaired.

All of this comes at a staggering cost. Maintaining prisons, funding courts, supporting the vast apparatus of the criminal justice system consumes billions of dollars each year—money that could be spent on education, healthcare, housing, and other programs that address the root causes of crime. The financial cost is enormous, but the social cost is even greater.

This is why a shift toward a more restorative and community-based approach to justice is not just desirable but necessary. Such an approach focuses on addressing the harm caused by crime and repairing the relationships between victim, offender, and community. It emphasizes the importance of including all stakeholders in the justice process. It aims to address the underlying causes of crime and promote social justice by providing opportunities for offenders to make amends and become active members of their communities.

Restorative justice practices—victim-offender mediation, community conferencing, family group conferencing, and others—have been shown to be effective in reducing recidivism rates and promoting healing for victims and offenders. These practices provide a more holistic approach to justice, taking into account the needs of all stakeholders and the community as a whole.

The traditional method of carrying out justice must be changed. We need a system that addresses root causes, promotes healing, and serves all members of the community. We need a system that prioritizes restoration over punishment, participation over exclusion, and community over bureaucracy.

Crime as Catalyst: Christie's Insight

Nils Christie, the Norwegian criminologist we encountered in earlier chapters, offered a powerful insight about the relationship between crime and community. He believed that crime could serve as a catalyst which, if channeled properly, could provide the motivation to empower the community to take a fuller and more direct responsibility for addressing it.

This idea is counterintuitive. We usually think of crime as purely destructive—a problem to be solved, a harm to be punished. Christie saw something else. He saw that crime, by its very nature, forces a community to confront its values, its relationships, and its responsibilities. It creates an opportunity for the community to come together, to address the harm that has been done, and to take action to prevent future harm.

Christie introduced the concept of "conflict resolution through social discipline" as an alternative to traditional criminal justice. He believed that crime is not only an individual act but a social phenomenon. Traditional criminal justice systems, by focusing on punishment and relying on law enforcement, fail to address the root causes of crime. They also remove conflicts from the communities where they occur, depriving those communities of the opportunity to learn and grow from them.

In Christie's approach, the community is empowered to take a more active role in addressing crime and conflict. Restorative justice processes seek to repair the harm caused by the offense and restore relationships between offender, victim, and community. Offenders are held accountable, but the goal is not punishment for its own sake. The goal is healing and reconciliation.

Crime serves as a catalyst for community empowerment because it forces individuals to confront the impact of crime on their community and to take action to address it. When a crime occurs, it cannot be ignored. It demands a response. In a restorative justice system, that response comes from the community itself. The community is the primary stakeholder, and justice is based on restoring relationships and repairing harm rather than on punishing offenders.

This approach also emphasizes the importance of social discipline—the informal social controls that exist within a community. These controls include family, friends, neighbors, and other community members who hold each other accountable for their actions. Christie argued that social discipline can be more effective than formal criminal justice systems because it is rooted in the community and based on shared values.

When a community takes responsibility for addressing crime, it develops its own capacity for maintaining order and promoting well-being. It becomes stronger, more cohesive, more resilient. Crime, rather than being purely destructive, becomes an occasion for growth and renewal.

This is not to romanticize crime or minimize its harms. Crime causes real suffering, and that suffering must be addressed. But Christie's insight reminds us that how we respond to crime matters. A response that excludes the community and relies solely on professionals deprives the community of an opportunity to grow. A response that involves the community and empowers it to take responsibility can transform crime from a source of division into a catalyst for unity.

Conceptual Models for Community-Based Practice

Over the years, scholars and practitioners have developed several conceptual models that provide frameworks for community-based practices in responding to crime. These models offer different perspectives on how communities can be involved in justice and how crime can be prevented and addressed. Let me name and briefly describe some of the most important ones.

Restorative Justice is perhaps the most familiar of these models. It is a philosophy that seeks to repair the harm caused by crime and conflict by involving all parties—the victim, the offender, and the community—in a process of dialogue, accountability, and restitution. The goal is to restore relationships and promote healing, rather than simply punishing offenders. Restorative justice programs include victim-offender mediation, community conferencing, circles, and other forms of dialogue and accountability.

Community Justice is a model that emphasizes the importance of involving the community in all aspects of the criminal justice system, from prevention and intervention to adjudication and reentry. The goal is to empower the community to take a more active role in addressing the root causes of crime and to promote community safety and well-being. Community justice initiatives include community courts, neighborhood probation, community prosecution, and other programs that bring justice closer to the people it serves.

Communitarianism is a political philosophy that emphasizes the importance of community values, social responsibility, and civic engagement. Communitarians believe that individual rights must be balanced with the needs and interests of the community, and that communities must take an active role in shaping social norms and values. This philosophy provides a foundation for many community-based approaches to justice, including restorative justice and community justice.

Communities That Care Programs are community-based initiatives that seek to prevent crime and delinquency by identifying and addressing risk factors in young people's lives. These programs involve a range of stakeholders—parents, schools, law enforcement, community organizations—and focus on building protective factors and promoting positive youth development. "Communities That Care PLUS," mentioned in your materials, is an example of this approach. It is the product of years of prevention science research and collaboration with states and communities across the country. These programs help communities use data to choose tested and effective programs tailored to their specific needs and to track progress over time. They represent a social development strategy that fosters the success of young people through every stage of development.

Community Policing is a law enforcement strategy that emphasizes partnerships between police and the community in preventing crime and promoting public safety. Community policing involves problem-solving, community engagement, and collaborative approaches to addressing the underlying conditions that contribute to crime. Officers are assigned to specific neighborhoods, where they build relationships with residents and work with them to identify and address concerns.

Civic Responsibility is the belief that individuals have a moral obligation to participate in the life of their community and to work for the common good. This includes participating in civic organizations, volunteering, voting, and taking an active role in community decision-making. When citizens embrace civic responsibility, they become partners in creating safe and just communities.

Devolution is the transfer of power and responsibility from central government to local communities. Devolution seeks to empower local communities to take an active role in addressing social and economic issues, including crime and justice. By bringing decision-making closer to the people affected by those decisions, devolution can make government more responsive and effective.

These conceptual models provide frameworks that can guide community-based practices in responding to crime. They emphasize the importance of community involvement, restorative approaches, problem-solving, and social responsibility. By using these models to inform policy and practice, communities can work together to promote safety, prevent crime, and advance social justice.

Crime Prevention Through Problem-Solving

One of the most distinctive features of restorative justice is its focus on crime prevention through problem-solving for the future, rather than solely establishing blame for past criminal behavior. The attitude behind crime prevention is simple: "Let's fix the problem so it doesn't happen again." Establishing blame is not crime prevention.

This represents a fundamental shift in thinking. The traditional retributive model looks backward. It asks: what crime was committed, who is responsible, and what punishment do they deserve? The focus is on the past—on establishing guilt and imposing consequences. Once the punishment has been administered, the system's work is done. Whether the offender changes, whether the victim heals, whether the community becomes safer—these questions are largely irrelevant to the legal process.

Restorative justice looks forward. It asks: what harm has been caused, what needs to be repaired, and what can be done to prevent this from happening again? The focus is on the future—on healing, restoration, and prevention. The goal is not simply to punish but to transform.

Restorative justice recognizes that crime is not just a legal problem but a social problem that affects the community as a whole. It emphasizes the importance of addressing the underlying causes of crime—poverty, lack of education, social inequality, family breakdown, addiction, mental illness. By involving the community in the restorative justice process, it creates an opportunity for the community to address these underlying issues and work together to prevent future crime.

In restorative justice, the focus is on repairing the harm caused by the crime rather than just punishing the offender. The victim is given a voice and is able to express how the crime has affected them. The offender is given an opportunity to take responsibility for their actions and make amends. By addressing the harm, restorative justice aims to prevent future crime by changing the behavior of the offender and creating a sense of accountability.

Restorative justice also emphasizes the importance of rehabilitation and reintegration. It recognizes that offenders are often products of their environment and that by providing them with the necessary support, they can become responsible members of society. This might include education, job training, counseling, substance abuse treatment, or other forms of support. By addressing the root causes of criminal behavior, restorative justice aims to prevent future crime.

Contrast this with retributive justice. Retributive justice is reactive. It responds to crime after it happens, and its primary tool is punishment. It is based on the belief that punishment serves as a deterrent to future crime. But research has shown that punishment alone is not an effective deterrent. Certainty of punishment matters more than severity, and our system is far from certain. Most crimes never result in arrest, let alone conviction and punishment.

Moreover, retributive justice does nothing to address the conditions that produce crime. It punishes offenders and returns them to the same environments, with the same problems, and expects different results. This is not justice. It is a revolving door.

Restorative justice offers a different path. By focusing on prevention through problem-solving, by addressing root causes, by involving the community, by promoting rehabilitation and reintegration, it seeks to break the cycle of crime and create safer, healthier communities.

Giving Victims a Voice and a Path to Healing

In the restorative justice process, victims are given the opportunity for input and healing by gaining a better understanding of what happened to them. This is essential because crime, viewed as a violation of one person by another, produces a wide range of emotions—anger, bitterness, fear, confusion, and more. A victim's emotions resulting from crime are a major concern in the restorative justice process.

In the traditional criminal justice system, victims often feel left out of the process. They are not heard. Their needs are not addressed. They are used as witnesses for the prosecution, then discarded once their testimony is given. The system processes their case, but it does not process their pain.

Restorative justice recognizes that victims play a critical role in the process of repairing harm. Their active participation is not optional; it is essential. In the restorative justice process, victims are given a voice and an opportunity to share their experiences and express how the crime has affected them.

Victims are encouraged to participate in the process and provide input on how to address the harm caused by the crime. They may be asked to provide a victim impact statement—a written or oral statement describing how the crime has affected them physically, emotionally, and financially. This statement is shared with the offender and the community, allowing them to understand the full impact of the crime.

Victims may also participate in a face-to-face meeting with the offender, known as a restorative conference or circle. In this meeting, the victim has the opportunity to express directly to the offender how the crime has affected them. The meeting is facilitated by a trained restorative justice practitioner and includes both parties, as well as any other affected individuals and community members. The goal is to promote healing for all involved and to develop a plan to repair the harm caused by the crime.

Through this process, victims gain a better understanding of what happened. They may learn about the offender's motivations for committing the crime, as well as any underlying issues that contributed to their behavior. This understanding can be an important part of the healing process. It helps victims see the offender as a human being rather than a monster. It can help them let go of anger and resentment.

Victims may also learn about the criminal justice system and how it works—the roles of police, prosecutors, and judges. This can be important for victims who feel frustrated or powerless. Restorative justice provides an opportunity for victims to have a more active role and to feel that their voices are being heard.

In addition to gaining understanding, victims receive support and resources to help them cope with the trauma of the crime. This may include counseling, financial assistance, or referrals to other support services. By addressing the needs of the victim, restorative justice promotes healing and can help prevent further victimization.

Understanding, Venting, and Input: The Path to Closure

Why does understanding bring closure and enable victims to move on with their lives? A good formula for closure is understanding plus venting plus input equals closure. It is imperative that the victim has a part in the justice process.

Victims of crime often experience feelings of anger, fear, and helplessness. These emotions can linger long after the crime has occurred and can have a significant impact on the victim's ability to move forward. Achieving closure requires addressing these emotions and regaining a sense of control.

Understanding is one of the most important aspects of achieving closure. Victims need to understand what happened and why. They need answers to their questions. Why was I targeted? What was the offender thinking? Could I have done anything differently? These questions can haunt victims for years if left unanswered.

In the restorative justice process, victims have the opportunity to gain this understanding. They learn about the offender's motivations and the circumstances surrounding the crime. This understanding helps victims make sense of their experience and integrate it into their life story. It can help them see that the crime was not their fault and that they are not alone.

Venting is another essential component. Victims need the opportunity to express their emotions—to vent their anger, their fear, their sadness. This venting can take place in therapy, in support groups, or in the restorative justice process itself. By venting their emotions, victims release pent-up feelings and experience a sense of relief and catharsis. They are able to process their trauma rather than suppressing it.

Input is the third component. Victims need to have a part in the justice process. They need to have a say in how the harm caused by the crime is addressed and what steps should be taken to prevent further victimization. This input can be provided through a victim impact statement, through participation in a restorative conference, or through advocacy efforts.

By having a part in the process, victims regain a sense of control over their lives. They are no longer passive recipients of whatever the system delivers. They are active participants in their own healing. This sense of agency is essential for moving forward.

Understanding, venting, and input together create the conditions for closure. Victims who have these opportunities are better able to heal and to move on with their lives. They are less likely to be stuck in a state of fear, anger, or resentment. They are more likely to find peace.

Teaching Offenders the Human Impact of Their Actions

In restorative justice, offenders are taught the real human impact of their criminal behavior and how to make restitution to victims. Making amends may include restitution for any financial loss caused by the offender, but it goes beyond that. It includes acknowledging the emotional and psychological harm as well.

Traditionally, the criminal justice system has focused on punishment as a means of holding offenders accountable. The assumption is that suffering somehow balances the scales, that the offender has "paid their debt" to society. But what debt has actually been paid? The victim has not been compensated. The community has not been restored. The offender has not been changed.

Restorative justice takes a different approach. It seeks to promote accountability through a process of repairing harm and restoring relationships. Through this process, offenders are given the opportunity to understand the real human impact of their criminal behavior.

This often involves meeting with the victim and hearing firsthand about the harm that was caused. This can be a powerful experience. It allows the offender to see the victim as a real person with feelings and emotions, rather than as a faceless entity. It breaks down the psychological barriers that allow offenders to minimize or justify their actions.

In addition to understanding the impact of their actions, offenders are taught how to make restitution. This may involve financial compensation for losses, but it may also involve community service, direct service to the victim, or other forms of repair. By making restitution, offenders take concrete steps to repair the harm and demonstrate their commitment to making things right.

Restorative justice also emphasizes the importance of reintegrating offenders back into the community. Rather than simply punishing offenders and sending them to prison, restorative justice seeks to help them become responsible members of society. This may involve education, job training, counseling, or other forms of support.

The goal is not just to hold offenders accountable but to transform them. By teaching them the human impact of their actions and providing opportunities for restitution, restorative justice offers a more meaningful and effective form of accountability than traditional punishment-based approaches.

The Community's Crucial Role

Within the restorative justice paradigm, the community plays a very crucial role by putting victims and offenders in active and interpersonal problem-solving roles. This is based on the recognition that crime is not just a violation of the law but also a violation of relationships and communities.

One of the main goals of restorative justice is to repair the harm caused by the crime and to restore relationships between victim, offender, and community. This can only be achieved through the active participation of all parties. By involving the community, victims and offenders are able to see the impact of their actions on a larger scale and to understand their roles within the community.

Through the restorative justice process, victims and offenders work together to identify the harm that was caused and to develop a plan for repairing it. The community provides a safe and supportive environment for this work. Community members may act as mediators or facilitators, or they may provide resources and support for the victim and offender.

By involving the community, victims and offenders also see the impact of their actions on the wider community. This can be a powerful motivator for change. Offenders come to understand that their actions have consequences beyond the immediate victim. They see that they have damaged the trust and cohesion of the community as a whole.

The community's role is not passive. It is active and engaged. Community members are not just observers; they are participants. They have a stake in the outcome and a responsibility to help make things right.

Specific Roles of the Community

The community plays several specific roles in a restorative justice paradigm. Let me name them.

First, **supporting crime victims**. The community can provide support and resources to help victims heal from the harm caused by the crime. This may include counseling services, financial assistance, and emotional support. When victims know that their community stands with them, they are better able to cope with their trauma.

Second, **setting standards of conduct**. The community can establish clear expectations for behavior and hold individuals accountable for their actions. This helps to prevent future crime by promoting a culture of respect and responsibility. When community norms are clear and consistently reinforced, individuals are more likely to internalize them.

Third, **providing opportunities for the offender to make amends**. The community can create opportunities for offenders to take responsibility for their actions and make amends to the victim and community. This may involve community service, restitution, or other forms of restorative justice. When offenders are given the chance to make things right, they are more likely to take that opportunity seriously.

Fourth, **establishing community harmony**. By promoting a sense of community and belonging, the community can help to reduce crime and create a more harmonious and peaceful society. This can be achieved through community-building activities, restorative justice programs, and other initiatives that bring people together.

Overall, the community plays a crucial role by providing support and resources to victims, holding individuals accountable, providing opportunities for offenders to make amends, and promoting community harmony. By working together to promote healing and repair harm, the community helps to create a safer, more just, and more cohesive society.

The Role of Elected Officials

Elected officials have an important role to play in serving the communities that elect them. One way they can do this is by providing assistance, information, and funds for community programs.

Elected officials have the ability to advocate for and allocate resources to support community programs that address issues such as crime prevention, education, job training, and social services. They can work with community leaders and organizations to identify needs and priorities and to develop strategies for addressing them.

Elected officials can also serve as a liaison between the community and government agencies, helping to facilitate communication and access to services. They can provide information and education to community members about government programs and policies, and they can advocate for their constituents' interests at all levels of government.

Through their role as elected officials, they have the ability to influence policy decisions that impact the well-being of their communities. They can work to promote policies that support community safety, economic development, and social justice.

It should be noted, however, that elected officials often serve the "loudest voice" in the community. This means that those who are most vocal and organized are most likely to be heard. Therefore, if we want our elected officials to support restorative justice and community programs, we must band together and make our voices heard. We must organize, advocate, and hold our officials accountable.

Building Familiarity, Bonding, and Trust Through Community Programs

Community programs, and the efforts of organizing them, bring about familiarity, bonding, and trust within the community. This is essential for creating the conditions in which restorative justice can flourish.

In recent years, the media has highlighted many unfortunate incidents between communities and law enforcement. When this is all the media focuses on, it can paint a falsely negative and often unfair picture of law enforcement, leading to a misplaced loss of trust by the public. While rebuilding that trust can be hard, it is not impossible. Community programs across the nation have taken measures to improve relationships between law enforcement and the communities they serve.

Community programs bring together individuals who may not have had the opportunity to interact before. They create opportunities for shared experiences, learning, and growth. When community members come together to work on a shared goal—organizing a neighborhood watch, creating a community garden, planning a block party—they form connections based on common interests and values. This shared purpose creates a sense of camaraderie and trust.

Community programs also provide opportunities for individuals to learn from each other and develop new skills. A neighborhood clean-up day might involve learning about recycling. A community art project might teach new artistic techniques. As individuals learn and grow together, they become more invested in the success of the community and more willing to contribute to its improvement.

Another important benefit is the building of social capital—the networks, norms, and trust that exist within a community. By participating in community programs, individuals build relationships and establish social connections. These connections lead to increased opportunities for civic engagement and greater social and economic mobility.

Community programs also provide a platform for community members to voice their opinions and concerns and to participate in decision-making processes that impact their lives. This sense of empowerment and ownership leads to greater investment in the community and a stronger sense of belonging.

Finally, community programs can promote cultural awareness and understanding. Programs that celebrate different cultural traditions or provide opportunities for cultural exchange help to break down barriers and promote mutual respect and appreciation.

Shared Responsibility for Managing Crime

Should the responsibility for managing crime conditions be assumed by the community? The answer is yes, but not exclusively. Crime management is a shared responsibility that involves a range of actors.

Law enforcement agencies are responsible for enforcing the law and maintaining public safety. They play a critical role in preventing and responding to criminal activity and in holding offenders accountable. Local government has a responsibility to provide resources and support for crime prevention and intervention programs and to develop and implement policies that promote public safety.

Community organizations and individual citizens also have a role to play. Community-based organizations can provide services and programs that address the root causes of crime—poverty, lack of education, substance abuse. They can help build social connections and support networks that promote community safety and well-being.

Individual citizens can contribute by being vigilant and reporting suspicious activity. They can take steps to prevent crime—securing their homes and vehicles, organizing neighborhood watch programs, participating in community cleanup efforts.

Ultimately, crime management is a collaborative effort that requires the involvement of all members of the community. By working together and assuming responsibility for their individual roles, community members can contribute to a safer and more secure environment for all.

The Emotional Impact of Crime on Communities

The effects of crime on the community are evidenced by feelings of anger, anxiety, and fear. Crime has a profound impact, and the effects can be felt long after the crime has been committed.

Anger is a common emotional response, particularly when crime is seen as a violation of community norms and values. Community members may feel angry that someone would commit a crime in their neighborhood or against someone they know. This anger can create frustration and helplessness.

Anxiety is another common response. Community members may feel anxious about their own safety, particularly if the crime was violent or if they believe they or their loved ones could be targeted. This anxiety can create hyper-vigilance, where community members are constantly on guard and may avoid certain areas or activities.

Fear is perhaps the most common response. When a crime is committed, community members may feel a sense of vulnerability and may worry that they or their loved ones could be the next victim. This fear can be particularly intense in communities that have experienced high levels of crime. Fear can create isolation, as community members hesitate to engage with neighbors or participate in community activities.

The range of emotions resulting from crime may include hatred, prejudice, depression, or even the desire for revenge. These emotions can have negative consequences, including reduced quality of life, decreased social cohesion, and increased stress and anxiety.

To address these emotional effects, it is important to provide support and resources for those who have been impacted. This may include counseling services for victims and their families, as well as community-based programs that promote safety and well-being.

How Negative Feelings Alter Community Behavior

The negative feelings resulting from crime have altered community behavior in significant ways. People begin to avoid social activities. They purchase alarm systems. They do not leave their houses at night. They watch their children more closely. Some purchase firearms for protection.

If you have ever driven through a neighborhood that has been violated by crime, you have seen the evidence. Tall fences. Aggressive guard dogs. Burglar bars on windows. Floodlights everywhere. Even the homeowners appear aggressive and unfriendly. The physical environment reflects the psychological state of the community.

These responses are understandable. When people feel threatened, they take measures to protect themselves and their loved ones. But these measures also have costs. They isolate people from each other. They create an atmosphere of suspicion and fear. They undermine the very community bonds that are essential for long-term safety and well-being.

The Tornado Effect

The effect of crime on a community has been illustrated as a tornado funnel having a type of "whirlwind effect." This is a powerful image that captures the far-reaching impact of crime.

At the center of the tornado funnel, there is a point of maximum destruction. In the case of crime, this is the victim and their immediate family. The victim suffers physical injuries, financial losses, and emotional trauma. Family members are also deeply impacted as they provide support and care.

As the tornado funnel moves outward, the impact becomes more diffuse. Neighbors and friends of the victim feel fear and anxiety. They worry about their own safety and the safety of their loved ones. Businesses in the area may be impacted as customers stay away.

The "whirlwind effect" also impacts institutions—schools, churches, community organizations. These institutions may see a decline in attendance or participation as community members hesitate to engage in activities that take them out of their homes.

The impact of crime on a community can be far-reaching and long-lasting. It creates fear and anxiety, disrupts social and economic activity, and undermines trust and social cohesion.

The Broad Range of Havoc

A tornado creates a broad range of havoc. At the point where it touches the ground, it causes the most damage—destroying buildings, uprooting trees, overturning vehicles. Beyond the point of ground contact, the winds have a far-reaching effect, causing damage even to structures not directly in the path. The tornado even produces fear and anxiety in areas away from its path.

Crime operates the same way. At the center is the direct victim, suffering the most intense harm. Beyond the center, the effects ripple outward—affecting family, friends, neighbors, and the broader community. The fear and anxiety created by crime are felt even by those who were not directly victimized.

The justice system has traditionally focused solely on the point of contact—the offender and, to a degree, the victim. Its primary goal has been to punish offenders and ensure public safety. Under this approach, the offender is the primary actor, and the victim's role is limited to that of a passive recipient of harm.

But this focus is incomplete. It ignores the broader impact of crime on the community. It fails to recognize that crime damages relationships and undermines social cohesion. It neglects the community's role as both a victim and a potential source of resolution.

The Community as Ignored Victim and Source of Resolution

The community has been widely ignored as both a key victim and a source of resolution for several reasons.

First, the criminal justice system has traditionally viewed crime as a problem between an individual offender and victim, with little consideration given to the broader community impact. This narrow focus has led to a neglect of the community's role.

Second, the system has often failed to engage with communities in meaningful ways. This has undermined trust and reduced the community's willingness to participate in justice processes.

Communities perceive that the system is not interested in their concerns, reinforcing their marginalization.

Third, there has been a lack of resources and support for community-based solutions. Communities have been left to deal with the impact of crime on their own, limiting their ability to develop effective responses.

Fourth, there has been a tendency to view crime as an individual problem rather than a social problem. This leads to a focus on punishing individual offenders rather than addressing underlying social and economic factors.

To effectively address crime and its impact, we must adopt a more holistic approach that recognizes the central role of communities in preventing crime and promoting safety.

What Restorative Justice Brings

Restorative justice has the potential to bring resolution, healing, and reconciliation to the problem of crime within the community.

First, it provides a framework for resolving conflicts that is more responsive to the needs and concerns of victims and communities. Rather than focusing primarily on punishing offenders, it seeks to repair harm and restore relationships. This leads to a greater sense of resolution for victims.

Second, it promotes healing by providing victims with the opportunity to share their experiences in a safe and supportive environment. This helps victims process their trauma and move forward. Victims receive acknowledgment and validation for their experiences.

Third, it promotes reconciliation by fostering a sense of community and shared responsibility for preventing and responding to crime. By engaging offenders and encouraging them to take responsibility, restorative justice creates accountability and a commitment to making amends.

The typical outcomes of restorative justice include victim-offender conferencing and mediation, victim assistance, restitution, service by offenders to victims, community service by offenders, and assistance to offenders.

By providing a more responsive and inclusive framework for addressing crime, restorative justice helps to repair harm and restore relationships. This leads to greater safety, trust, and social cohesion, which helps to prevent future crime and promote the well-being of the community as a whole.

CHAPTER 05

PROMISING PRACTICES OF RESTORATIVE JUSTICE

We have journeyed a long way together in this book. We have examined the traditional view of justice and found it wanting—costly, ineffective, and damaging to victims, offenders, and communities alike. We have explored why the system must be restructured, seeing how it isolates the public, steals conflicts from those to whom they belong, and leaves everyone frustrated and unsatisfied. We have considered a different view of justice, one that focuses on repairing harm rather than inflicting punishment, on restoring relationships rather than breaking them, on healing rather than hurting.

In the previous chapter, we examined the conceptual frameworks that undergird restorative justice—the ideas, theories, and models that give it shape and substance. We saw how thinkers like Nils Christie have helped us understand crime as a catalyst for community empowerment, and how various conceptual models provide frameworks for community-based practice.

Now we turn to something practical. We turn to the promising practices that have emerged as communities around the world have embraced the principles of restorative justice. These practices are not abstract theories. They are real programs, real processes, real interventions that are being used every day to address harm, heal relationships, and restore communities. They represent the best of what restorative justice has to offer—concrete ways of putting principles into practice.

In this chapter, we will explore these practices in depth. We will look at sentencing circles, victim impact statements, community reparation boards, community service, restitution, victim-offender mediation, family group conferencing, victim impact panels, victim impact classes, and a range of community-based initiatives that connect the justice system with the public. We will see how each of these practices works, what goals they serve, and what makes them effective. And we will consider how they can be implemented in ways that honor the principles of restorative justice and serve the needs of victims, offenders, and communities.

Restoring Harmony Through Community Involvement

Let us begin with a fundamental question: why do community-based and restorative-minded practices seek to restore harmony at the community level by directly involving the public in the justice process?

The answer lies in the nature of crime itself. Crime is not simply an act against an individual. It is an act against relationships, against community, against the social fabric that holds us together. When a crime occurs, the harm radiates outward from the victim to affect family members, neighbors, and the broader community. Trust is damaged. Fear increases. Social cohesion is undermined.

If crime affects the community, then the response to crime must involve the community. This is the insight at the heart of restorative justice. Traditional justice systems treat crime as a matter between the state and the offender, with the community relegated to the sidelines. Restorative justice recognizes that this exclusion is itself a form of harm. It deprives the community of the opportunity to address the harm, to support those affected, and to take responsibility for preventing future crime.

By involving the public in the justice process, community-based and restorative-minded practices seek to restore harmony. They bring together victims, offenders, and community members to discuss what happened, to understand the harm that was caused, and to work together to make things right. This process does not just address the immediate harm; it strengthens the community's capacity to prevent future harm. It builds relationships, fosters understanding, and creates a sense of shared responsibility.

Restorative justice is a prime example of this approach. It brings together the victim, the offender, and members of the community affected by the crime to discuss the harm caused and how to make amends. The goal is not punishment but repair—repairing harm, restoring relationships, and rebuilding trust. This approach is rooted in indigenous justice practices that have understood for millennia the importance of community involvement in resolving conflicts.

Research has shown that restorative justice is effective. It reduces recidivism rates. It increases victim satisfaction with the justice system. It provides a more inclusive and transparent approach to justice, involving all stakeholders in the process. Victims have a voice and a say in how the harm is addressed. Offenders take responsibility for their actions and make amends.

Community justice is another example. This approach involves the community in the decision-making process of the justice system. It recognizes that crime and harm are not just individual issues but community issues that require community solutions. Community justice programs take many forms—community courts, community policing, community mediation. Community courts involve community members in sentencing and rehabilitation. Community policing involves officers working closely with residents to address crime collaboratively. Community mediation involves community members acting as mediators to resolve conflicts peacefully.

These approaches have been shown to reduce crime and increase community engagement with the justice system. By involving the community, they increase trust and promote a sense of ownership over community safety.

In conclusion, community-based and restorative-minded practices seek to restore harmony by involving the public in the justice process. They recognize that crime affects the wider community and requires community solutions. By involving the public, they repair harm and restore relationships, rather than simply punishing offenders.

Bringing Justice to the Community

The goal of the restorative justice process is to bring the justice system to the community, rather than stripping them of this responsibility. This is a fundamental shift in how we think about justice.

In traditional criminal justice systems, the focus is on punishment and retribution. The needs and perspectives of victims and the community are largely ignored. This approach is alienating. Those directly affected by crime feel disconnected from the process. The wider community feels that justice is something done to them, not something they participate in.

Restorative justice seeks to change this. It involves all stakeholders—victim, offender, and community—in the process. This allows for a more inclusive and transparent justice process that is better able to address the needs of all involved.

Restorative justice recognizes that communities have a stake in the justice process and can play an important role in addressing harm and preventing further harm. Community members have a unique understanding of the social and cultural context in which the harm occurred. They can provide valuable insights into the needs and concerns of all involved. By involving the community, the justice system is able to draw on this knowledge and expertise to develop solutions tailored to the specific needs of the community.

Moreover, by bringing the justice system to the community, restorative justice promotes a sense of ownership and accountability among community members. When community members are involved in the justice process, they are more likely to feel invested in the outcomes and to take an active role in preventing future harm. This helps to create a more cohesive and resilient community, better able to address the underlying causes of crime and harm.

The goal is not to strip the community of responsibility but to restore it. In traditional systems, responsibility has been taken away from communities and given to professionals. Restorative justice seeks to give it back.

Features of a Community-Based and Restorative Approach

A community-based and restorative approach to justice involves several key features. Let me name them.

First, **providing full information to those affected by crime**. This includes victims, offenders, and the wider community.

Everyone who has a stake in the outcome has a right to know what is happening, why, and what options are available.

Second, **giving full access to decision-making processes**. All stakeholders are allowed to participate in the development of solutions. Their voices are heard. Their perspectives are considered.

Third, **using processes that are comfortable and understandable to those involved**. This might include dialogue, mediation, or circles—processes that feel natural and accessible, not foreign and intimidating.

Fourth, **being consensual in nature**. When necessary, all parties agree to the terms of the restorative process. No one is coerced. No one is forced to participate against their will.

Fifth, **bringing together the community and the justice system** to work collaboratively in addressing harm and preventing further harm. This is not a competition but a partnership.

Sixth, **using the justice system to bring healing to the community**, rather than just punishing offenders. Healing becomes the goal, not an afterthought.

Seventh, **being empowering in nature**. All stakeholders have a voice and play an active role in the justice process. They are not passive recipients but active participants.

Thus, a community-based and restorative approach prioritizes repairing harm, restoring relationships, and promoting community involvement and empowerment. It is not just about punishing offenders but about making things right for everyone.

Bridges Connecting System and Community

The promising practices of restorative justice serve as bridges to connect the system and community objectives in such a way that they blend into one indistinguishable outcome—a better justice system.

Restorative justice focuses on repairing harm caused by crime or conflict and restoring relationships between individuals and the community. Unlike the traditional punitive system, it seeks to involve all parties affected by a crime or conflict in a collaborative process to address the harm and find ways to prevent it from happening again.

These practices serve as bridges in several ways.

First, they create a space for dialogue and collaboration between the justice system and the community. Restorative justice recognizes that the community is an important stakeholder, and its involvement leads to more effective and sustainable outcomes.

Second, they empower community members to participate in the justice process. Restorative justice programs often involve community members as mediators, facilitators, and members of decision-making panels. This involvement gives community members a voice and helps build trust and understanding between the justice system and the community.

Third, they address the root causes of crime and conflict. Restorative justice recognizes that crime and conflict are often the result of underlying issues—poverty, trauma, social inequality. By addressing these issues, restorative justice helps prevent crime and conflict from happening in the first place.

Fourth, they promote accountability and responsibility among offenders. By involving offenders in the process of repairing harm, restorative justice gives them a sense of ownership and responsibility for their behavior. This helps prevent future offending and promotes positive behavior change.

In summary, the promising practices of restorative justice serve as bridges connecting system and community objectives. By empowering community members, addressing root causes, and promoting accountability, they help create a better justice system—more effective, sustainable, and responsive to community needs.

Many Promising Practices

As communities embrace the principles of restorative justice, many promising practices are being developed. Let me name and describe some of the most important ones.

Sentencing Circles are one of the best-known practices. The Hollow Water First Nations Community Holistic Healing Circle provides a powerful example. Community members used circles to deal with high levels of alcoholism. In the safety of those circles, many began to disclose experiences with sexual abuse. This led to the development of healing circles as a way of dealing with the harm created by offenders, healing victims, and restoring the community.

Victim Impact Statements are written or oral information from crime victims, in their own words, about how a crime has affected them. All fifty states allow victim impact statements at some phase of the sentencing process. Most states permit them at parole hearings, and victim impact information is generally included in the pre-sentencing report presented to the judge.

Community Restorative Boards involve trained community members coming together to resolve conflicts and address harm caused by crime or conflict. The board helps facilitate communication and decision-making between all parties involved.

Community Service requires individuals who have committed a crime to perform unpaid work as a way of repairing harm caused by their actions. This promotes positive behavior change and reduces the likelihood of future offending.

Restitution requires offenders to pay compensation to the victim as a way of repairing the harm caused. This promotes accountability and responsibility.

Victim Offender Mediation brings victim and offender together face-to-face to discuss the harm caused by the offense and work together to find a way to repair it. This process can lead to greater understanding and empathy and can promote healing.

Family Group Conferencing brings together family members and friends to discuss an issue or problem. The aim is to find a solution that works for everyone and to promote healing and understanding.

Victim Impact Panels provide a platform for victims of crime to share their experiences with offenders. The aim is to promote understanding and empathy among offenders and to promote positive behavior change.

Victim Impact Classes are programs designed to help offenders understand the impact of their actions on victims. The aim is to promote empathy and accountability and to encourage positive behavior change.

Beyond these, there are many other promising practices. **Restorative Circles** bring individuals together in a circle to discuss a particular issue or problem, guided by a facilitator, with the aim of building relationships, resolving conflicts, and promoting healing. **Community Reparations** involve the community coming together to address harm caused by a particular issue or problem, working together to find ways to repair the harm, prevent future harm, and promote healing. **Restorative Justice in Schools** uses restorative practices to address disciplinary issues, focusing on repairing harm caused by student behavior, promoting positive behavior change, and building a positive school community.

Each of these practices is designed to promote healing, understanding, and accountability while addressing harm caused by crime or conflict.

Understanding Sentencing Circles

What is a sentencing circle? A sentencing circle is a community-directed process, conducted in partnership with the criminal justice system, to develop an agreement on an appropriate sentencing plan that addresses the concerns of all interested parties.

A sentencing circle brings together the victim, the offender, their families, and other community members to collectively determine an appropriate sentencing plan. The process is conducted in partnership with the criminal justice system, typically with the involvement of a judge or other legal official, but it is community-directed and focused on repairing harm and promoting healing rather than solely on punishment.

The goal is to provide a space for all interested parties to come together to discuss the harm that has been caused by the crime, the needs of the victim, the responsibility of the offender, and the needs of the community. Through dialogue and discussion, the group works to develop an agreement on an appropriate sentencing plan that addresses the concerns of all parties involved.

The process typically involves several stages. First, the group establishes guidelines for the discussion, including a commitment to listening to one another with respect and empathy. Then, the victim and the offender are given the opportunity to share their perspectives on the crime, including how it has impacted them and their families. This is followed by a discussion among all participants about the harm that has been caused and the ways in which the offender can make amends.

The group then works together to develop a sentencing plan that addresses the needs of the victim, the responsibility of the offender, and the needs of the community. This can include a range of restorative measures—community service, restitution, counseling, education. The plan is typically presented to a judge or other legal official, who has the final say in the sentencing but takes into account the recommendations of the group.

The benefits of sentencing circles are numerous. They provide an opportunity for the victim to have a say in the sentencing process and to receive restitution or other forms of amends from the offender. They promote accountability and responsibility among offenders. They can help reduce recidivism rates by addressing the root causes of criminal behavior. And they can help restore trust and build relationships within the community, as the group works together to develop a plan that addresses the needs of all parties.

It should be noted that a sentencing circle is NOT a "lynch mob." It is a group of individuals truly concerned about developing appropriate steps to promote the healing of all affected parties and to prevent future crimes.

Who Participates in Sentencing Circles

Sentencing circles are structured to involve the victim, the offender, police, prosecutor, defense counsel, judge, and all interested community members.

No one in the sentencing circle is a spectator. All are active participants in the justice process, with equal opportunity to offer input. The process is facilitated by a trained facilitator and conducted in partnership with the criminal justice system. The goal is to promote healing, accountability, and repair of the harm caused by the crime, while ensuring that the needs and concerns of all parties are addressed.

What a Successful Sentencing Circle Encourages

A successful sentencing circle encourages participants to resolve conflicts, share responsibility for outcomes, develop constructive relationships, enhance respect and understanding, and discover innovative solutions.

By involving all parties in the process, sentencing circles provide an opportunity for the offender to take responsibility for their actions, make amends to the victim and community, and receive support to address underlying issues that may have contributed to their behavior. Victims have the opportunity to share their experiences and have their needs and concerns addressed.

Through this process, participants can build understanding, empathy, and trust, leading to positive relationships and the potential for long-term healing and transformation. By engaging in a collaborative and community-directed process, participants can also develop innovative and effective solutions that may not have been possible through traditional justice processes.

The Multi-Step Procedure of Sentencing Circles

Typically, a sentencing circle involves a multi-step procedure.

First, there is **the participation of the offender in the circle process**. The offender is given the opportunity to take responsibility for their actions and address the harm they caused. They are also encouraged to identify and address any underlying issues that may have contributed to their behavior.

Second, there is **a healing circle for the victim**. The victim is given the opportunity to share their experiences and have their needs and concerns addressed. This can help them to heal and move forward.

Third, there is **a healing circle for the offender**. The offender is given the opportunity to receive support and guidance to address any underlying issues that may have contributed to their behavior.

Fourth, there is **a sentencing circle to develop an agreement** on the elements of a sentencing plan. The circle process is used to develop an appropriate sentencing plan that addresses the needs and concerns of all parties involved. This can include elements such as restitution, community service, or other forms of accountability.

Fifth, there are **follow-up circles to monitor the offender**. The circle process may include follow-up circles to monitor the offender's progress and ensure that they are fulfilling the terms of their sentencing plan. This helps to ensure that the offender continues to take responsibility for their actions and work to repair the harm caused.

The Role of Community Justice Committees

A community justice committee provides direction and leadership, deciding which cases to accept and establishing circles and support groups for the victim and offender.

A community justice committee is a group of community members who come together to support and address the needs of individuals impacted by the criminal justice system. The committee provides direction and leadership by deciding which cases to accept, establishing circles and support groups for the victim and offender, and coordinating with the justice system.

Why is a community justice committee important?

First, it provides an opportunity for community members to take an active role in the justice system. By serving on a committee, community members can provide their perspectives and insights into the needs of the community and individuals impacted by the justice system. This helps to ensure that justice is delivered in a way that is responsive to community needs, rather than being imposed from outside.

Second, it helps build trust and relationships between the justice system and the community. By involving community members in the justice process, the committee increases transparency and accountability, demonstrating that the justice system is responsive to community needs. This reduces tension and conflict and fosters greater cooperation and understanding.

Third, it helps address underlying issues that may contribute to criminal behavior. By establishing circles and support groups for the victim and offender, the committee promotes healing, accountability, and rehabilitation. It helps offenders address underlying issues and supports them in making positive changes.

Fourth, it helps reduce the burden on the justice system. By diverting cases away from the traditional justice system, the committee reduces the workload of courts and other justice system actors, freeing up resources to focus on more serious cases.

A community justice committee is an important tool for promoting justice and healing in the community. It is an important component of a restorative justice approach, which seeks to build safer, healthier communities by addressing the root causes of criminal behavior and promoting healing and reconciliation.

Determining Appropriateness for Sentencing Circles

Several key factors determine whether a case is appropriate for a sentencing circle.

First, **the nature of the offense**. Sentencing circles are typically used for non-violent offenses—property crimes, drug offenses—and may not be appropriate for crimes involving violence or sexual assault.

Second, **the willingness of the offender to take responsibility**. The offender must be willing to admit wrongdoing and take responsibility for their actions. If the offender denies the offense or shows no remorse, a sentencing circle may not be appropriate.

Third, **the victim's willingness to participate**. The victim must be willing to participate in the process and engage in dialogue with the offender.

Fourth, **the level of community support**. The community must be willing to participate in the process and support the restorative justice approach. This includes the involvement of community members in the circle and their commitment to monitor the offender's progress and support their rehabilitation.

Fifth, **the availability of resources**. A successful sentencing circle requires significant resources—trained facilitators, support services for the victim and offender, follow-up support for the offender. If these resources are not available, a sentencing circle may not be appropriate.

The success of a sentencing circle depends on the willingness of all parties to participate and work toward a restorative outcome. The community justice committee plays a key role in determining whether a case is appropriate and providing the necessary support and resources.

The Importance of Justice System Participation

Representatives of the justice system must participate in circles to ensure fair treatment of both victims and offenders.

The presence of justice system representatives—police officers, prosecutors, defense attorneys, judges—helps ensure that the process is conducted in a fair and impartial manner. These representatives help ensure that the offender's rights are protected and that the victim's needs and concerns are addressed. The involvement of the justice system also helps ensure that the outcome of the circle is in compliance with the law.

The participation of justice system representatives also helps build trust between the community and the justice system. By involving representatives in the circle, it helps bridge the gap between the justice system and the community, promoting a greater sense of trust and understanding.

Additionally, the involvement of justice system representatives helps educate the community on the legal process and the role of the justice system. By participating in the circle, they can help explain legal concepts to community members who may not be familiar with the legal system, promoting greater understanding and acceptance.

However, it is important that justice system representatives participate in a way that is supportive of the restorative justice approach. They must be willing to embrace the principles of restorative justice—the focus on repairing harm, the involvement of all parties. If they approach the circle with a punitive mindset, it can undermine the effectiveness of the restorative justice approach.

Goals of the Sentencing Circle

The goals of the sentencing circle are multiple.

First, **encouraging dialogue**. The circle process is designed to encourage open dialogue between the victim, offender, and community members. The goal is to create a safe space where all parties can share their perspectives and concerns and work together to find a resolution acceptable to everyone.

Second, **developing a fair and just sentencing plan**. The circle process is intended to create a sentencing plan that addresses the harm caused by the offense and takes into account the needs of the victim, the offender, and the community. The goal is to create a plan that is fair and just for all parties.

Third, **promoting healing and restoration**. Sentencing circles are designed to promote healing and restoration for all parties. The circle process can help the victim feel heard and understood, and can help the offender take responsibility and make amends. The goal is to help everyone move forward in a positive way.

Fourth, **reducing recidivism**. By focusing on the underlying causes of the offense and addressing the harm caused, the circle process can help reduce the likelihood of the offender reoffending. The goal is to create a plan that promotes accountability and helps the offender make positive changes.

Fifth, **building community relationships**. Sentencing circles are designed to promote community involvement and engagement in the justice system. By involving community members in the circle process, it helps build stronger relationships between the community and the justice system.

The goal is to create a more collaborative and effective justice system that works for everyone.

The Victim Impact Statement

Through a Victim Impact Statement, the victim offers a description of the crime and how it affected their life and the lives of their loved ones.

A Victim Impact Statement is a written or oral statement prepared by a victim of a crime, or their family members, describing the impact the crime has had on their lives. It is an opportunity for victims to share their experiences with the court and provide information that may be considered during the sentencing process.

The VIS is an important tool in the criminal justice system because it provides a voice for victims who may otherwise feel unheard. It allows them to express their feelings, thoughts, and concerns about the impact of the crime on their lives. The VIS also helps the court understand the emotional and physical harm caused by the offense, which can be used to determine an appropriate sentence.

The VIS typically includes a description of the crime, the physical and emotional impact on the victim and their loved ones, and a statement about the victim's opinions and recommendations regarding the sentence. The victim may also describe any financial losses—medical expenses, lost income—that resulted from the crime.

The VIS can be given in either written or oral form. In some jurisdictions, victims may read their statement aloud in court; in others, the statement may be read by a victim advocate or the prosecutor. Regardless of the form, the VIS is a powerful tool that can have a significant impact on the sentencing process.

The VIS serves several important purposes. First, it helps ensure that victims are heard and their experiences are taken into account during sentencing. This can provide victims with a sense of closure and validation, helping them feel more empowered in the aftermath of crime.

Second, the VIS can help humanize the victim in the eyes of the court and the defendant. It can help the defendant understand the harm they have caused and the impact of their actions on others. This can promote empathy and accountability, reducing the likelihood of recidivism.

Third, the VIS can help promote transparency and accountability in the criminal justice system. By providing victims with an opportunity to share their experiences, it helps build trust between victims and the justice system and promotes greater public understanding of the impact of crime.

When the VIS Provides Vital Information

The victim impact statement provides authorities with vital information during several stages of the criminal justice process.

During the **pre-sentencing investigation phase**, the VIS is used by the probation officer or other officials to prepare a pre-sentencing report for the judge. The VIS helps inform the judge about the impact of the crime on the victim—emotional, physical, and financial harm. This information can influence the judge's decision on the appropriate sentence, taking into account the harm caused to the victim and the community.

During the **sentencing phase**, the VIS is often read aloud in court, allowing the victim to share their story directly with the judge and the offender. This can have a powerful impact on both, as they hear firsthand the effects of the crime on the victim and their loved ones.

The VIS can also be used as part of **pre-parole investigations**, conducted before an offender's release from prison to determine suitability for release and to establish conditions of parole. The VIS can inform the parole board about the ongoing impact of the crime on the victim and their need for protection and support. It can also inform the board about the offender's level of remorse and rehabilitation efforts.

Finally, the VIS can be used in **parole revocation hearings**, held when an offender violates the conditions of their parole. The VIS can inform the parole board about the ongoing impact of the crime on the victim and their continued need for protection and support, as well as the offender's lack of compliance.

In all these stages, the VIS plays an important role in ensuring that the voice of the victim is heard and taken into account. It provides a platform for victims to share their experiences and the impact of the crime on their lives, helping to ensure that the criminal justice system considers the harm caused to victims and their ongoing needs for support and protection.

How Victim Impact Panels Can Help

Victim impact panels are restorative justice programs that provide a platform for victims of crimes to share their experiences and the impact the crimes have had on their lives. These panels are usually held for a group of offenders who have committed similar crimes—drunk driving, drug offenses—and are required to attend as part of their sentence or rehabilitation program. The panels typically consist of several victims or family members who speak to the offenders about how the crimes affected them personally, emotionally, and financially.

Victim impact panels can be helpful in several ways.

First, they allow victims to express their feelings and experiences in a safe and supportive environment. Many victims, especially those who have suffered from violent crimes or sexual assault, often feel isolated and unable to discuss their experiences. Victim impact panels provide a forum for these individuals to express their emotions and share their stories with others who have experienced similar situations.

Second, they can be a powerful tool for changing offender behavior. By hearing firsthand from victims about the impact of their crimes, offenders can gain a deeper understanding of the harm they have caused and the long-term consequences of their actions. This promotes empathy and accountability, essential components of restorative justice.

Third, they can help promote healing and closure for victims and their families. By providing an opportunity to share their experiences and feelings with others, victims can begin to process their trauma and move forward in their recovery. The panels can also help victims feel empowered by giving them a voice in the criminal justice system and the opportunity to make a positive impact on others.

Fourth, they can be an effective way to educate offenders about the impact of their crimes on the broader community. By hearing from a variety of victims and family members, offenders gain a broader perspective on the harm caused by their actions and the need to take responsibility. This promotes community safety by reducing the likelihood of recidivism and promoting positive behavior change.

Victim Impact Panels were introduced by Mothers Against Drunk Driving in 1982 and have since spread throughout the United States in an attempt to reduce drunk driving. The objective is to expose DUI offenders to the pain and suffering caused by drunk driving without necessarily condemning the offender.

Making Victim Impact Statements Effective

For a victim impact statement to be an effective tool, several things need to be done.

First, **proper notification**. Victims should be informed about their right to make a VIS and the opportunity to present it at the appropriate stage of the criminal justice process. Notification should be timely, and victims should receive assistance in preparing their statements if needed.

Second, **confidentiality and safety**. Victims should be assured that their VIS will be treated with confidentiality and not disclosed to the public or media. They should be provided with adequate protection and support during the process, especially if they fear retaliation or intimidation.

Third, **clarity and accuracy**. The VIS should be written in a clear and concise manner, using simple language that is easy to understand. The victim should describe the impact of the crime on their life and the lives of their loved ones in a factual and objective way, avoiding emotional or inflammatory language. The statement should be based on accurate and verifiable information, supported by evidence or documentation if possible.

Fourth, **focus on impact**. The VIS should focus on the harm caused by the crime rather than on the offender's character or motives. The victim should describe how the crime has affected their physical, emotional, and financial well-being, as well as their sense of security, trust, and dignity. They should also address the impact on their relationships, work, and community involvement.

Fifth, **respectful and constructive tone**. The VIS should be written in a respectful and constructive tone, acknowledging the offender's right to a fair trial and due process while expressing the victim's perspective and feelings in a non-confrontational way. The statement should aim to educate and sensitize the court or parole board about the human cost of crime and the need for accountability, restitution, and rehabilitation.

Sixth, **follow-up and feedback**. Victims should be informed about the outcome of the case and the use of their VIS in the decision-making process. They should also be offered the opportunity to provide feedback on their experience of making a VIS and the support they received. This feedback can be used to improve victim services and enhance the effectiveness of restorative justice practices.

Additionally, probation officials must diligently seek to locate victims and document VIS information as part of pre-sentencing investigations. Correction officials need to maintain records of the VIS for review by parole authorities and notify victims of their right to VIS input at parole hearings. Parole boards should encourage the use of VIS by victims for parole hearings and revocation proceedings.

Increased Satisfaction Through VIS

The use of the victim's VIS in the justice process reportedly has increased their satisfaction with the entire criminal justice system. Not only does the victim's VIS increase satisfaction, it also promotes healing in the aftermath of crime.

One of the primary benefits of VIS is that they give victims a voice in the criminal justice process. Prior to the widespread use of VIS, victims often felt ignored or powerless in the face of a justice system focused on punishing offenders. By allowing victims to describe the impact of the crime on their lives, VIS validate their experiences and emotions and give them a sense of control over the process.

Research has shown that the use of VIS can have a positive impact on victims' satisfaction with the criminal justice system. Victims who are allowed to provide a VIS are more likely to report feeling that the court process was fair and just, and that their voice was heard. They are also more likely to feel that they received a measure of justice and closure, even if the sentence was not as severe as they had hoped.

In addition to improving victim satisfaction, the use of VIS can also have a positive impact on the sentencing process itself. Judges and other legal professionals are often limited in their understanding of the full impact of a crime on a victim's life. VIS provide a more complete picture of the harm caused by the crime and can help judges make more informed decisions about appropriate sentences.

However, for VIS to be effective, several considerations must be taken into account. Victims must be given the opportunity to provide a statement and must feel safe and supported in doing so. VIS must be taken seriously by judges and other legal professionals, viewed as a vital part of the sentencing process, not just a perfunctory exercise. And VIS must be used in a way that is fair and equitable for all parties, not to inflame passions or encourage harsher sentences than warranted.

When used appropriately, VIS can provide victims with a sense of empowerment and closure and help ensure that justice is served in a way that reflects the true impact of the crime.

Four Factors That Increase Victim Satisfaction

Research suggests that four factors increase the victim's overall satisfaction with the justice system and reduce victim trauma.

First, **participation and involvement**. Victims who are actively involved in the justice process—through victim impact statements or other restorative practices—are more likely to feel that their voices are heard and that they have some control over the outcome. This leads to increased satisfaction and reduced trauma.

Second, **empathy and understanding**. When victims feel that justice system professionals—judges, prosecutors, police officers—are empathetic and understanding, they are more likely to feel supported and less traumatized. This can be achieved through training for justice professionals and by ensuring that victims are treated with respect and dignity throughout the process.

Third, **timeliness**. Victims who experience a timely resolution to their case are more likely to feel satisfied and less traumatized. Delays in the justice process can cause additional stress and trauma, particularly if victims are required to attend multiple court hearings or if the case drags on for months or years.

Fourth, **communication and information**. Victims who are kept informed about the progress of their case and the decisions made by justice professionals are more likely to feel satisfied and less traumatized. This can be achieved through regular updates, clear communication, and providing victims with information about their rights and options.

These factors highlight the importance of a victim-centered approach to the justice system, one that prioritizes the needs and experiences of victims to promote their healing and well-being. When victims are treated with respect and empathy and given opportunities to participate, they are more likely to feel satisfied with the outcome and less traumatized by the experience.

The Two Main Goals of VIS

The two main goals of a victim impact statement are clear.

First, to provide the victim with an opportunity to describe the impact of the crime on their lives and the lives of their loved ones, in their own words. This allows the victim to have a voice in the justice process and to express their emotions, feelings, and concerns about the crime.

Second, to provide the court with information about the harm caused by the crime, which can be used to determine an appropriate sentence for the offender. The VIS helps the court understand the full extent of the harm caused and to make a more informed decision about the sentence.

Community Reparation Boards

A strategy for involving the community in the justice process is the establishment of community reparation boards. While these boards are often used with offenders convicted of non-violent crimes and minor offenses, they can be established to address a wide range of offenses, including serious and violent crimes.

The focus of community reparation boards is to involve the community in the justice process and provide opportunities for offenders to make amends for their actions by completing meaningful acts of reparation. These boards typically consist of community members who work with offenders to identify appropriate acts of reparation that will benefit both the offender and the community. These acts may include community service, restitution, and other forms of restorative justice.

By involving the community in the process, community reparation boards aim to increase public trust in the justice system and provide a more balanced and restorative approach to justice. They can also help address underlying issues that may have contributed to the offender's behavior—substance abuse, mental health issues—by providing a more holistic approach to addressing crime and helping offenders reintegrate into society.

The Function of a Community Reparation Board

A community reparation board is a restorative justice approach that involves community members in the rehabilitation of an offender. The board is made up of volunteers from the local community who work with the offender to develop a plan of action to make amends for their actions.

The function of a community reparation board is to provide a forum for the offender to take responsibility for their actions and make amends for the harm they have caused to the community. The board works with the offender to develop a reparation plan designed to repair the harm caused by the offender's actions.

The reparation plan can include a variety of activities—community service, financial restitution, education and training programs. The board monitors the offender's progress in carrying out their reparation plan and provides support and guidance as needed.

The community reparation board provides an opportunity for the offender to engage with the community and make meaningful contributions. It also helps build trust and understanding between the offender and the community.

The board serves as an alternative to traditional forms of punishment such as incarceration, which can be costly and often do not address the root causes of the offender's behavior. By involving the community in the rehabilitation process, the community reparation board can provide a more effective and sustainable solution.

The process typically involves one-on-one meetings with offenders sentenced by the court to participate. Board members and the offender discuss the nature of the crime, its impact on the victim and community, and its consequences. The board members then develop a set of proposed sanctions which are presented to the offender.

A community restoration board may also address the root causes of the crime and offer instruction or education on the matter. For instance, a drug dealer may not recognize that they have a lazy spirit and that the responsible thing is to get a job.

Factors for Successful Community-Driven Reparation Boards

Several factors have been determined as important elements of implementing a successful community-driven reparation board program.

First, **cooperation of the criminal justice system**. For a community reparation board program to be effective, there needs to be cooperation and coordination with the criminal justice system—law enforcement, prosecutors, judges. This ensures that the program operates within the legal framework and that offenders are held accountable.

Second, **well-trained staff that is committed**. Staff trained in restorative justice principles and practices, as well as in the specific procedures of the reparation board program, are essential. Staff members must be committed to the goals of the program and able to work effectively with both offenders and community members.

Third, **working with victim organizations** and ensuring that victims are represented and provided adequate opportunity to participate. Victims must have a voice in the reparation board process, and their input must be taken into account when developing agreements. Victim organizations can help ensure that victims are informed about the program and have access to support services.

Fourth, **processing cases expeditiously** and in a manner that is simple for community members to understand. Cases must be processed in a timely manner, and the procedures must be clear and easy to understand for all participants. This ensures that the program operates efficiently and that community members feel their time and efforts are valued.

Fifth, **facilitating a positive experience for board members**. Board members must have a positive experience in the reparation board process so that they will be willing to participate in future cases. This includes providing training and support and ensuring that their contributions are recognized and appreciated.

Sixth, **supporting the program with adequate resources**. Adequate resources—funding, staff, facilities—are essential for success. Without sufficient resources, the program may not be able to operate effectively or serve all cases referred to it.

Seventh, **striving for success and healing** for victims, community, and offender participants. The ultimate goal is to achieve success and healing for all participants. This requires a commitment to restorative justice principles and a willingness to work collaboratively toward a shared goal.

Promise of Community Reparation Boards

Experiential and anecdotal information show much promise for community reparation boards as an effective response to non-violent crime. These boards are an innovative way to involve the community in the criminal justice process and offer an alternative to traditional forms of punishment.

One key advantage is that they allow community members to be actively involved in the resolution of crime. This participation leads to greater community ownership of the justice process and a deeper sense of responsibility for addressing crime.

Additionally, community reparation boards can help restore trust between offenders and their community, creating a greater sense of accountability.

Furthermore, community reparation boards can offer a more effective and efficient way of resolving non-violent crimes. By involving community members in the resolution, they reduce the burden on the criminal justice system and save valuable resources. This alternative approach can also help reduce the likelihood of recidivism and prevent the escalation of minor offenses to more serious crimes.

Community reparation boards can provide a safe and supportive environment for victims to be heard and have their needs met. This approach helps restore the harm caused by the offender, promotes healing, and helps the victim move forward. Additionally, they provide an opportunity for offenders to take responsibility for their actions and make amends directly to those they have harmed.

However, implementation requires careful consideration and attention to detail. It is essential to ensure that community members participating in the board have adequate training and support. It is also important to establish clear guidelines and procedures for handling cases to ensure fairness and consistency.

While this approach requires significant effort and resources to implement, the potential benefits for victims, offenders, and communities make it a valuable alternative to traditional forms of punishment.

Goals of Community Restorative Boards

Community restorative boards aim to accomplish several goals.

First, **promote citizen ownership of the criminal justice system** by involving them directly in the justice process. When citizens participate, they develop a sense of investment and responsibility.

Second, **provide opportunities for victims and community members to confront offenders** in a constructive manner about their criminal behavior. This confrontation is not about humiliation but about accountability and understanding.

Third, **provide opportunities for offenders to take personal responsibility** and be held directly accountable for the harm caused to victims and communities. This is accountability in its truest sense—not passive suffering but active repair.

Fourth, **generate meaningful "community-driven" consequences** for criminal behavior that reduce costly reliance on formal criminal justice processing. Community-driven consequences are often more effective and less expensive than traditional sanctions.

Additionally, community restorative boards aim to encourage offender accountability by involving the offender in the process and encouraging them to take responsibility and work toward repairing harm. They empower victims by providing an opportunity to participate in the justice process and have a say in the outcome, as well as providing support and resources for healing. They build community relationships by fostering positive relationships between offender, victim, and community, encouraging community members to work together to find solutions. They reduce recidivism by providing offenders with more meaningful and restorative consequences, reducing the likelihood of reoffending. And they provide a cost-effective alternative to traditional justice systems, often less costly than traditional court proceedings.

The main focus in this intervention measure is the satisfaction of the victim.

Community Service as Restorative Practice

Community service is a restorative practice that offers a way an offender can be held accountable to repair some of the harm caused by their criminal behavior. Community service should NOT be a practice sanctioned to humiliate the offender. The programs should be meaningful and contribute to the community's improvement.

What is community service? Community service is a form of restorative justice that involves an offender performing a set number of hours of unpaid work for the benefit of the community. This work is typically performed as part of a court-ordered sentence or as a condition of probation or parole. The goal is to provide offenders with a way to make amends for their actions and to give back to the community affected by their wrongdoing.

Community service can take many forms—picking up litter, cleaning up parks, volunteering at a local charity, assisting with community events. The type of service is usually determined by the nature of the offense and the needs of the community. The number of hours required is typically based on the severity of the offense and the discretion of the sentencing judge or probation officer.

Community service is often seen as a more rehabilitative form of punishment compared to incarceration or fines. It allows offenders to take responsibility for their actions, make amends, and develop a sense of civic responsibility. Additionally, it can provide offenders with valuable job skills and work experience, which can help them secure future employment and reduce their likelihood of reoffending.

However, community service is not a one-size-fits-all solution and may not be appropriate for all offenders or offenses. It is also important to ensure that community service does not become a form of exploitation or a way to exploit free labor from offenders. Proper oversight and monitoring are necessary to ensure that community service is carried out in a fair and equitable manner and that offenders are given meaningful opportunities to make amends and give back to the community.

Partnership for Successful Community Service

A successful community service program requires a close partnership between justice officials and community members. Justice officials play a critical role in setting up the program, identifying appropriate projects, and monitoring compliance. Community members play a vital role in identifying needs and opportunities for service projects, providing supervision and support for offenders, and evaluating the impact of the program on the community.

Close collaboration between these two groups is necessary to ensure that the program is effective, sustainable, and meets the needs of both the justice system and the community. Effective communication and trust-building between justice officials and community members are essential to overcome any potential barriers or challenges in implementing the program.

Examples of Community Service

Community service can take various forms, including but not limited to:

Cleaning up litter from public areas like parks, beaches, and streets. Planting trees or beautifying public spaces with gardening. Serving food at a soup kitchen or food bank. Helping out at a homeless shelter. Assisting with the care of animals at an animal shelter. Assisting at a nursing home or hospital. Tutoring or mentoring children in schools or after-school programs. Assisting with disaster relief efforts. Helping with youth sports programs or other community events. Performing administrative work for non-profit organizations. Assisting with community recycling programs. Providing support at community centers or libraries. Painting or refurbishing community buildings or structures. Assisting with community clean-up efforts after natural disasters. Helping to maintain community gardens or urban farming projects.

These are just some examples. Community service opportunities can vary widely depending on the needs of the community and the interests and skills of the offender.

Community service programs began in the United States with female traffic offenders in Alameda County, California, in 1966, and local initiatives followed in several counties throughout the United States. In the United Kingdom, Parliament enacted legislation in the early 1970s giving courts specific powers to order community service as a sentencing sanction, not just a condition of probation.

Goals of Community Service

The goals of community service are multiple.

First, **hold offenders accountable** for the harm they have caused to victims and the community. Accountability means taking responsibility and making amends.

Second, **provide communities with human resources** that can improve the quality of life in public environments. Community service benefits the community directly.

Third, **help offenders develop new skills** through supervised work activities. This promotes rehabilitation and employability.

Fourth, **allow victims a voice** in the type of community service performed. Victims can have input into what would constitute meaningful reparation.

In addition, community service provides restitution to the community, offering a way for offenders to give back to the community they have harmed. It encourages responsibility, helping offenders take responsibility for their actions and make amends. It promotes personal growth and development, providing an opportunity to develop new skills, gain work experience, and build self-confidence. It fosters community involvement, encouraging offenders to become more involved in their community, promoting a sense of belonging and connection. It reduces recidivism by providing a positive outlet for time and energy and helping offenders build positive relationships with community members. And it can help offenders develop better work habits.

Effectiveness of Community Service

Community service is effectively used in all states and at the federal level as a component of criminal sentences involving diversion, probation, and parole. It is a form of punishment that requires offenders to perform unpaid work in their local communities as a way of repaying society for their crimes.

One benefit of community service is that it allows offenders to give back to the community and make amends for their actions. It can also provide a sense of accomplishment and self-worth to those completing the work. Additionally, community service can help offenders build new skills, develop a sense of responsibility and accountability, and gain valuable work experience, which can help them become more employable in the future.

At the state level, community service is often used as an alternative to traditional incarceration, especially for low-level offenders who do not pose a serious threat to public safety. In many cases, community service can be more cost-effective than incarceration and can help reduce overcrowding in prisons and jails.

At the federal level, community service is often used as a component of criminal sentences involving diversion, probation, and parole. Diversion programs are designed to divert nonviolent offenders away from the criminal justice system and into community-based programs that address the root causes of their criminal behavior. Probation and parole programs are designed to provide supervision and support to offenders returning to the community after serving time in prison.

Community service has proven to be an effective form of punishment that benefits both the offender and the community. By requiring offenders to give back to their communities, community service can help reduce recidivism rates and promote public safety. Additionally, it can provide offenders with valuable skills and work experience that can help them successfully reintegrate into society.

Restitution as Restorative Process

Restitution is a restorative process by which offenders are held accountable for the financial losses they have caused the victims of their crime. This process involves the offender making financial payments or providing other forms of compensation to the victim as a way of repairing the harm that was done.

Restitution can be a powerful tool in the criminal justice system. It helps ensure that offenders are held accountable for their actions and that victims receive some form of justice. It can also be an important part of the healing process for victims, providing a sense of closure and helping them recover from financial losses.

One key benefit of restitution is that it allows offenders to take responsibility for their actions and make amends for the harm they have caused. By requiring offenders to pay restitution, it sends a message that their actions have consequences and that they are accountable for the financial losses they have caused.

Restitution can also be beneficial for offenders, providing them with a sense of accomplishment and helping them make positive changes in their lives. By making financial payments and taking steps to repair the harm they have caused, offenders may gain a sense of self-worth and personal responsibility that can help them avoid future criminal behavior.

Additionally, restitution can be an effective alternative to traditional forms of punishment such as incarceration or fines. Restitution can be less costly to the criminal justice system and can also be a more effective way of reducing recidivism rates by addressing the underlying issues that led to the offender's criminal behavior.

Appropriate Restitution Orders

Appropriate restitution orders are based on information gathered through either victim impact statements or pre-sentencing investigations. They should be made after a careful assessment of the victim's losses and the offender's earning capacity.

Restitution orders are an important part of the criminal justice system, requiring offenders to compensate their victims for the financial losses they have caused. To ensure that restitution orders are appropriate and based on accurate information, the criminal justice system relies on either victim impact statements or pre-sentencing investigations.

Victim impact statements provide important information about the harm caused by the crime and the financial losses incurred. This information can be used to determine the appropriate amount of restitution that the offender should be required to pay.

Pre-sentencing investigations, conducted by probation officers, provide judges with detailed information about the offender's background, criminal history, and current circumstances. These reports can also include information about the financial losses incurred by the victim as a result of the crime. Based on this information, judges can make informed decisions about the appropriate amount of restitution.

Both victim impact statements and pre-sentencing investigations are important tools in ensuring that restitution orders are appropriate and based on accurate information. In cases where there may be disputes about the amount of restitution, judges may hold hearings to gather additional information and make a determination.

Restitution as Essential Victim's Right

Restitution is considered to be an essential victim's right, which helps victims reconstruct their lives in the aftermath of a crime. When a crime is committed, victims can suffer significant financial losses—medical expenses, lost wages, property damage. Restitution provides a way for victims to recover these losses and receive compensation for the harm that was caused.

In addition to providing financial compensation, restitution serves an important psychological function for victims. It can help victims feel that they have regained some control over their lives and that justice has been served. It can also help victims feel that they have been heard and that their experiences have been taken seriously.

Furthermore, restitution is often seen as a more just and equitable form of punishment than fines or other financial penalties. Fines are typically paid to the government, while restitution is paid directly to the victim. This helps ensure that the victim is compensated for their losses and that the offender is held accountable for the harm they have caused.

Finally, restitution can be an important tool in reducing recidivism rates. By requiring offenders to take responsibility for their actions and make amends for the harm they have caused, restitution can help prevent future criminal behavior. This can ultimately lead to safer communities and a more effective criminal justice system.

Receiving Restitution

Receiving restitution payment can make a victim feel that the justice system is working on their behalf to ensure that they are justly compensated for their losses. Restitution provides victims with a sense of justice and accountability. When offenders are required to pay restitution, it sends a message that they are being held responsible for the harm they have caused and that the justice system is taking steps to address the victim's financial losses.

Victims who receive restitution payments can also feel a sense of closure and satisfaction, knowing that they have been compensated for the harm they have suffered. This can help ease their financial burdens and allow them to move forward with their lives.

However, not all victims will receive restitution payments. In some cases, offenders may not have the financial means to make restitution, or they may refuse to pay. In these situations, victims may need to seek alternative forms of compensation, such as civil lawsuits or victim compensation programs.

Despite these challenges, restitution remains an important component of the criminal justice system. In its traditional sense, restitution has been defined as a monetary payment by the offender to the victim for the harm reasonably resulting from the offense. Restitution can be either monetary payments or in-kind services to the victim. The main purpose of institutionalized restitution was to prevent retaliatory violence for wrongdoing, providing a more "civilized" means of reparation.

Remedies for Non-Compliance

Remedies for non-compliance to restitution orders may include several options.

Converting restitution orders to civil judgments allows the victim to pursue collection through civil court. Extending sentence periods until restitution is paid means that the offender will remain under supervision until the restitution is fully paid. Forfeiture of assets means that the offender's assets—property, vehicles—can be seized and sold to pay the restitution. Income garnishment orders mean that a portion of the offender's wages can be withheld and applied toward the restitution. Revocation of the offender's driver's license can serve as a deterrent and incentive for the offender to comply. Revocation of probation and parole means that the offender may be returned to prison for violating the terms of their release.

The specific remedies may vary depending on the jurisdiction and the nature of the offense. In some cases, additional penalties or sanctions may be imposed, such as fines or community service. The goal of these remedies is to ensure that the offender is held accountable for their actions and that the victim receives the compensation they are owed.

Goals of Restitution

The goals of restitution are multiple.

Providing financial compensation is the primary goal—reimbursement for expenses related to medical treatment, property damage, lost wages, and other financial losses.

Holding offenders accountable is another goal. By requiring them to pay restitution, they are taking responsibility for the harm they have caused and working to make things right.

Deterrence is a third goal. Knowing that they will be required to pay restitution if they commit a crime can discourage some offenders from engaging in criminal activity.

Restoration is a fourth goal. Restitution can be part of a restorative justice approach, aiming to restore the harm caused by a crime. By compensating victims for their losses, restitution can help restore their sense of security and well-being.

Promoting justice is a fifth goal. Restitution ensures that offenders are held accountable for their actions and that victims are compensated for the harm they have suffered.

Victim Offender Mediation

Victim offender mediation provides interested victims the opportunity to meet their offender in a safe, structured, and supervised setting to engage in meaningful mediated discussion of the crime. This type of mediation is a form of restorative justice based on the principles of healing, reconciliation, and accountability.

The goal of victim offender mediation is to provide victims with a voice in the justice system and to promote healing and closure for both the victim and the offender. Through mediated discussions, victims are able to express how the crime has impacted their lives and to ask questions of the offender. Offenders are also given the opportunity to take responsibility for their actions and to make amends for the harm they have caused.

The mediation process is structured and supervised to ensure the safety and well-being of all participants. Mediators are trained professionals who facilitate the discussion and ensure that both parties have an opportunity to be heard. The process is voluntary, and both the victim and the offender must agree to participate.

Research has shown that victim offender mediation can have positive outcomes for both victims and offenders. Victims who participate in mediation may experience a sense of empowerment, healing, and closure. Offenders may gain a greater understanding of the harm they have caused and may be more likely to take responsibility for their actions and make amends.

Victim offender mediation is a valuable tool in the criminal justice system that can help promote healing, reconciliation, and accountability. This program should not be court ordered but voluntary for both the victim and offender. The success of this service will largely depend on the willingness of the victim and offender to settle the issues resulting from the crime.

Referral System for Victim Offender Mediation

The victim offender mediation program typically operates on a referral system, meaning that the program is not open to all victims and offenders but only those who are referred by a judge, prosecutor, or other criminal justice official.

The referral process typically involves several steps. First, identification: Criminal justice officials identify cases that may be appropriate for victim offender mediation. This may include cases in which the offender has admitted guilt, the victim is interested in participating, and there is no history of violence or abuse. Second, assessment: The victim and offender are assessed to determine their suitability for mediation. This may involve interviews with both parties to assess their willingness and ability to participate. Third, referral: If both parties are found suitable, they are referred to a trained mediator who will facilitate the process. Fourth, mediation: The mediator facilitates a face-to-face meeting between the victim and offender in a safe and structured environment. During the mediation, the parties discuss the offense and its impact on the victim, and the offender takes responsibility and makes amends. Fifth, follow-up: After the mediation, the parties may be required to follow up with the mediator or other officials to ensure that the terms of the agreement are being met.

By operating on a referral system, the victim offender mediation program is able to ensure that only cases that are appropriate for mediation are referred. This helps ensure the safety and well-being of all participants and promotes positive outcomes for both victims and offenders.

Goals of Victim Offender Mediation

The goals of victim offender mediation are multiple.

First, **support the healing process** by providing a safe, controlled setting for victims and offenders to meet and speak on a strictly voluntary basis.

Second, **allow the offender to learn about the impact** of the crime on the victim and to take direct responsibility for their behavior.

Third, **provide an opportunity for the victim and offender to develop a mutually acceptable plan** that addresses the harm caused by their crime.

In addition, victim offender mediation aims to empower victims by giving them an opportunity to be heard, to express how the crime has affected them, and to ask questions of the offender. It holds offenders accountable by encouraging them to take responsibility and make amends. It promotes healing and closure for both parties. It can help restore relationships by promoting understanding, empathy, and forgiveness. And it may help reduce recidivism by addressing underlying issues and promoting accountability.

Family Group Conferencing

Family group conferencing is a process of intervention whereby the community members most affected by the crime come together to meet with the victim and the offender to discuss the resolution of the criminal incident. This particular intervention process can have a great impact on the offender who is sensitive to the voice of family members and relatives.

Family group conferencing brings together the community members most affected by a crime—including the victim, offender, and their families—to discuss the resolution of the incident. The purpose is to provide a forum for open dialogue and problem-solving and to create a plan for repairing the harm caused by the crime.

While family group conferencing is often used in cases involving juvenile offenders, it can also be used in cases involving adult offenders. The process typically involves referral, preparation, conference, and follow-up.

The goals of family group conferencing are similar to those of victim offender mediation—empowering victims, holding offenders accountable, promoting healing and closure, restoring relationships, and reducing recidivism. Family group conferencing is based on the principles of restorative justice and seeks to create a sense of community involvement and responsibility for addressing crime and its impact.

The Conferencing Group

The conferencing group in family group conferencing may include several participants.

The victim—the person who was directly harmed by the crime. The offender—the person who committed the crime. Family members or support persons of the victim—parents, siblings, partners, friends who can provide emotional support and guidance. Family members or support persons of the offender—parents, siblings, partners, friends who can provide support and guidance. Community members—representatives from the local community who have been affected by the crime or who can provide support and guidance. And a conference facilitator—a neutral third party who guides the conference process and ensures that everyone has an opportunity to speak and be heard.

The specific makeup of the conferencing group may vary depending on the case and the preferences of the participants. The goal is to create a safe and supportive environment where everyone has a voice and is able to contribute to the resolution.

Who Runs the Conferencing Group

The family group conferencing process is typically facilitated by a trained facilitator or coordinator who is neutral and impartial. The coordinator is responsible for guiding the conference process and ensuring that everyone has an opportunity to speak and be heard. The coordinator may be a trained mediator, social worker, or other professional with experience in restorative justice practices. In some cases, the coordinator may be a member of the community or a volunteer who has been trained to facilitate family group conferences. The coordinator's role is to ensure that the conference is conducted in a safe and respectful manner and that the needs of all participants are taken into consideration.

How the Conference Begins

The conference typically begins with the offender admitting guilt and accepting responsibility for their actions. This is an important step in the restorative justice process, as it allows the victim and the community to see that the offender is taking responsibility for their behavior and is committed to making things right. By admitting guilt, the offender acknowledges the harm they have caused and signals a willingness to work toward repairing the harm. This can be an important first step in the process of healing and restoration for all parties involved.

Conferencing is used only when the offender admits guilt (or in some jurisdictions, admits liability or declines to deny guilt). It is not used to determine guilt, and at any time during the process the offender may choose to bring the conference to a halt and proceed to court for a traditional determination of guilt or innocence.

How a Successful Conference Ends

A successful family group conferencing session ends when participants reach and sign an agreement outlining their expectations and commitments. The goal is to come to a resolution that is satisfactory to all participants—the victim, the offender, and the community. This resolution is typically outlined in a written agreement that is signed by all parties involved.

The agreement may include a range of commitments and expectations. Restitution: The offender may agree to make restitution to the victim, either through monetary payments or through other means such as community service. Apology: The offender may agree to apologize to the victim for their behavior, either in writing or in person. Counseling or therapy: The offender may agree to participate in counseling or therapy to address underlying issues that contributed to their behavior. Future behavior: The offender may agree to avoid certain behaviors in the future or to take specific steps to prevent similar incidents. Community service: The offender may agree to participate in community service as a way of making amends to the community.

Once the agreement has been reached and signed, the coordinator or facilitator will typically follow up with all participants to ensure that the commitments are being fulfilled. This follow-up process is an important part of restorative justice, helping to ensure that the resolution is meaningful and effective for all parties.

Family Group Conferencing is a means of involving family members, including extended family and friends, in decision-making and planning for children about whom concerns have been expressed in relation to their safety or well-being.

Where Family Group Conferencing Is Used

Family group conferencing is currently used in schools, police departments, probation offices, and neighborhood groups. Its application continues to expand as communities recognize its value in addressing conflict and harm.

Benefits of Family Group Conferencing

Studies have shown that family group conferencing can be an effective way of building community skills in conflict resolution and participatory decision-making. By involving members of the community in the process of resolving conflicts and addressing criminal behavior, family group conferencing can help strengthen social ties and promote a sense of collective responsibility for maintaining safe and healthy communities.

One key benefit is that it allows all participants to have a voice in the decision-making process. By bringing together the victim, the offender, and community members, family group conferencing encourages open and honest dialogue and provides an opportunity for all parties to be heard. This can be a powerful tool for building community cohesion and promoting positive social interactions.

In addition to promoting community skills in conflict resolution and decision-making, family group conferencing has been shown to have other benefits. For example, it can be an effective way of reducing recidivism rates among offenders, as it provides a more holistic approach to addressing criminal behavior. By focusing on the underlying causes of criminal behavior and working to repair harm to the victim and the community, family group conferencing can help break the cycle of crime and reduce the likelihood of future offenses.

Family group conferencing is a valuable tool for promoting restorative justice and building stronger, more resilient communities. By involving all stakeholders in the process of resolving conflicts and addressing criminal behavior, it can help create a sense of shared responsibility and promote positive social change.

Goals of Family Group Conferencing

The goals of family group conferencing are multiple.

First, **provide an opportunity for the victim to be directly involved** in the discussion of the offense and in decisions regarding appropriate sanctions.

Second, **increase the offender's awareness of the human impact** of their behavior and provide an opportunity to take full responsibility.

Third, **engage the collective responsibility of the offender's support system** for making amends and shaping the offender's future behavior.

Fourth, **allow both offender and victim to reconnect to key community support systems**.

In addition, family group conferencing aims to encourage open and honest dialogue, providing a safe and structured environment for all parties to discuss the impact of the crime and work toward a resolution. It aims to restore harm caused by the crime to the victim and the community, developing a plan to make restitution, apologize, or take other steps to make things right. It empowers all participants to be actively involved in the process of resolving the conflict, promoting participation, decision-making, and ownership of the outcome. It aims to reduce recidivism by addressing the underlying causes of criminal behavior. And it helps build and strengthen relationships among participants.

Victim Impact Panels

Victim impact panels are designed to educate offender groups about the negative consequences and impact of criminal behavior on their lives and on the lives of their families, friends, and other members of the community.

Victim impact panels are an important component of many criminal justice systems. They are typically structured as educational sessions where offenders hear from victims or family members of victims who have been impacted by crime. These sessions may take place in-person or online and are often mandatory for offenders as part of their sentence or as a condition of their release.

The primary goal of victim impact panels is to educate offenders about the real-world consequences of their criminal behavior. This can include hearing about the physical, emotional, and financial impact of crime on victims, as well as the broader impact on families, friends, and the community. By increasing awareness and empathy, victim impact panels can help deter future criminal behavior and promote positive social change.

Victim impact panels rely on the participation of victims or their family members to share their experiences and provide a personal perspective on the impact of crime. This participation is entirely voluntary, and victims are typically given support and guidance throughout the process to ensure their comfort and safety.

While the effectiveness of victim impact panels can be difficult to measure, many studies have shown that they can be a powerful tool for reducing recidivism and promoting offender accountability. By providing a human face to the impact of criminal behavior and increasing awareness of real-world consequences, victim impact panels can help promote positive behavioral change and reduce the likelihood of future offending.

Victim impact panels offer offender groups a wide range of views or perspectives on the type of crime being discussed. A panel group speaking collectively can have a greater chance of impacting the offenders.

Crimes Addressed by Victim Impact Panels

Victim impact panels have been used in a wide range of criminal cases, including robbery, assault, domestic violence, child abuse, elder abuse, DUI/DWI, manslaughter, homicide, sexual assault, hate crimes, white-collar crime, and property crimes.

The purpose is to provide a forum for victims or their family members to share the impact of the crime on their lives with offenders, increasing offender awareness of the human impact of their actions, promoting empathy, and reducing the likelihood of future offending.

Utilization of Victim Impact Panels

Victim impact panels are utilized in various settings—in jail and prison settings, treatment programs, defensive driving schools, youth education programs, and training forums for criminal justice professionals to help them better understand the scope and trauma of victimization.

They are typically utilized as a component of a criminal sentence or as part of a diversion or rehabilitation program. Offenders who are required to attend may be mandated by a judge, as a condition of probation, or as part of a plea agreement.

During the panel, victims or their family members share their personal experiences of victimization and the impact it has had on their lives. The panel may also feature presentations from law enforcement officials, victim advocates, or other experts on the effects of crime.

The goal is to provide a powerful and emotional reminder to offenders of the harm that their actions have caused. By hearing directly from those affected, offenders may be more likely to take responsibility, show remorse, and commit to making positive changes. The panel also serves as community education, raising awareness of the impact of crime.

Goals of Victim Impact Panels

The goals of victim impact panels can be summarized as follows.

First, **to increase offender awareness** of the human impact of their actions. By hearing directly from victims, offenders may better understand the harm they have caused and the need to take responsibility.

Second, **to promote empathy** in offenders, encouraging them to see the world from the victim's perspective. This can reduce the likelihood of future offending.

Third, **to facilitate healing** for victims or their family members. The panel can be a cathartic experience, providing an opportunity to express feelings and share experiences in a supportive environment.

Fourth, **to raise community awareness** of the impact of crime on victims and the community. By bringing victims and offenders together, the panel fosters a sense of community responsibility for preventing crime and supporting victims.

Victim Impact Classes

The victim impact class is an educational program designed to teach offenders the human consequences and impact of crime. The term may be used interchangeably with "victim impact panel" or "victim impact program," but generally refers to a specific type of educational program designed to provide offenders with a deeper understanding of the impact of their crimes on victims and society.

The goal is to help offenders develop empathy and understanding for their victims, as well as a sense of accountability for their actions. These classes typically involve lectures, videos, and interactive activities intended to demonstrate the real-world consequences of criminal behavior.

Offenders may be required to attend as a condition of their sentence or as part of a diversion or rehabilitation program. The specific content and format may vary depending on the jurisdiction and the type of crime committed.

The main focus in victim impact classes is on how the crime affected the victim and the victim's family.

Types of Crimes Addressed

The curriculum of a victim impact class can address a wide range of crimes—property crimes, sexual assault, domestic violence, child abuse and neglect, elder abuse and neglect, drunk driving, drug-related crimes, gang violence, homicide.

In addition to specific types of crimes, victim impact classes may also address broader topics such as the impact of crime on victims and their families, the criminal justice system, and the role of rehabilitation and treatment in preventing recidivism.

The curriculum is designed to help offenders understand the consequences of their actions and to promote empathy and accountability. By educating offenders about the impact of their crimes, victim impact classes aim to prevent future criminal behavior and promote community safety.

Success Factors for Victim Impact Classes

The success of a victim impact class program depends largely on strong support and involvement from crime victims, victim service providers, and community members. But it's a two-way street. The success also depends on criminals' willingness to acknowledge the effects that their actions had on the victim and the victim's family, and how it damaged the community's sense of security.

The active participation of offenders is crucial. Offenders who are willing to engage in the program, listen to victims' stories, and reflect on the impact of their behavior are more likely to benefit and reduce their risk of reoffending.

Victims who participate play a critical role in educating offenders about the impact of their crimes and promoting accountability and empathy. Their involvement also provides an opportunity for them to share their experiences and heal from their own victimization.

Criminal justice professionals—judges, prosecutors, defense attorneys, probation officers—play a critical role in referring offenders, monitoring progress, and ensuring compliance. Victim advocates assist with program administration and provide support to victims. Program facilitators—trained professionals with expertise in trauma-informed care and group therapy—are essential. Community organizations provide support for program promotion, volunteer recruitment, and fundraising.

Settings for Victim Impact Classes

The victim impact class is currently being implemented in a variety of settings—diversion programs, probation, prison, pre-release, detention, and parole supervised settings. It is often used as a condition of probation or parole and may be required as part of a court-ordered sentence for certain crimes. Additionally, some schools and community organizations offer victim impact classes as a preventative measure to educate youth about the impact of crime and encourage pro-social behavior.

Goals of Victim Impact Classes

The goals of victim impact classes are multiple.

First, **to teach offenders about the short- and long-term trauma of victimization**. Understanding trauma is essential for developing empathy.

Second, **to increase offenders' awareness of the negative impact** of their crime on victims and other community members.

Third, **to encourage offenders to accept responsibility** for their past criminal behaviors.

Fourth, **to provide victims and victim service providers with a forum** to educate offenders about the consequences of their criminal actions, with the hope that it will help prevent future offending.

Fifth, **to build linkages between criminal justice agencies, victims, and victim service organizations**.

Additional goals include increasing awareness and empathy, encouraging accountability, reducing recidivism, and promoting healing. Victim Impact Classes assist offenders in learning the true nature of crime and how crime harms and damages real people and communities.

Connecting the Justice System and the Public

Restorative-minded practices aim to promote healing, accountability, and community involvement in the criminal justice system, bridging the gap between the system and the public.

Victim Offender Mediation provides an opportunity for victims to meet their offender in a safe and structured setting to discuss the impact of the crime and work toward a resolution. By involving both parties, it promotes communication and empathy, helping to rebuild relationships. This process can also help restore trust and confidence in the criminal justice system and promote community involvement.

Family Group Conferencing brings together the community members most affected by a crime to discuss a resolution. This process allows community members to participate in decision-making and helps build community skills in conflict resolution and participatory decision-making. It encourages community involvement, promoting transparency and accountability.

Victim Impact Panels educate offenders about the impact of their crimes on victims and the community. By providing offenders with a better understanding of the harm they have caused, they promote empathy, accountability, and responsibility. They also promote community involvement by bringing victims and offenders together, creating opportunities for dialogue, and increasing public awareness.

Victim Impact Classes educate offenders about the human consequences and impact of crime. By providing an understanding of the impact on victims and society, they promote empathy and accountability. They also promote community involvement by educating offenders, which can reduce recidivism and help build safer communities.

Community Policing involves the establishment of "mini-stations" in neighborhoods and the assignment of law enforcement officers to specific geographic areas. In recent years, tragic deaths of black youths in confrontations with police have sown distrust for law enforcement. This perception is not fair to the vast majority of dedicated, well-meaning officers, but it has shaken the connection between law enforcement and the neighborhoods they serve. Community policing is not new—an estimated 58% of law enforcement agencies reported having dedicated community-oriented officers in 2003. Since then, many more have adopted transparent models involving neighborhood businesses, nonprofits, media outlets, and other community groups in keeping their municipality safe.

Neighborhood Probation is similar to community policing, with probation officers assigned to specific geographic areas instead of having dispersed caseloads. These officers establish community partnerships, joining area neighborhoods in working with offenders to prevent recidivism, deal with community "hot spots," gang intimidation, drug houses, and other concerns. Efforts are made to collaborate with other service agencies—public health, social services, churches.

School Based Probation involves placing juvenile probation officers in schools, assigned to the same geographic area as the schools. These officers provide problem-solving assistance to the school for students on probation. The objective is to monitor probationers while seeking ways to increase the likelihood of school success through improved grades, reduced truancy and expulsion, and increased high school graduation.

Community Prosecution helps communities resolve crime-related problems identified by residents, using prosecutors assigned to specific neighborhoods. This practice can also assist communities by explaining legal constraints that prevent law enforcement from acting and devising alternative tools citizens and police can use when conventional ones fail.

Community Defense involves accessible community-based defense attorneys representing individuals accused of crime. They also represent clients before an arrest is made to avoid problems. The main objective is to provide legal services for solving problems that foster crime and injustice before crime occurs. It seeks to address structural problems in many communities, offering assistance to families and community members experiencing difficulties that can be addressed with legal assistance.

Community Courts are established in neighborhoods to be closer to community needs. By decentralizing court facilities, citizens have access to remote locations where they can file forms, pay fines, and participate in the court process more conveniently. Court decentralization, also known as devolution, requires collaboration between the court and community groups to forge a more broadly based connection between the court and community.

These promising practices represent the living reality of restorative justice. They are not abstract theories but concrete programs being implemented in communities across the country and around the world. They offer hope for a different kind of justice—one that heals rather than hurts, restores rather than destroys, and involves rather than excludes. In the chapters that follow, we will explore how these practices can be implemented and how the Church can play a role in this transformative work.

CHAPTER 06

SHOULD THE CHURCH GET INVOLVED IN RESTORATIVE JUSTICE?

We have traveled a long and winding road together in this book. We began by examining the traditional view of justice—its ancient roots in the law of retaliation, its psychological appeal, and its troubling consequences. We saw how a system designed to punish has grown into a massive enterprise that incarcerates more of its citizens than any other nation on earth, at enormous cost and with little to show for it.

We then explored why this system must be restructured. We looked at the soaring costs, the public's fear and frustration, the isolation of communities, and the way the system steals conflicts from those to whom they belong. We saw how the traditional model fails victims, fails offenders, and fails communities.

In the third chapter, we began to glimpse a different view of justice. We explored restorative justice—what it is, how it differs from the traditional model, and why it offers hope for healing and reconciliation. We considered the principles and practices that make restorative justice unique, and we saw how it centers victims, holds offenders accountable through repair, and involves communities in the process of justice.

In the fourth chapter, we examined the conceptual frameworks that undergird restorative justice—the ideas, theories, and models that give it shape and substance. We saw how thinkers like Nils Christie have helped us understand crime as a catalyst for community empowerment, and how various conceptual models provide frameworks for community-based practice.

In the fifth chapter, we explored the promising practices that have emerged as communities embrace restorative justice. We looked at sentencing circles, victim impact statements, community reparation boards, community service, restitution, victim-offender mediation, family group conferencing, victim impact panels, victim impact classes, and a range of community-based initiatives that connect the justice system with the public.

Now we come to a question that may be on your mind. Perhaps you have been reading this book and thinking about all that restorative justice entails—the principles, the practices, the conceptual frameworks—and you have been wondering: what does this have to do with me? What does this have to do with the Church?

The answer is simple and profound: everything.

In this chapter, we will explore the relationship between the Church and restorative justice. We will see that restorative justice is not merely a secular alternative to traditional punishment but is deeply rooted in biblical principles and the very character of God. We will examine the clear mandate that Scripture gives to the people of God to engage in criminal justice ministry. We will consider the questions this mandate raises and the challenges it presents. And we will see that the Church, far from being a bystander to the work of justice, is called to be its primary agent—an agent of reconciliation, healing, and restoration in a broken and hurting world.

God's Chosen Instrument

Let us begin with a bold assertion: God has selected the Church as His primary instrument of restorative justice, and has given it a clear mandate to do criminal justice ministry.

This is not a statement based on wishful thinking or political activism. It is based on the clear teaching of Scripture. In Matthew 25:36, Jesus Himself taught that it is His will for the Church to minister to those in prison: "I was in prison and you visited Me." This mandate has been reaffirmed in Hebrews 13:3: "Remember them that are in bonds, as bound with them."

Think about the implications of these verses. Jesus does not say that visiting prisoners is optional for His followers. He does not say that it is a good idea for those who feel called to it. He presents it as a criterion of judgment. In the Matthew passage, the righteous are those who visited Him in prison, and the unrighteous are those who did not. When we visit those in prison, we are visiting Christ Himself. When we neglect those in prison, we are neglecting Christ.

This is a staggering thought. The sovereign Lord of the universe, the King who will sit on His glorious throne and judge the nations, identifies Himself with the incarcerated. He counts their treatment as His own. This means that criminal justice ministry is not a peripheral activity for the Church—a nice thing to do if we have extra time and resources. It is central to our identity as followers of Jesus.

The Bible is filled with passages that emphasize the importance of caring for prisoners and those who are marginalized or oppressed. In Isaiah 61:1, the prophet declares that God has anointed him to "preach good tidings unto the meek; he hath sent me to bind up the brokenhearted, to proclaim liberty to the captives, and the opening of the prison to them that are bound." Jesus Himself quoted this passage at the beginning of His ministry, announcing that it was fulfilled in Him.

In Matthew 5:7, Jesus says, "Blessed are the merciful, for they shall obtain mercy." Mercy is not an abstract concept. It is expressed in concrete actions toward those who are suffering, including those who are incarcerated. Throughout the New Testament, we see examples of Christ's compassion for prisoners and His call to His followers to care for them.

Consider the story of Paul and Silas in Acts 16. They were thrown into prison for preaching the gospel. They had every reason to be discouraged and bitter. Instead, they used their time in prison to worship and pray. And their witness led to the conversion of their jailer and his entire household. This is a powerful example of how the presence of God's people in prison can bring about transformation—not only for themselves but for others.

The Church has an important role to play not only in ministering to prisoners but also in advocating for criminal justice reform and promoting restorative justice practices. The Church can provide a powerful witness to the world by modeling forgiveness, reconciliation, and healing, even in the midst of brokenness and injustice. When the Church lives out its calling, it becomes a sign of the Kingdom of God—a kingdom where justice and mercy embrace, where the last are first, and where the prisoners are set free.

Questions Raised by the Mandate

The mandate to do criminal justice ministry raises several important questions. These are questions that every believer and every church must grapple with if they are to take this calling seriously.

First, **is my view of justice consistent with the biblical view?** This is the foundational question. Many of us have absorbed the dominant cultural view of justice without ever examining it in light of Scripture. We assume that justice means punishment, that offenders should suffer for their crimes, that the system exists to make people pay. But is this what the Bible teaches? As we have seen throughout this book, the biblical view of justice is far richer and more complex. It includes punishment, to be sure, but it also includes restoration, reconciliation, and healing. It is not content with making offenders suffer; it seeks to make them whole.

Second, **does a commitment to restorative justice suggest that I do not support retributive efforts to administer justice?** This is a common concern. Some worry that embracing restorative justice means abandoning accountability and letting offenders off the hook. But this is a misunderstanding.

Restorative justice does not reject accountability; it redefines it. Accountability in the restorative paradigm means taking responsibility for harm and working to repair it. This is a higher standard of accountability than simply serving time. It requires offenders to face their victims, to acknowledge the harm they have caused, and to take concrete steps to make things right.

Third, **what should be my goal and from what perspective do I view my work within the criminal justice system?** This question gets at motivation and worldview. Are we working to punish offenders or to restore them? Are we viewing them through the lens of the world—as criminals defined by their worst actions—or through the eyes of Jesus—as human beings made in God's image, capable of change, worthy of love? Our goal and our perspective will shape everything we do.

Fourth, **do I preach Jesus only and leave past behavior alone, or do I deal with both behavior and faith, and in dealing with both, in what sequence do I approach the two?** This is a practical question for those engaged in prison ministry. Some approaches focus exclusively on spiritual matters, never addressing the criminal behavior that led to incarceration. Others focus on behavior change without addressing the spiritual dimension. The restorative justice paradigm suggests that both are important and that they are interconnected. Genuine transformation involves both a change of heart and a change of behavior. The question of sequence may vary from person to person, but both must be addressed.

Beyond these personal questions, there are broader questions about how the Church should fulfill this mandate.

What specific actions should the Church take to fulfill this mandate? The answer will vary depending on context, resources, and calling. Some churches may focus on visiting prisoners and providing pastoral care. Others may start reentry programs to help former inmates transition back into society. Others may advocate for policy changes at the local, state, or national level. Still others may partner with restorative justice programs in their communities. The important thing is to do something—to respond to the mandate rather than ignoring it.

How can the Church balance its role as a spiritual institution with the practical aspects of criminal justice ministry? This is an ongoing tension. The Church is called to proclaim the gospel and make disciples. But the gospel has implications for every area of life, including how we treat those who have been incarcerated. A church that preaches spiritual salvation while ignoring the physical, emotional, and social needs of prisoners is not fully living out the gospel. At the same time, a church that focuses exclusively on practical needs without addressing spiritual realities is missing its primary calling. The two must be held together.

How can the Church work collaboratively with the criminal justice system, while also advocating for systemic change? This requires wisdom and discernment. The Church must be willing to partner with government agencies and justice professionals where possible, building relationships and working together for the good of offenders, victims, and communities. At the same time, the Church must be willing to speak truth to power, advocating for changes that reflect biblical values of justice, mercy, and restoration. This is not always easy, but it is necessary.

What types of support and resources are necessary for the Church to effectively carry out its mandate? Churches need training, education, and ongoing support to engage in criminal justice ministry effectively. They need volunteers who are committed and equipped. They need partnerships with other organizations. They need prayer and spiritual covering. Without these resources, even well-intentioned efforts can falter.

How can the Church ensure that its criminal justice ministry is inclusive and equitable, and does not perpetuate systemic biases or discrimination? This is a critical question. The criminal justice system is marked by significant racial and socioeconomic disparities. The Church must be aware of these realities and ensure that its ministry does not reinforce them. This means being intentional about reaching out to all who are affected by crime, regardless of race, class, or background. It means examining our own biases and working to overcome them. It means advocating for justice and equity at every level.

How can the Church help to address the root causes of crime, such as poverty, inequality, and lack of access to education and employment opportunities? This requires a holistic approach. The Church cannot simply respond to crime after it happens; it must also work to prevent crime by addressing the conditions that produce it. This means engaging in ministries that alleviate poverty, provide education and job training, strengthen families, and build community. It means advocating for policies that create opportunities for all people, especially those who are most vulnerable.

How can the Church support both victims and offenders in the restorative justice process, while also upholding the principles of accountability and justice? This requires balance and wisdom. The Church must care for victims, providing comfort, support, and advocacy. It must also care for offenders, offering opportunities for repentance, restoration, and reintegration. Both are essential. Neither can be neglected. And throughout, the Church must uphold the principles of accountability and justice, ensuring that harm is acknowledged and addressed.

These are not easy questions. They require prayer, study, dialogue, and discernment. But they are questions that must be asked if the Church is to take seriously its mandate to engage in criminal justice ministry.

Restorative Justice as a Biblical Paradigm

Restorative justice is not merely a secular concept that Christians can choose to support or ignore. It is a biblical-based paradigm, founded in the call to the ministry of reconciliation.

Second Corinthians 5:18 refers to the ministry of reconciliation, assigned to all believers. The verse says: "All this is from God, who reconciled us to himself through Christ and gave us the ministry of reconciliation." The message we must declare is that we can have a restored relationship with God through Jesus.

This is the heart of the gospel. God, who was wronged by our sin, did not simply punish us. He did not extract retribution. Instead, He initiated reconciliation. He sent His Son to absorb the cost of our wrongdoing, to pay the penalty we deserved, and to open the way for us to be restored to relationship with Him. This is the ultimate model of restorative justice.

Restorative justice is rooted in the biblical principles of forgiveness, mercy, and justice. In the Old Testament, the concept of justice is central to God's character and His relationship with His people. Justice is not only about punishment but also about restoring relationships, reconciling people to God and each other, and making things right. The Hebrew word for justice, *mishpat*, appears throughout the Scriptures and carries this rich meaning.

In the New Testament, Jesus taught and modeled restorative justice in His interactions with individuals who were considered outcasts by society. Consider the woman caught in adultery (John 8:1-11). The religious leaders brought her to Jesus, ready to stone her according to the law of Moses. They were focused on punishment, on retribution. Jesus responded by challenging them: "He who is without sin among you, let him be the first to throw a stone at her." One by one, they left. Then Jesus said to the woman, "Neither do I condemn you. Go and sin no more."

This is restorative justice in action. Jesus did not minimize the woman's sin. He did not say that what she did was acceptable. But He also did not condemn her. Instead, He offered her forgiveness and a path to transformation. He restored her dignity and called her to a new way of living.

Consider Zacchaeus, the tax collector (Luke 19:1-10). Zacchaeus was a collaborator with the Roman occupiers, a man who had enriched himself by cheating his own people. When Jesus came to his house, the crowd murmured that He would associate with such a sinner. But Jesus' presence transformed Zacchaeus. He stood up and said, "Behold, Lord, the half of my goods I give to the poor. And if I have defrauded anyone of anything, I restore it fourfold." Jesus responded, "Today salvation has come to this house."

Again, we see restorative justice. Jesus did not demand restitution from Zacchaeus. He did not threaten punishment. Instead, His presence and acceptance created the conditions for Zacchaeus to take responsibility for his actions and make amends. The offender became a restorer.

The Apostle Paul also emphasized the importance of reconciliation and restoration in his letters to the early Christian communities. He called on them to forgive one another, to reconcile their differences, and to work together for the common good. In Colossians 3:12-13, he wrote: "Therefore, as God's chosen people, holy and dearly loved, clothe yourselves with compassion, kindness, humility, gentleness and patience. Bear with each other and forgive one another if any of you has a grievance against someone. Forgive as the Lord forgave you."

Restorative justice seeks to build on these biblical principles by providing a framework for addressing harm, restoring relationships, and promoting healing and reconciliation. Rather than focusing solely on punishment and retribution, restorative justice encourages offenders to take responsibility for their actions, to make amends for the harm they have caused, and to work toward repairing the harm done to the victim and the community.

In summary, restorative justice is grounded in the biblical call to the ministry of reconciliation, which emphasizes the importance of forgiveness, mercy, and justice in addressing harm and restoring relationships.

Viewing Man Through the Eyes of Jesus

The ministry of reconciliation requires that we view man through the eyes of Jesus, rather than as the world views him. This is a radical shift in perspective.

Jesus made a profound statement in John 3:17: "God did not send His Son into the world to condemn the world, but that the world through Him might be saved." When He comes again, He will come in judgment upon those who refuse His offer of salvation. But until then, we must remember that mankind is so important to Jesus that He died for them (John 3:16).

Think about what this means. The Son of God, the second person of the Trinity, left the glory of heaven and took on human flesh. He lived a perfect life, was betrayed, beaten, and crucified. He suffered and died—for sinners. For those who rejected Him. For those who mocked Him. For those who crucified Him. While we were still sinners, Christ died for us (Romans 5:8).

This is the measure of God's love for humanity. And this love is not based on our merit or worthiness. It is not because we are good that God loves us. It is because He is good. He loves us because He is love.

The ministry of reconciliation is grounded in this belief: human beings are created in the image of God, and their worth and dignity must be recognized and affirmed. This means that we must view individuals through the eyes of Jesus, who saw them as valuable and worthy of love and redemption, regardless of their past actions.

In contrast, the world often views individuals based on their actions or social status. The world stigmatizes and marginalizes those who have been involved in the criminal justice system. They are labeled as criminals, offenders, ex-cons. They are defined by their worst moments. This creates a cycle of shame and despair that can hinder their ability to make positive changes and reintegrate into society.

The restorative justice paradigm seeks to shift the focus from punishment and retribution to healing and restoration, both for victims and offenders. This requires us to see individuals not just as perpetrators of crime, but as human beings who have the potential to change and be restored to their communities.

When we view offenders through the eyes of Jesus, we see beyond their crimes. We see people who are broken, who have made terrible choices, who have caused great harm—but who are still loved by God, still capable of change, still worthy of dignity and respect. This does not mean we minimize their actions or ignore the harm they have caused. It means we hold them accountable while also offering them hope.

By viewing individuals through the eyes of Jesus and embracing the restorative justice paradigm, we can promote healing, reconciliation, and transformation for all those impacted by crime.

The Legacy of Adam's Sin

To understand why restorative justice is necessary, we must understand the human condition. As a result of Adam's sin, what has he passed on to the human race? The answer is physical and spiritual death for everyone.

Death has three distinct manifestations in Scripture. First, there is spiritual death or separation from God (Ephesians 2:1-2; 4:18). This is the condition of every person apart from Christ. We are dead in our trespasses and sins, alienated from the life of God.

Second, there is physical death (Hebrews 9:27). It is appointed for men to die once, and after this comes judgment. Physical death is the consequence of sin entering the world, and it is the lot of every human being.

Third, there is eternal death, also known as the second death. This includes not only eternal separation from God but eternal torment in the lake of fire (Revelation 20:11-15). This is the ultimate destiny of those who reject God's offer of salvation in Christ.

In Christian theology, this state of sinfulness passed from Adam to all humanity is commonly referred to as "original sin." The idea is based on the biblical account in Genesis where Adam and Eve disobeyed God by eating the forbidden fruit from the tree of the knowledge of good and evil.

The concept of original sin teaches that as a result of Adam's disobedience, human nature has been corrupted and inclined toward sin. This means that all human beings are born with a natural tendency toward sin and a predisposition to rebel against God. This sin nature affects every aspect of human life, including thoughts, emotions, and actions.

The Bible teaches that the only way to overcome this state of sinfulness is through faith in Jesus Christ. Through His death and resurrection, Jesus provides a way for human beings to be reconciled to God and to be set free from the power of sin.

Restorative justice, therefore, is seen as a means of embodying the ministry of reconciliation by extending forgiveness and restoration to those who have committed offenses, just as Christ has done for us. When we participate in restorative justice, we are acting as agents of God's grace, offering to others what we have received from Him.

Jesus, the Great Mediator

Although punishment is deserved, Jesus, the Great Mediator between God and man, brings restorative justice to the earth. Rather than condemn the world, "God was in Christ reconciling the world to Himself, not imputing their trespasses to them" (2 Corinthians 5:19).

As the Bible teaches, all humans have sinned and fall short of the glory of God (Romans 3:23). The punishment for sin is death (Romans 6:23). But God, in His love and mercy, provided a way for humans to be reconciled to Him through the sacrifice of His Son Jesus Christ (John 3:16).

Jesus' death on the cross provided a way for humans to be forgiven of their sins and restored to a right relationship with God. Through faith in Jesus, individuals can receive the forgiveness and reconciliation that He offers (Romans 5:10-11; 2 Corinthians 5:18-19).

In this sense, Jesus brings restorative justice to the earth by reconciling individuals to God and restoring relationships that have been broken by sin. This restorative justice is not limited to the spiritual realm. It can also be extended to the earthly realm through practices such as forgiveness, reconciliation, and restoration. In this way, restorative justice can be seen as an expression of Jesus' love and mercy toward humanity, as well as a way to bring healing and wholeness to broken individuals and communities.

The cross is the ultimate demonstration of restorative justice. It shows us that God takes sin seriously—seriously enough to require a sacrifice. But it also shows us that God's response to sin is not merely punitive. It is redemptive. He provides a way for sinners to be restored. He absorbs the cost of justice Himself so that we can be reconciled.

This is the model for our own engagement with justice. We must take sin seriously. We must hold offenders accountable. But our ultimate goal must be restoration, not merely punishment. We must be willing to absorb costs, to extend forgiveness, to work for reconciliation. This is what it means to follow Jesus.

The New Justice of God

The new justice of God is not retributive in nature, but redemptive. God's new justice brings healing because of its redemptive nature. Notice how Paul described God's redemptive justice in Titus 2:14: "Our great God and Savior Jesus Christ, who gave Himself for us, that He might redeem us from every lawless deed and purify for Himself His own special people."

The concept of restorative justice emphasizes repairing the harm caused by a crime rather than merely punishing the offender. In contrast to traditional retributive justice, which focuses on punishing the offender for breaking the law, restorative justice seeks to restore the harm caused by the offender's actions and promote healing and reconciliation between the offender, victim, and community.

In this sense, the new justice of God is not retributive but redemptive. The Bible teaches that God's justice is rooted in His love and mercy for humanity. Instead of simply punishing humanity for their sins, God seeks to redeem them through His Son Jesus Christ. Through His death and resurrection, Jesus paid the penalty for humanity's sins and offers the gift of salvation to all who repent and believe in Him.

As followers of Christ, we are called to imitate His example of restorative justice. This involves seeking the good of all parties involved, including the offender, victim, and community. Restorative justice recognizes the humanity of all individuals, including those who have committed crimes, and seeks to help them become fully restored members of society. This approach acknowledges that all individuals have inherent value and are capable of change and growth.

The new justice of God is redemptive, seeking to restore and reconcile all parties involved in a crime. This approach emphasizes love, mercy, and the potential for growth and transformation, rather than punishment and retribution.

Healing Relationships with God and Community

God's new justice brings healing to relationships with God and the community of man. This restorative justice seeks to bring healing and reconciliation to relationships between God and humanity, as well as among people. This is reflected in the life and teachings of Jesus, who taught His followers to love one another, to forgive their enemies, and to seek reconciliation with those they had wronged.

Through Jesus' death and resurrection, He made it possible for humanity to be reconciled to God and to one another. This reconciliation is not simply a matter of forgiving sins and moving on. It is about restoring broken relationships and building new ones based on love, trust, and mutual respect.

In this way, restorative justice seeks to bring healing to the harm caused by crime, rather than simply punishing the offender. It recognizes the dignity and worth of every human being and seeks to restore the harm done to the victim, the offender, and the community as a whole.

Restorative justice practices, such as victim-offender mediation and family group conferencing, provide opportunities for those affected by crime to come together, share their experiences, and work toward healing and reconciliation. These practices seek to empower victims, hold offenders accountable, and promote community healing and restoration.

Ultimately, the goal of restorative justice is not simply to punish offenders, but to create a more just and peaceful society, where relationships are characterized by love, forgiveness, and mutual respect, and where harm is transformed into healing and growth.

Crime as Injury

The restorative justice paradigm suggests that crime is an injury to God, individuals, relationships, and the community, rather than just a violation of laws and rules. It views crime as a harm done to people and relationships, rather than simply as a violation of the state's laws and rules. It emphasizes repairing the harm done to victims and restoring relationships between the offender, victim, and the community, rather than focusing solely on punishing the offender.

In addition, crime causes injury to the criminal him or herself, when you consider all the opportunity costs associated with the criminal's choice to engage in illegal rather than legal and productive activities. The offender is also harmed—by their own actions, by the consequences they face, by the separation from community, by the damage to their own character and potential.

This understanding of crime as injury to multiple parties is essential for a biblical view of justice. When we sin, we harm God by violating His law and dishonoring His name. We harm others by causing them pain, loss, and suffering. We harm the community by damaging trust and social cohesion. And we harm ourselves by corrupting our own hearts and wasting our potential.

A just response to crime must address all of these injuries. It must seek to repair the harm done to God, to victims, to community, and to offenders themselves. This is what restorative justice aims to do.

The Goal of Restorative Justice

The goal of restorative justice is to repair the harm caused by the crime, promote healing for the victim and community, and hold the offender accountable while giving them an opportunity to make amends and reintegrate into society. It focuses on addressing the root causes of the crime and finding ways to prevent future harm, rather than just punishing the offender. Restorative justice seeks to restore relationships and promote reconciliation between the parties involved, and to empower individuals and communities to take an active role in resolving conflicts and repairing harm.

This goal is deeply biblical. Throughout Scripture, God reveals Himself as one who repairs, restores, and reconciles. He heals the brokenhearted. He binds up wounds. He restores the years that the locusts have eaten. He reconciles the world to Himself. This is the God we serve, and this is the work He calls us to do.

When we engage in restorative justice, we are participating in God's own work of restoration. We are being agents of His healing grace in a broken world.

Justice in Indigenous Communities

In indigenous communities around the world, the responsibility for the administration of justice is often held by the community itself, rather than by external authorities. This approach to justice is rooted in the community's traditions, values, and cultural practices. Indigenous communities view justice not only as a response to crime or wrongdoing but also as a way of restoring relationships and promoting harmony within the community.

In these communities, the administration of justice is often carried out by a council of elders or other community members who are respected for their wisdom, knowledge, and experience. These individuals are selected based on their understanding of the community's customs and values and their ability to make fair and just decisions. The council may also include representatives from the victim's family and the offender's family, as well as other members of the community who are affected by the incident.

The process of administering justice in indigenous communities often involves dialogue and consensus-building rather than punishment. The goal is to restore the relationships that have been damaged by the wrongdoing and to find a resolution that benefits everyone involved. This may involve restitution, compensation, or other forms of reparation, as well as efforts to address the root causes of the problem and prevent similar incidents from occurring in the future.

This indigenous approach to justice has much to teach us. It reminds us that justice is not something that should be monopolized by professionals and institutions. It is something that belongs to the community. It is something that we all have a stake in and a responsibility for.

The responsibility for the administration of justice in indigenous communities is an important aspect of maintaining cultural identity and promoting social harmony. It serves as a reminder that justice is not just about punishing offenders but also about healing relationships and promoting community well-being.

The Community Facilitates Healing

In the restorative justice paradigm, the community plays a critical role in facilitating the healing process between the broken relationship caused by crime. Rather than leaving the criminal justice process solely to the legal system, the community takes responsibility for addressing the harm caused by crime and promoting healing.

The community's involvement in the restorative justice process is important for several reasons.

First, it helps to rebuild trust between the victim, offender, and the community. When the community comes together to address the harm caused by the crime, it sends a powerful message of solidarity and support to both the victim and offender. This can help to promote a sense of community and foster a sense of accountability for everyone involved.

Second, the community's involvement can help to promote healing and closure for the victim. In traditional criminal justice systems, victims are often left feeling isolated and powerless. However, when the community comes together to support the victim and hold the offender accountable, it can help the victim to regain a sense of control over their life and promote healing.

Third, the community's involvement can help to reduce recidivism rates. By providing the offender with support and guidance, the community can help to address the underlying issues that may have contributed to their criminal behavior. This can help to reduce the likelihood of future offenses and promote rehabilitation.

Thus, the community's involvement in restorative justice is critical for promoting healing, accountability, and rehabilitation. By working together to address the harm caused by crime, the community can play an important role in building a safer and more just society.

Punishment and Restoration

Punishment is not restorative if it is done out of revenge or through retribution. Restorative justice focuses on repairing harm and restoring relationships between victims, offenders, and the community. Punishment, on the other hand, often focuses on retribution and deterrence rather than restoration. Punishment can be a necessary response to criminal behavior, but it is not inherently restorative.

When punishment is done out of revenge or a desire for retribution, it can perpetuate cycles of harm and violence. Instead of addressing the root causes of the behavior and working to repair the harm done, punitive responses may simply escalate the conflict and create new victims. Punishment that is not focused on restoration can also perpetuate societal inequalities and injustices by disproportionately affecting marginalized and oppressed populations.

Restorative justice, on the other hand, offers an alternative to punitive responses by prioritizing the needs of the victim, the offender, and the community. This approach seeks to understand the underlying causes of criminal behavior and to address the harm done through a process of dialogue, accountability, and repair.

Restorative justice can provide healing and closure for victims, as they are given the opportunity to share their experiences and have a say in the resolution of the harm done to them. Offenders are also given the chance to take responsibility for their actions and to make amends for the harm they have caused. The community is involved in the process and is given the opportunity to address underlying issues and to work toward preventing future harm.

Punishment is not restorative if it is done out of revenge or through retribution. Restorative justice offers an alternative approach that focuses on repairing harm, restoring relationships, and preventing future harm.

Questions for Ministry

In a restorative justice paradigm for ministry, several important questions can be addressed.

What is God's view of justice? The concept of justice is central to the character of God as described in the Bible. According to Scripture, God's view of justice is that it is impartial, fair, and righteous. God's justice is not influenced by any human biases or prejudices, and it is based on His unchanging moral standards. God's justice is also described as restorative, meaning that it seeks to repair the damage caused by wrongdoing and restore right relationships.

What does He expect of us? God expects us to pursue justice and righteousness in all areas of our lives. This includes treating others fairly, advocating for the oppressed and marginalized, and working toward systems and structures that promote justice and equity. The Bible also emphasizes the importance of mercy and forgiveness, even in the context of justice.

How should we view the unrighteous acts of the offenders? As Christians, we are called to hate sin but love sinners. This means that we should condemn and resist unrighteous acts, but also seek to offer grace, forgiveness, and the opportunity for redemption to those who have committed them. We should strive to see offenders through God's eyes, recognizing that they too are made in His image and are in need of His love and mercy.

Does biblical justice include something other than punishment of wrongs committed against God and man? Yes, biblical justice includes more than just punishment for wrongs committed against God and man. It also includes restorative justice, which seeks to repair the harm caused by wrongdoing and restore relationships between the offender and the victim. Restorative justice emphasizes the importance of accountability, but also focuses on healing and reconciliation.

How do I minister through a biblical paradigm of justice? To minister through a biblical paradigm of justice, it is important to first cultivate a deep understanding of God's character and His view of justice. This can be done through prayer, study of Scripture, and engagement with the broader Christian community. From there, it is important to seek out opportunities to advocate for justice and mercy in our communities and to work toward building systems and structures that reflect God's vision of justice. This can involve supporting organizations that are doing this work, volunteering time and resources, and engaging in advocacy and activism. Ultimately, ministering through a biblical paradigm of justice involves a commitment to love, mercy, and restoration, even in the face of great injustice and pain.

In a ministry context, restorative justice can be applied to a variety of situations. How can we respond to harm caused within our faith community in a way that promotes accountability, healing, and reconciliation? How can we address the root causes of injustice in our society and work toward systemic change? How can we create a culture of empathy, compassion, and forgiveness within our faith community? How can we support those who have experienced trauma and help them to find healing and wholeness? How can we engage in dialogue with those who hold different beliefs or have been harmed by our community, with a focus on understanding and relationship-building? How can we integrate restorative justice principles into our worship and spiritual practices, such as confession, forgiveness, and reconciliation? How can we work toward repairing harm caused by historical injustices, such as colonization or racism? How can we support individuals who have been impacted by the criminal justice system, including those who have been incarcerated and their families? How can we promote a restorative approach to conflict resolution within our faith community and in our wider society? How can we work collaboratively with other organizations and faith communities to promote restorative justice principles and practices in our communities?

These are the questions that should guide our ministry as we seek to embody God's restorative justice.

Job's Discovery About God's Justice

The book of Job offers profound insights into the nature of God's justice. Job discovered that God's justice was more complicated than simply receiving punishment for wrongs he had done and blessings for living a righteous life.

Job is a book that tells the story of a man who experiences great suffering and loss. Throughout the book, Job struggles to understand why he is suffering and questions the justice of God. In the end, Job has an encounter with God that leads him to a deeper understanding of God's justice.

One of the key things that Job discovers is that God's justice is not always predictable or easily understood. Job had assumed that if he was righteous, he would be rewarded, and if he sinned, he would be punished. However, his suffering seemed to contradict this understanding of justice. Through his conversations with his friends and with God, Job begins to realize that God's justice is more complex than a simple cause-and-effect relationship between behavior and outcome.

Job also discovers that God's justice is rooted in God's wisdom and sovereignty. Job realizes that God's ways are beyond his understanding, and that God is not obligated to explain or justify His actions. Job humbly submits to God's authority, recognizing that God's justice is ultimately trustworthy and good, even if it is not always easy to understand.

Consequently, Job's experience leads him to a deeper appreciation of God's justice, which is not simply about rewarding the righteous and punishing the wicked, but is rooted in God's wisdom, sovereignty, and goodness.

God's Questions to Job

In Job 40:8, God asks Job two questions that suggest he knew little about the justice of God: "Would you discredit my justice? Would you condemn me to justify yourself?"

These two questions suggest that Job had a limited understanding of the justice of God and that he had been trying to justify himself rather than trust in God's wisdom and sovereignty.

The first question, "Would you discredit my justice?" implies that Job may have been questioning the fairness or goodness of God's justice. Job had experienced great suffering and loss, and he may have been struggling to reconcile his understanding of justice with his own experiences. God's question challenges Job to trust in God's justice, even when it is difficult to understand.

The second question, "Would you condemn me to justify yourself?" suggests that Job may have been trying to justify his own righteousness in the face of his suffering. Job had maintained his innocence throughout his trials, and he may have been tempted to criticize God's justice in order to make his own case. God's question challenges Job to trust in God's righteousness and sovereignty, even when it challenges his own sense of justice.

Together, these two questions remind Job that God's justice is not limited by human understanding or perspective. Job is called to trust in God's wisdom and righteousness, even when it challenges his own assumptions and beliefs.

Job's Response

After God revealed His concept of justice in chapter 42, Job responded by acknowledging his own limited understanding and submitting to God's sovereignty. He said, "I know that you can do all things, and that no purpose of yours can be thwarted... I had heard of you by the hearing of the ear, but now my eye sees you" (Job 42:2,5). Job confessed that he had spoken without understanding and repented in dust and ashes.

God then rebuked Job's friends for their misguided attempts to explain Job's suffering and instructed them to offer burnt offerings and have Job pray for them, indicating that Job's faithfulness and repentance had led to his restoration.

Job's response to God's concept of justice is one of humility and submission, acknowledging that he did not fully comprehend

God's ways and trusting in His sovereignty. Job did repent and admit that he did not understand or know God's concept of justice.

Seeing Righteousness and Justice

When Job saw the righteousness of God, he also saw the justice of God. Throughout his trials, Job never lost his faith in God, but he did question the justice of his situation. He demanded an explanation for his suffering, and his friends offered various theories, including that Job must have sinned and brought his misfortune upon himself.

However, in the end, God spoke directly to Job and revealed His ultimate plan and purpose. Job was humbled by the experience and realized that he could not fully comprehend the justice and righteousness of God. He acknowledged that God's ways were beyond his understanding and that he had spoken about things he did not understand.

Therefore, when Job saw the righteousness of God, he also saw the justice of God. He recognized that God's justice was not necessarily based on the human understanding of fairness and punishment. Instead, God's justice was rooted in His ultimate plan and purpose, which was beyond human comprehension.

Job's story demonstrates that justice is not always straightforward, and the human understanding of justice is limited. Ultimately, justice is grounded in the divine plan and purpose, and it is only through faith and trust in God that we can truly understand it.

The Unity of God's Attributes

It is important to know that God's attributes are one. In Christianity, God's attributes are often described as being unified or inseparable. This means that each attribute, such as God's love, mercy, justice, and righteousness, are not separate or distinct qualities, but rather they are interconnected and flow from God's essential nature.

For example, God's justice is not arbitrary or separate from God's love and mercy. Instead, God's justice is grounded in His love and mercy and works in harmony with these attributes. God's justice is not punitive, but restorative, and seeks to bring about the healing and redemption of individuals and society.

Similarly, God's righteousness is not a separate attribute from His justice, but rather flows from it. God's righteousness is the standard by which justice is measured and the foundation of His dealings with humanity.

Thus, the unity of God's attributes is a fundamental concept in Christian theology and helps to shape our understanding of God's character and actions in the world.

Jesus as Justice and Righteousness

In Scripture, Jesus is spoken of as both the justice and righteousness of God. He embodies these attributes in His teachings and actions. Jesus taught about the importance of justice and how it should be carried out with compassion and mercy. He challenged the corrupt authorities of His time and defended the marginalized and oppressed.

Jesus also lived a life of perfect righteousness, obeying God's laws and fulfilling the prophecies of the Old Testament. Through His death and resurrection, Jesus provided a way for humanity to be reconciled with God and receive salvation. This act was both just and righteous, as it fulfilled the requirement of justice for sin while demonstrating God's love and mercy for His creation.

Therefore, when Jesus is referred to as the justice and righteousness of God, it highlights the fact that He embodies these attributes fully and perfectly. It also emphasizes the importance of justice and righteousness in the Christian faith and how they are central to understanding God's character and plan for humanity.

Justice and Righteousness Revealed

When justice came to the nations, it brought the righteousness of God, which reconciles those who receive Jesus Christ as Savior. The concept of justice and righteousness is a common theme throughout the Bible, both in the Old and New

Testaments. The justice of God is often described as a characteristic that is synonymous with righteousness, mercy, and compassion. In the Old Testament, justice was typically administered through the law, and the consequences of disobedience were severe. However, God's ultimate goal was always to restore and reconcile His people to Himself.

In the New Testament, the justice and righteousness of God were fully revealed through Jesus Christ. Jesus came to fulfill the law and to reconcile sinners to God through His death on the cross. The Apostle Paul wrote in Romans 3:21-26: "But now apart from the law the righteousness of God has been made known, to which the Law and the Prophets testify. This righteousness is given through faith in Jesus Christ to all who believe. There is no difference between Jew and Gentile, for all have sinned and fall short of the glory of God, and all are justified freely by his grace through the redemption that came by Christ Jesus. God presented Christ as a sacrifice of atonement, through the shedding of his blood—to be received by faith. He did this to demonstrate his righteousness, because in his forbearance he had left the sins committed beforehand unpunished—he did it to demonstrate his righteousness at the present time, so as to be just and the one who justifies those who have faith in Jesus."

Through faith in Jesus Christ, God's justice and righteousness are revealed in a way that reconciles us to Him. This reconciliation brings about a transformation of our lives, as we are empowered to live in a way that is pleasing to God and brings about justice and righteousness in our relationships and communities. Ultimately, the justice and righteousness of God are inseparable and are fully revealed through Jesus Christ.

The Responsibility of Every Believer

Second Corinthians 5:18 states, "All this is from God, who reconciled us to himself through Christ and gave us the ministry of reconciliation." This verse highlights the responsibility of every believer to be involved in the ministry of reconciliation.

The passage emphasizes that it is God who has initiated reconciliation through Jesus Christ. As believers, we have received this gift of reconciliation and are now called to extend it to others. This involves actively participating in the work of bringing people into a restored relationship with God and with one another.

The phrase "ministry of reconciliation" means that believers are called to be ambassadors of Christ, working toward the restoration of relationships and the healing of brokenness. This can take many forms, including sharing the gospel with others, seeking to reconcile broken relationships, working for social justice, and demonstrating love and compassion toward others.

The responsibility of every believer is not just to receive the gift of reconciliation but to actively participate in extending it to others. This requires a commitment to living out our faith in practical ways, both individually and collectively as the body of Christ. It is a call to be agents of change in a broken world, working toward the restoration of all things through the power of the Holy Spirit.

Furthermore, we have been given the ministry of reconciliation. In other words, as ambassadors for Christ, we have the responsibility of bringing others to Christ so they can reconcile with God.

Restoration in the Old and New Testaments

Restoration is reflected in the Law that was given in the Old Testament and the new commandment Jesus gave in the New Testament. In the Old Testament, the Law included provisions for restitution and restoration for victims of crime. For example, Exodus 22:1 states, "If a man steals an ox or a sheep and slaughters it or sells it, he must pay back five head of cattle for the ox and four sheep for the sheep." This shows that the offender had to not only return the stolen property but also provide additional compensation for the harm caused to the victim.

In the New Testament, Jesus gave a new commandment to His disciples in John 13:34: "A new commandment I give to you, that you love one another: just as I have loved you, you also are to love one another." This commandment emphasizes the importance of love and forgiveness in relationships and is reflected in the principles of restorative justice which aim to repair harm and restore relationships.

Furthermore, the ultimate act of restoration is seen in the death and resurrection of Jesus Christ. Through His sacrifice, He made it possible for individuals to be restored to a right relationship with God and to experience healing and reconciliation in their relationships with others. This concept is central to the Christian faith and underlies the principles of restorative justice, which seek to restore broken relationships and promote healing and reconciliation.

The Purpose of the Law

What purpose did the Law serve? Galatians 3:24 states, "Therefore the law was our tutor to bring us to Christ, that we might be justified by faith." The purpose of the Law was to serve as a guardian or tutor, guiding the Israelites and teaching them about God's standards of righteousness. The Law revealed God's moral and ethical standards and demonstrated humanity's inability to perfectly keep them. It exposed the need for a savior and pointed toward Jesus Christ, who fulfilled the Law and made a way for justification by faith. The Law also served as a temporary measure until the coming of Christ, who established a new covenant and fulfilled the requirements of the Law. Therefore, the Law served to reveal humanity's need for redemption, guide them in righteousness, and ultimately point toward Jesus Christ as the solution to the problem of sin.

A schoolmaster or tutor in ancient Greek culture would accompany the children in his care, instructing and disciplining them when necessary. The law was like a schoolmaster which, by showing us our sins, was escorting us to Christ.

The Word Made Flesh

When the Word of God became flesh and lived among us, the consummation of the justice of God in the earth yielded righteousness. This statement highlights the idea that when

Jesus Christ, who is referred to as the "Word of God," came to live among human beings, it marked the ultimate fulfillment of God's justice on earth. In other words, God's justice was made complete and perfect through Jesus Christ, who through His life, death, and resurrection reconciled humanity to God and made it possible for people to receive forgiveness and salvation.

The justice of God is a fundamental aspect of God's character, which requires that all wrongdoing is punished and righteousness is upheld. The law of God, as revealed in the Old Testament, serves as a standard for righteousness and justice, but it also highlights the impossibility of human beings being able to perfectly keep the law. As a result, humanity became separated from God due to sin and was in need of redemption.

Through Jesus Christ, however, God's justice was satisfied, and the gap between humanity and God was bridged. Christ's death on the cross paid the penalty for sin, and His resurrection defeated death, which is the ultimate consequence of sin. As a result, those who believe in Jesus Christ and follow Him can experience the righteousness of God and be reconciled to God.

The justice of God finds its ultimate fulfillment in the person of Jesus Christ, who through His life, death, and resurrection reconciled humanity to God and made it possible for people to experience the righteousness of God.

The Law of Lex Talionis

The law of "lex talionis" was given to limit the revenges of a people without Christ. This Latin term translates to "law of retaliation" or "law of retribution." It is often associated with the Old Testament law of "an eye for an eye, a tooth for a tooth" found in Exodus 21:24, Leviticus 24:20, and Deuteronomy 19:21. This law was given to the ancient Israelites to regulate the concept of justice in their society, particularly in relation to crimes committed against one another.

The law of "lex talionis" sought to limit the revenge of a people without Christ by instituting a proportionate punishment for the harm done. In essence, it prevented individuals from taking excessive vengeance on others and encouraged them to seek justice through legal means. For example, if someone caused harm to another person, they were required to compensate them in a proportionate manner, rather than inflicting greater harm or taking excessive revenge.

However, the "lex talionis" was not perfect, and it had limitations. It did not address the underlying causes of the crimes committed or seek to restore relationships between offenders and victims. It was primarily concerned with ensuring justice was served by punishing the offender.

With the coming of Christ, the concept of justice was transformed from retribution to restoration. Jesus taught the importance of forgiveness, mercy, and love, and He demonstrated these qualities in His own life and ministry. Through His death and resurrection, Jesus provided a way for all people to be reconciled with God and with one another.

While the "lex talionis" served a purpose in regulating justice in ancient Israel, it was limited in its ability to address the underlying issues and restore relationships. Through Christ, the concept of justice was transformed into one of restoration, emphasizing forgiveness, mercy, and love as the means to bring about reconciliation between individuals and with God.

The Law of Retaliation and God's Justice

The law of retaliation began to teach that revenge was not part of God's justice, and that punishment did not yield righteousness. This law, also known as "lex talionis," was a principle of justice common in many ancient cultures. It allowed for retaliation in kind—"an eye for an eye" and "a tooth for a tooth." This law was given to limit the revenges of a people without Christ and to ensure that justice was served in a fair and proportionate manner.

However, with the coming of Christ, the law of retaliation began to be seen in a new light. Jesus taught that revenge was not part of God's justice and that punishment did not yield righteousness. Instead, He called for forgiveness and reconciliation and taught that the greatest commandment was to love God and love our neighbors as ourselves.

The apostle Paul also emphasized the importance of forgiveness and reconciliation in his teachings. In his letter to the Romans, he wrote, "Do not repay anyone evil for evil. Be careful to do what is right in the eyes of everyone. If it is possible, as far as it depends on you, live at peace with everyone" (Romans 12:17-18). Paul also wrote to the Corinthians that "God was reconciling the world to himself in Christ, not counting people's sins against them" (2 Corinthians 5:19).

In light of these teachings, it is clear that the law of retaliation was given to limit revenge in a world without Christ, but that the coming of Christ brought a new way of thinking about justice and righteousness. Forgiveness and reconciliation became the central focus, and the law of retaliation was seen as a limited and imperfect means of achieving justice.

Jesus Fulfills the Law

Jesus came to fulfill the Law and to provide a higher standard for those needing restoration. The concept of restoration has been a part of God's plan since the beginning of time, as seen in the Law given to the Israelites in the Old Testament. However, the people's inability to keep the Law perfectly revealed the need for a higher standard and a means of true restoration. This is where Jesus Christ comes in.

Jesus came not to abolish the Law, but to fulfill it (Matthew 5:17). He provided the perfect example of righteousness and obedience to God's will, serving as the ultimate sacrifice for the forgiveness of sins and offering a path to true restoration. Through faith in Jesus, believers can experience reconciliation with God and the transformation necessary to live a life of righteousness.

Furthermore, Jesus elevated the concept of restoration beyond just physical or material compensation to include emotional and spiritual healing. In the Sermon on the Mount, He taught that those who have been wronged should not seek revenge but rather seek to love and serve their enemies (Matthew 5:43-48).

He also emphasized the importance of forgiveness, instructing His followers to forgive others as they have been forgiven by God (Matthew 6:14-15).

In this way, Jesus provided a higher standard of justice and restoration that goes beyond mere legalistic compliance with the Law. He showed that true restoration involves not only the settling of debts and the restoration of relationships but also the healing of emotional and spiritual wounds. Through faith in Him, believers can experience the transformative power of God's love and grace, leading to true restoration and righteousness.

The Fulfillment of Justice

The fulfillment of justice was not intended to give offenders what they deserved, but to move them toward restoration through the power of love. Romans 6:23 describes two inexorable absolutes: spiritual death is the paycheck for every man's sin, and eternal life is a loving free gift God gives undeserving sinners who believe in His Son.

The concept of justice in Christianity is closely related to restoration, which involves the transformation of the offender and the healing of the community affected by the offense. Jesus came to fulfill the law of justice, not by simply punishing offenders, but by providing a higher standard for restoration. The ultimate goal of justice, therefore, is not to give offenders what they deserve, but to restore them through the power of love.

Jesus demonstrated this approach to justice in His teachings and actions. For example, when the Pharisees brought to Him a woman caught in adultery and asked if she should be stoned according to the Law of Moses, Jesus did not condemn her, but instead offered forgiveness and restoration (John 8:1-11). He also taught that forgiveness should be offered not just seven times, but seventy-seven times (Matthew 18:21-22).

Furthermore, Jesus' death and resurrection provided the ultimate demonstration of restorative justice. Through His sacrifice, He provided a way for offenders to be reconciled to God and restored to their rightful place in the community. This is exemplified in 2 Corinthians 5:18-19, which states, "All this is from God, who reconciled us to himself through Christ and gave us the ministry of reconciliation: that God was reconciling the world to himself in Christ, not counting people's sins against them."

The fulfillment of justice in Christianity is not about punishment or revenge, but about restoration through love and forgiveness. This approach requires a shift in focus from the offender to the victim and the community, and a willingness to work toward healing and reconciliation.

The Goal of Restorative Justice Ministry

What is the goal of restorative justice ministry? Most ministries today do not address all the parties that are affected by the crime. They either focus on the offender while neglecting the victim and community, or they focus only on the victim.

Complete healing and restoration only occur when the injuries to all parties are addressed.

The goal of restorative justice ministry is to promote healing, reconciliation, and restoration for all parties affected by crime or harm. This approach recognizes that crime is not just a violation of law, but a violation of relationships and the community. Therefore, restorative justice ministry seeks to repair the harm caused by crime by bringing together the victim, the offender, and the community to address the needs of all involved.

Restorative justice ministry aims to shift the focus from punishment to restoration, offering a more holistic approach to justice that takes into account the emotional, psychological, and spiritual needs of all parties involved. This involves creating a safe space for open dialogue, empathy, and understanding, and facilitating a process of healing and transformation that leads to greater accountability, responsibility, and meaningful restitution.

The goal of restorative justice ministry is not just to resolve conflicts, but to promote social justice and community well-being. This means addressing the root causes of crime and working toward systemic change that promotes equity, fairness, and respect for all individuals. Restorative justice ministry also seeks to empower individuals and communities to take an active role in shaping the justice system and promoting a more compassionate and restorative approach to justice.

Therefore, the goal of restorative justice ministry is to foster healing, reconciliation, and restoration for all involved, promoting a more just and peaceful society for all.

Loving One Another

God requires that we love one another, as Jesus loved us, and to love our neighbor as ourselves. This requirement is derived from two key teachings of Jesus. In John 13:34-35, Jesus says, "A new commandment I give to you, that you love one another: just as I have loved you, you also are to love one another. By this all people will know that you are my disciples, if you have love for one another." This commandment to love one another is rooted in Jesus' own love for His disciples, which was selfless, sacrificial, and unconditional.

The second teaching comes from Mark 12:31, where Jesus answers a question about which commandment is the most important. He replies, "The most important is, 'Hear, O Israel: The Lord our God, the Lord is one. And you shall love the Lord your God with all your heart and with all your soul and with all your mind and with all your strength.' The second is this: 'You shall love your neighbor as yourself.' There is no other commandment greater than these."

Together, these teachings call us to love others with the same love that God has shown us, and to love our neighbors as ourselves. This love is not based on merit or worthiness, but is a reflection of the unconditional love that God has for all people. As Christians, we are called to live out this love in our relationships with others, seeking to show kindness, compassion, and forgiveness to all, regardless of their background, beliefs, or actions. Ultimately, the goal of this love is to bring healing, restoration, and reconciliation to broken relationships and a hurting world.

Who Is Our Neighbor?

Our neighbor is the prisoner who offended, the victim who is brokenhearted, and the community which was blinded by a need for revenge. In the Bible, Jesus tells us to love our neighbor as ourselves. This commandment includes all people, even those who have committed crimes and are incarcerated. When we show love and compassion to those who have offended, we are fulfilling this commandment and demonstrating the love of Christ.

The victim of a crime is also our neighbor, and we are called to show them love and support as they heal from the trauma they have experienced. Restorative justice seeks to bring healing to both the offender and the victim, recognizing that both have been affected by the crime in different ways.

Furthermore, when a community is affected by crime, it is important to remember that the members of that community are also our neighbors. Restorative justice principles aim to involve the community in the process of addressing the harm caused by the crime and developing solutions that promote healing and prevention.

Ultimately, restorative justice ministry recognizes that all people are created in the image of God and have inherent dignity and worth. By loving our neighbor, including those who have offended, those who have been victimized, and the wider community, we can work toward a more just and compassionate society.

Biblical Justice as Restoration

Biblical justice is restoration through righteousness to all who receive Christ. Paul described this view in Romans 3:22: "the righteousness of God, through faith in Jesus Christ, to all and on all who believe."

Biblical justice can be defined as the restoration of what is broken or wrong, to bring about righteousness in all aspects of life. The ultimate source of justice is God, and He has revealed His perfect standard of justice in the Bible. The Bible teaches that justice is an important part of God's character, and that He desires justice for all people. This includes both the victim and the offender.

Restoration is the key to biblical justice. When a wrong has been committed, restoration involves making things right between the offender and the victim, and also between the offender and God. This restoration is made possible through the sacrifice of Jesus Christ, who paid the penalty for our sins and made it possible for us to be reconciled to God.

Restorative justice ministry, therefore, seeks to bring about this restoration through various means such as restitution, reconciliation, and rehabilitation. It seeks to involve all parties affected by the crime, including the offender, the victim, and the community.

The goal of restorative justice ministry is not only to hold offenders accountable for their actions but also to bring about healing and reconciliation for all involved. It aims to address the root causes of crime and to provide opportunities for offenders to take responsibility for their actions, make amends, and move toward a better future.

Biblical justice is about restoring what is broken or wrong to bring about righteousness for all involved, and this is made possible through the sacrifice of Jesus Christ. Restorative justice ministry seeks to bring about this restoration by involving all parties affected by the crime and providing opportunities for healing, reconciliation, and rehabilitation.

The Epistle to Philemon

Which epistle of the Apostle Paul serves as a fine example of restorative justice? The answer is Philemon. Paul's letter to Philemon serves as a fine example of restorative justice.

In this letter, Paul writes to Philemon, a slave owner, regarding his slave Onesimus who had run away and then come to faith in Christ through Paul's ministry. Paul writes to appeal to Philemon to receive Onesimus back not just as a slave, but as a brother in Christ.

Paul could have simply ordered Philemon to release Onesimus, or could have taken legal action against him for mistreating his slave. Instead, Paul takes a restorative justice approach by appealing to Philemon's Christian values and urging him to do what is right, not just what is legally required.

In his letter, Paul acknowledges that Onesimus had wronged Philemon, and offers to make things right by paying for any damage caused by his escape. He also reminds Philemon that they are brothers in Christ, and that he should receive Onesimus back as he would receive Paul himself.

This approach emphasizes reconciliation and restoration rather than punishment and retribution. It shows how restorative justice can be applied even in situations that involve societal structures of oppression, such as slavery.

Concepts in Philemon

The epistle to Philemon demonstrates several principles of restorative justice, including the concepts of rehabilitation (verses 10, 16), restoration (verse 17), and restitution (verses 18-19).

Until I read this letter to Philemon, I didn't realize what a talented leader Paul was. I knew he was a great theologian, an incredible author, a successful businessman and church planter, and a compelling speaker. But in this letter, we see his leadership skills as he competently addressed the situation. He left the decision completely up to Philemon and didn't trample all over his rights as the slave's owner. And yet, as we see throughout this letter, Paul arranged things so it would be very difficult for Philemon to say no without losing face among his brothers and sisters in Christ.

The epistle demonstrates several principles of restorative justice. First, **forgiveness**—Paul encourages Philemon to forgive his runaway slave, Onesimus, who has since become a Christian. Second, **reconciliation**—Paul writes to Philemon, asking him to receive Onesimus back as a brother in Christ, rather than as a slave. Third, **restitution**—Paul offers to pay any debts or damages owed by Onesimus to Philemon, as a way of making things right between them. Fourth, **healing**—Paul acknowledges the hurt and pain caused by Onesimus' actions, but seeks to bring healing and restoration through forgiveness and reconciliation. Fifth, **community involvement**—Paul asks the church in Colossae to support Philemon and Onesimus in their journey toward reconciliation, showing the importance of community involvement in restorative justice.

Thus, the epistle to Philemon demonstrates how restorative justice principles can be applied in personal relationships, leading to reconciliation and restoration.

The Crime of Onesimus

What crime did the slave, Onesimus, commit against his owner, Philemon? Onesimus stole from his master and ran away. This very heart-warming letter was written by Paul for the purpose of interceding for the runaway slave who had become a faithful Christian. He not only was pleading for mercy for him from his master, Philemon—he was also reminding Philemon of his duty as a fellow Christian toward this man.

Paul's Recommendation

What course of action did Paul recommend to Onesimus after he became a Christian? It was agreed that Onesimus would return to Philemon to make amends, even though under Roman law he could face the death penalty.

In the Epistle to Philemon, Paul recommended that Onesimus should return to his master, Philemon, and reconcile with him. Paul urged Philemon to welcome Onesimus back not as a slave, but as a brother in Christ. He offered to personally pay for any wrong that Onesimus had committed and asked Philemon to receive him with forgiveness and love. Paul's message was that true restoration and justice can only be achieved through forgiveness and reconciliation, rather than punishment and retribution.

This was a volatile situation. Onesimus was a changed man, but he must have been nervous about going back to Philemon. After all, Roman law gave slave owners the right to brand the forehead of runaway slaves, lock them in chains, or simply execute them. Onesimus knew he deserved any one of these punishments because he had not only run away from Philemon but had stolen from him as well. Anything could happen.

A Brother Beloved

The Epistle to Philemon is Paul's plea that Onesimus no longer be viewed as a runaway slave, but rather as a brother beloved. If a man is a stranger, I might make him my slave. But how can I make my brother be my slave? In this relationship as brothers and not slaves, Paul effectively abolished the sting of the "master-slave" relationship.

In the ancient Roman world, slavery was a common institution and it was not uncommon for slaves to run away from their masters. When Onesimus, a slave of Philemon, ran away and later met Paul, he became a Christian and a changed man. Paul recognized that Onesimus was now a brother in Christ and not just a slave, and as such, he encouraged Philemon to see him in the same light.

In his letter to Philemon, Paul writes in verse 16, "no longer as a slave but more than a slave, a beloved brother, especially to me but how much more to you, both in the flesh and in the Lord." This statement makes it clear that Paul is urging Philemon to see Onesimus as more than just a slave, but as a fellow Christian and beloved brother.

Furthermore, Paul also offered to take responsibility for any debt that Onesimus owed to Philemon, indicating that he was willing to make things right between them and reconcile them as brothers in Christ.

Paul's message in the Epistle to Philemon is one of reconciliation and restoration, urging Philemon to see Onesimus not as a slave who had wronged him, but as a brother who had been transformed by the power of Christ.

The Way of the Cross

While the world pursues power and glory, Christians are to pursue the way of the Cross—the way of forgiveness, restoration, and love.

The way of the Cross, as exemplified by Jesus Christ, is a way of sacrificial love and humility. It is a path that goes against the values of the world, which often prioritize power, prestige, and personal gain. Instead of seeking these things, Christians are called to imitate Christ by putting the needs of others before their own and seeking restoration and reconciliation rather than revenge.

Forgiveness is a key aspect of the way of the Cross. Just as Christ forgave those who crucified Him, Christians are called to forgive those who have wronged them. This does not mean that justice should not be sought or that wrongs should be ignored, but rather that forgiveness should be extended even to those who do not deserve it. In this way, forgiveness can lead to restoration and healing, both for the individual who forgives and for the one who is forgiven.

Restoration is also a crucial aspect of the way of the Cross. Rather than seeking revenge or punishment, Christians are called to seek restoration and reconciliation with those who have wronged them. This means working toward repairing relationships and restoring the dignity of those who have been hurt. Restoration requires humility and a willingness to admit fault and seek forgiveness.

Love is the foundation of the way of the Cross. Christ's sacrificial love on the Cross is the ultimate example of love in action, and Christians are called to love others in the same way. This means seeking the good of others, even at personal cost, and putting the needs of others before one's own desires. Love is a transformative force that can bring healing, restoration, and reconciliation.

The way of the Cross is a path of forgiveness, restoration, and love. It is a way that goes against the values of the world, but leads to true healing and transformation. As Christians, we are called to imitate Christ in all things, including the way we interact with others. By following the way of the Cross, we can be agents of God's love and restoration in the world.

The Hope of Restorative Justice

No matter what a person has done in the past, God calls them to Himself and offers them the hope of restorative justice. Paul recognized this fact when he recorded these words in First Timothy 1:15: "Christ Jesus came into the world to save sinners, of whom I am chief." Paul had been a persecutor and murderer of the followers of Christ, but God called him to Himself and offered him the hope of restorative justice.

The message of the gospel is one of hope and redemption. It is a message that God loves us, despite our failures and sins, and desires to restore us to a right relationship with Him. This hope is available to all people, no matter what they have done in the past.

Throughout the Bible, we see examples of individuals who were given a second chance by God. David, for example, committed adultery and murder, but when he repented, God forgave him and restored him to his position as king. The apostle Paul, who persecuted Christians before his conversion, went on to become one of the greatest evangelists in history.

God's desire for restorative justice is seen in His provision of a way for our sins to be forgiven through Jesus Christ. When we repent and turn to Him, He forgives us and begins the process of restoring us to a right relationship with Him. This process may involve discipline and correction, but it is ultimately for our good and His glory.

As Christians, we are called to extend this message of restorative justice to others. We are called to love our neighbors and to seek to restore those who have been broken by sin and injustice. This may involve advocating for the rights of the oppressed, providing support to victims of crime, and working toward reconciliation between offenders and their victims.

In all of our efforts toward restorative justice, we must remember that it is only through the power of God's love and grace that true restoration can take place. We are not called to be judges or to seek revenge, but to extend the same forgiveness and mercy that we have received from God to others.

Forgiveness Makes Restoration Possible

The forgiveness granted by God and by others is what makes restoration possible. Forgiveness is an essential component of restorative justice because it allows for healing and reconciliation to take place. When someone has wronged another person, the relationship between them is damaged, and forgiveness is necessary for that relationship to be restored. Without forgiveness, the wronged person may hold onto anger, bitterness, and resentment toward the offender, preventing any chance of restoration.

God's forgiveness is offered freely to all who come to Him in repentance, acknowledging their wrongdoing and asking for His forgiveness. This forgiveness is not based on our own merit or worthiness but on God's grace and love for us. Similarly, when someone wrongs us, forgiving them is an act of grace and love, not based on their merit or worthiness, but on our desire to restore the relationship and move forward in love and reconciliation.

In the context of restorative justice, forgiveness allows both the offender and the victim to move toward healing and restoration. The offender can acknowledge their wrongdoing, seek forgiveness, and work toward making amends and rebuilding trust. The victim can choose to forgive and release their anger and bitterness toward the offender, allowing them to move forward in healing and reconciliation. Overall, forgiveness is a crucial aspect of restorative justice as it allows for the possibility of restoration and healing for all parties involved.

The Church has been given a clear mandate to engage in criminal justice ministry. This mandate is not optional. It is not peripheral. It is central to our identity as followers of Jesus Christ. We are called to be agents of reconciliation, to extend the same forgiveness and restoration that we have received from God to others, including those who have been incarcerated.

The question is not whether the Church should get involved in restorative justice. The question is whether we will be faithful to the calling we have been given. The world is watching. The prisoners are waiting. The victims are hoping. And Christ Himself, who identifies with the least of these, is calling us to action.

In the chapters that follow, we will explore how the Church can put these principles into practice. We will look at the restorative justice ministry paradigm, how the Church can impact corrections, and the process of organizational change. The call has been issued. The question remains: will we answer?

CHAPTER 07

THE RESTORATIVE JUSTICE MINISTRY PARADIGM

We have journeyed together through six chapters, each building upon the last. We began by examining the traditional view of justice—its ancient roots in the law of retaliation, its psychological appeal, and its troubling consequences. We saw how a system designed to punish has grown into a massive enterprise that incarcerates more of its citizens than any other nation on earth, at enormous cost and with little to show for it.

We explored why this system must be restructured. We looked at the soaring costs, the public's fear and frustration, the isolation of communities, and the way the system steals conflicts from those to whom they belong. We saw how the traditional model fails victims, fails offenders, and fails communities.

We then began to glimpse a different view of justice. We explored restorative justice—what it is, how it differs from the traditional model, and why it offers hope for healing and reconciliation. We considered the principles and practices that make restorative justice unique, and we saw how it centers victims, holds offenders accountable through repair, and involves communities in the process of justice.

We examined the conceptual frameworks that undergird restorative justice—the ideas, theories, and models that give it shape and substance. We saw how thinkers like Nils Christie have helped us understand crime as a catalyst for community empowerment, and how various conceptual models provide frameworks for community-based practice.

We explored the promising practices that have emerged as communities embrace restorative justice. We looked at sentencing circles, victim impact statements, community reparation boards, community service, restitution, victim-offender mediation, family group conferencing, victim impact panels, victim impact classes, and a range of community-based initiatives that connect the justice system with the public.

And in the previous chapter, we considered whether the Church should get involved in restorative justice. We saw that God has selected the Church as His primary instrument of restorative justice and has given it a clear mandate to do criminal justice ministry. We explored the biblical foundations of this calling and the questions it raises for those who would answer it.

Now, in this chapter, we turn to the practical outworking of all that we have learned. We turn to the restorative justice ministry paradigm—a framework for how the Church can actually do this work. This is not abstract theory. It is not distant policy. It is the hands-on, day-by-day, person-by-person ministry of bringing healing and restoration to those affected by crime.

In this chapter, we will explore what it means to minister to offenders, to victims, to families, and to communities. We will consider the role of repentance, the importance of addressing harm, the necessity of forgiveness, and the goal of restoration for all parties. We will see that restorative justice ministry is not simple or easy, but it is deeply rewarding and profoundly biblical.

Beyond the Regeneration of the Offender

Let us begin with an important truth. Although the primary goal of restorative justice ministry is the regeneration of the offender, other issues concerning their crime and the impact of that behavior need to be addressed. This is a point that is often missed, even by well-meaning ministries.

Here is what happens. An offender comes to faith in prison. They accept Christ. They experience genuine conversion. They are regenerated—born again. And when they are released, they may believe that society owes them something. After all, they have found Jesus. They have changed. Shouldn't everyone celebrate? Shouldn't doors open for them?

But this attitude, however understandable, is problematic. It ignores the fact that their crime caused real harm to real people. Victims are still suffering. Families are still broken. Communities are still fearful. The offender may have been transformed, but the consequences of their actions remain.

This is why crime and the impact of that behavior must be addressed. It is vital to the restorative justice process. Most regenerated offenders who come out of prison without having addressed the impact of their criminal behavior will often believe that society owes them something. They need to understand that while God's grace is free, the consequences of their actions still need to be addressed.

Restorative justice is a multifaceted approach to crime that focuses on healing and restoration, rather than solely on punishment. While the regeneration of the offender is a primary goal of restorative justice ministry, it is not the only issue that needs to be addressed.

When a crime is committed, it affects not only the offender but also the victim and the community. Therefore, restorative justice also seeks to address the harm caused by the crime and to make amends for the damage done. This includes addressing issues of accountability and responsibility, repairing harm, and reconciling relationships.

Restorative justice ministry recognizes that offenders must be held accountable for their actions and that they must make amends for the harm they have caused. This can take various forms, such as restitution, community service, or counseling. Additionally, offenders must acknowledge their responsibility for their actions and express remorse for the harm they have caused.

Restorative justice ministry also recognizes the importance of supporting the victim and addressing their needs. This can involve providing emotional support, financial assistance, or other forms of restitution. Victims must also be given a voice in the process, allowing them to express their feelings and concerns and to participate in the restoration process.

Finally, restorative justice ministry recognizes that crimes have a broader impact on the community as a whole. Therefore, the restoration process must involve the community, including community leaders and other stakeholders, in addressing the root causes of crime and working together to promote healing and reconciliation.

While the regeneration of the offender is an important goal of restorative justice ministry, it is only one aspect of a broader process that seeks to address the harm caused by the crime and to promote healing and restoration for all parties involved.

Ministering to the Needs of the Offender

When you minister to the needs of the offender, you must not forget that one of their needs is to be healed of the injury of the crime. This may sound strange. We usually think of offenders as causing injury, not suffering it. But the truth is that crime injures everyone it touches, including the person who committed it.

When ministering to the needs of an offender in a restorative justice context, it is important to acknowledge and address the harm that their actions have caused to others. This requires a focus not only on the offender's rehabilitation and restoration, but also on the needs of the victim and the wider community.

The offender may need to make amends for their actions, both through restitution and through actions that seek to repair the harm caused. This may involve making reparations to the victim, such as paying for damages or providing other forms of compensation. It may also involve participating in community service or other activities that benefit those affected by their behavior.

Additionally, the offender may need to address any underlying issues that contributed to their behavior, such as addiction, mental health problems, or a history of trauma. This may involve connecting them with appropriate resources and support, such as counseling, treatment programs, or support groups.

The offender may also need to heal from the ways in which they themselves have been harmed. Many offenders have experienced trauma, abuse, neglect, and other forms of victimization long before they ever committed a crime. They may carry deep wounds that have never been addressed. Part of restorative justice ministry is helping them find healing for these wounds as well.

A restorative justice approach seeks to address the needs of all parties involved, with a focus on healing and restoration rather than punishment and retribution. By ministering to the needs of the offender in a holistic way, we can work towards building a more just and compassionate society.

The Beginning of the Restorative Justice Process

What marks the beginning of the restorative justice process in the offender's life? Part of that healing process is to right the wrongs as much as it is in the power of the offender to do so.

The beginning of the restorative justice process in the offender's life is when they take responsibility for their actions and show genuine remorse for the harm they have caused. This may involve admitting guilt, making restitution, and seeking forgiveness from those affected by their actions. It is important for the offender to acknowledge the harm they have caused and to take steps towards making things right. Only then can the process of restoration begin.

This is not a small thing. Taking responsibility requires humility. It requires courage. It requires the offender to look squarely at what they have done and to own it completely. This is difficult for anyone, but it is especially difficult for those who have spent years, perhaps decades, avoiding responsibility and blaming others for their problems.

But it is essential. Without this step, there can be no genuine restoration. The offender may go through the motions of religious observance. They may attend Bible studies and prayer meetings. They may even experience moments of emotional release. But if they have not taken responsibility for the harm they have caused, the work is not done.

The beginning of restorative justice is marked by a genuine recognition of harm, a deep sense of remorse, and a willingness to take responsibility for one's actions and make things right.

Recognition, Remorse, and Repentance

In a restorative justice paradigm, the offender at some point recognizes the hurt he has caused, and experiences shame for his actions, a shame and sorrow which leads to repentance. This is a crucial distinction.

In 2 Corinthians 7:10, Paul explained that repentance is a result of "godly sorrow," which is very different from human remorse that has no redemptive capability. Human remorse is nothing more than the wounded pride of getting caught in a sin and having one's lusts go unfulfilled. This kind of sorrow leads only to guilt, shame, despair, depression, self-pity, hopelessness and death.

Think about the difference. Human remorse says, "I feel terrible that I got caught. I feel terrible that people are angry at me. I feel terrible about the consequences I'm facing." The focus is on self. The concern is about personal discomfort.

Godly sorrow says, "I feel terrible that I hurt that person. I feel terrible about the pain I caused. I feel terrible that I dishonored God and damaged my relationships." The focus is on others and on God. The concern is about the harm done, not the consequences faced.

In a restorative justice paradigm, the offender is not only held accountable for their actions, but is also given the opportunity to take responsibility for their actions and make amends. This can only happen when the offender recognizes the harm they have caused and experiences genuine remorse for their actions.

This recognition and remorse often come through a process of deep reflection and self-examination. The offender may be encouraged to acknowledge the full extent of the harm they have caused, and to understand how their actions have affected not only their victim, but also their family, their community, and themselves. Through this process, the offender may come to understand the gravity of their actions and the need for accountability.

This recognition and remorse can lead to genuine repentance, which involves not only feeling sorry for one's actions, but also taking concrete steps to make things right. This can include making restitution to the victim, participating in counseling or treatment programs to address underlying issues that led to the offense, and engaging in community service or other activities to make amends for the harm caused.

The beginning of the restorative justice process in the offender's life is marked by a genuine recognition of the harm caused, a deep sense of remorse, and a willingness to take responsibility for one's actions and make things right.

Repentance Beyond Conversion

Repentance goes far beyond accepting Christ as one's personal Savior; it is a decision to change behavior, attitudes, and beliefs that are not in agreement with the Word of God. This is a crucial understanding for restorative justice ministry.

Repentance is a crucial aspect of the Christian faith and a necessary step in the process of restorative justice. It is a decision to turn away from one's old way of life and turn towards God's way of living. It involves a change in behavior, attitudes, and beliefs that are not in agreement with the Word of God.

True repentance is not just about feeling sorry for one's actions; it is a genuine desire to change and make amends for the harm caused. In the context of restorative justice, repentance is the first step towards making things right with the victim and the community. It is a recognition that one's actions have hurt others and a willingness to take responsibility for the harm caused.

Repentance involves confessing one's wrongdoing and seeking forgiveness from God and those who have been hurt. It requires humility, vulnerability, and a willingness to face the consequences of one's actions. It is only through genuine repentance that the offender can begin the process of restoration and reconciliation.

Repentance is not a one-time event but an ongoing orientation of the heart. It is a continual turning away from sin and towards God. It is a daily decision to live differently, to think differently, to act differently. For the offender, this means that even after they have made amends for their past crimes, they must continue to walk in repentance, guarding against the attitudes and behaviors that led them astray.

Repentance is a vital part of the restorative justice process. It is a decision to turn away from one's old way of life and turn towards God's way of living. It involves a change in behavior, attitudes, and beliefs that are not in agreement with the Word of God. Repentance is the first step towards making things right with the victim and the community and is necessary for true restoration and reconciliation to take place.

From Restored to Restorer

The restorative justice paradigm suggests that the offender not only has to be restored through repentance, but also must become a restorer through restoration. This is a powerful and transformative concept.

It is very common for even regenerated offenders to harbor bitterness, hatred, and resentment toward members of the criminal justice community. They may even view this as a right resulting from the way they were treated while serving time. According to Hebrews 12:15, these types of feelings "cause trouble"; therefore, the offender must learn to forgive.

Restorative justice is a philosophy and approach to justice that focuses on repairing harm caused by criminal behavior rather than punishing the offender. It seeks to restore relationships between the offender, victim, and community, rather than simply punishing the offender. One of the key principles of restorative justice is the idea that the offender should not only be restored through repentance, but also become a restorer through restoration.

Restoration in the context of restorative justice involves repairing the harm caused by the offense. This can involve several steps, including acknowledging the harm done, taking responsibility for the offense, making amends to the victim, and working to prevent similar harm from occurring in the future. Restoration aims to bring about healing and reconciliation between the offender, victim, and community.

The idea that the offender should become a restorer through restoration means that the offender must not only be restored but also play an active role in restoring the harm they caused. This involves taking steps to make amends, such as apologizing to the victim, offering restitution, or engaging in community service. It also involves working to prevent future harm by addressing the underlying causes of the offense and taking steps to avoid similar behavior in the future.

By becoming a restorer through restoration, the offender can demonstrate their commitment to repairing the harm they caused and to making positive changes in their life. This can help to rebuild trust between the offender, victim, and community and can contribute to a sense of justice and healing.

The offender becomes a restorer when they move beyond their own healing to participate in the healing of others. They may share their story with at-risk youth, warning them of the consequences of criminal behavior. They may mentor other offenders who are just beginning their own journey of restoration. They may speak to community groups about the importance of forgiveness and reconciliation. In these ways and more, the restored offender becomes an agent of restoration for others.

The restorative justice paradigm suggests that the offender not only has to be restored through repentance, but also must become a restorer through restoration. This involves taking responsibility for the harm caused, making amends, and working to prevent future harm. By becoming a restorer, the offender can demonstrate their commitment to repairing the harm and making positive changes in their life, which can contribute to healing and reconciliation.

Addressing the Injury to the Victim

Ministry from a restorative justice paradigm has to address the issues concerning the injury to the victim of the offense(s). This is not optional. It is essential.

Restorative justice is a philosophy and approach to justice that focuses on repairing harm caused by criminal behavior rather than punishing the offender. It seeks to restore relationships between the offender, victim, and community, rather than simply punishing the offender. One of the key principles of restorative justice is the idea that ministry from this paradigm must address the issues concerning the injury to the victim(s) of the offense(s).

When ministry is approached from a restorative justice paradigm, the needs of the victim(s) are given priority. This involves addressing the injury caused by the offense(s) and working to repair the harm. The goal of restorative justice ministry is to bring about healing and reconciliation between the offender, victim, and community.

To address the issues concerning the injury to the victim(s) of the offense(s), restorative justice ministry may involve several steps.

Acknowledging the harm done is the first step. This involves recognizing and acknowledging the impact of the offense(s) on the victim(s). It involves listening to their experiences and feelings, and validating their pain. Victims need to know that their suffering has been seen and understood.

Offering support and care is the second step. Restorative justice ministry must provide care and support to the victim(s). This can include emotional support, practical assistance, and access to resources to help them heal. Victims may need counseling, financial assistance, help navigating the justice system, or simply a compassionate presence.

Facilitating communication is the third step. Restorative justice ministry can facilitate communication between the offender and victim(s). This can help the offender to take responsibility for their actions, apologize for the harm caused, and work to make amends. For victims, this communication can be healing, allowing them to express their pain and receive acknowledgment from the one who caused it.

Providing opportunities for the victim(s) to participate in the justice process is the fourth step. Restorative justice ministry can provide opportunities for the victim(s) to participate in the justice process. This can include offering input on the terms of restitution or community service, or participating in a restorative justice conference or circle. Victims should not be passive observers but active participants in their own healing.

Supporting the victim(s) throughout the process is the fifth step. Restorative justice ministry must continue to support the victim(s) throughout the process of healing and reconciliation. This can involve follow-up care, ongoing support, and advocacy for their needs. Healing is not a one-time event but a journey, and victims need companions on that journey.

Ministry from a restorative justice paradigm must address the issues concerning the injury to the victim(s) of the offense(s). This involves prioritizing the needs of the victim(s), acknowledging the harm done, providing support and care, facilitating communication, providing opportunities for the victim(s) to participate in the justice process, and supporting them throughout the process. By addressing the needs of the victim(s), restorative justice ministry can contribute to healing and reconciliation between the offender, victim(s), and community.

The Victim Is Not an Abstraction

The victim cannot be the system or the State, which are only abstractions. This is a crucial distinction that must be understood.

In the context of restorative justice, the victim is the person who has been directly harmed or affected by the offense committed by the offender. This can be an individual, a group, or a community. The focus of restorative justice is on repairing the harm caused by the offense and restoring the relationships between the offender, victim(s), and the community.

The system or the state, on the other hand, are abstractions that do not have feelings, emotions, or experiences. While the justice system and the state may have a role in responding to crime and addressing harm, they cannot be the victim(s) of the offense(s). Rather, they are responsible for upholding the law and administering justice in a fair and impartial manner.

In the traditional criminal justice system, the state is treated as the victim. The case is styled as "The People versus the Defendant" or "The State versus the Offender." The actual human victim becomes secondary, a witness for the prosecution rather than a party to the proceedings. This is a profound distortion.

It is important to recognize the difference between the victim(s) and the justice system or state in the context of restorative justice. By focusing on the needs of the victim(s), restorative justice seeks to provide a more human-centered approach to justice that prioritizes repairing harm and restoring relationships. This approach recognizes the emotional and psychological impact of crime on individuals and communities, and seeks to address these impacts through a process of healing and reconciliation.

The victim cannot be the system or the state, which are only abstractions. Rather, the focus of restorative justice is on repairing the harm caused to the victim(s) and restoring relationships between the offender, victim(s), and community. By recognizing the difference between the victim(s) and the justice system or state, restorative justice provides a more human-centered approach to justice that seeks to address the emotional and psychological impact of crime.

Crime Impacts Human Beings

Crime has an impact on human beings, who have feelings and emotions. This seems obvious, but it is often forgotten in the abstract procedures of the justice system.

Crime has an impact on human beings who have feelings and emotions because it involves the violation of one's physical or psychological integrity, sense of safety, and personal autonomy. When a person becomes a victim of crime, they may experience a range of emotions, including fear, anger, sadness, and anxiety.

For example, if someone is physically assaulted, they may suffer physical injuries and trauma, which can lead to pain, fear, and a loss of sense of control over their own body. Similarly, if someone's property is stolen or damaged, they may feel violated and experience a sense of loss or grief.

In addition to the direct impact on the victim(s), crime can also have an impact on their family, friends, and community. The fear of crime can lead to a loss of trust, a sense of vulnerability, and a decreased quality of life. It can also affect people's sense of safety and well-being, leading to social isolation, anxiety, and depression.

The emotional and psychological impact of crime is often long-lasting, and can have a significant impact on a person's quality of life. Victims may struggle with post-traumatic stress, depression, anxiety disorders, and other mental health challenges. They may have difficulty trusting others, forming relationships, or feeling safe in their own homes.

Restorative justice recognizes the importance of addressing these impacts and seeks to provide a more human-centered approach to justice that focuses on repairing harm and restoring relationships between the offender, victim(s), and community.

Crime has an impact on human beings who have feelings and emotions because it involves the violation of one's physical or psychological integrity, sense of safety, and personal autonomy. The emotional and psychological impact of crime can be long-lasting, and can have a significant impact on a person's quality of life. Restorative justice seeks to address these impacts by providing a more human-centered approach to justice that focuses on repairing harm and restoring relationships.

Addressing the Victim's Pain

Whenever there is a direct victim, their pain needs to be addressed so the offender can see how his/her actions affected and damaged the lives of other people. This step is so vital because it teaches the offender how to become a caring member of the community.

The statement that whenever there is a direct victim, their pain needs to be addressed so the offender can see how his/her actions affected and damaged the lives of other people is a central tenet of restorative justice. Restorative justice is an approach to justice that focuses on repairing the harm caused by crime and restoring relationships between the offender, victim(s), and community.

In a restorative justice process, the offender is given an opportunity to take responsibility for their actions, acknowledge the harm they have caused, and make amends to the victim(s) and community. This process requires the offender to confront the impact of their actions on others, including the pain and suffering of the victim(s).

When the pain of the victim(s) is addressed, it can have a powerful impact on the offender. Seeing and understanding the direct impact of their actions on others can help the offender develop empathy and understanding, leading to a greater sense of remorse and accountability for their actions. This, in turn, can lead to a greater likelihood of the offender taking steps to make amends, and less likely to reoffend.

Addressing the pain of the victim(s) is also an important aspect of healing and recovery for the victim(s). By being given a voice and having their pain acknowledged, victims can feel empowered and validated. They may also be more likely to forgive the offender and move forward in their own healing process.

This step transforms the offender's understanding of their crime. They may have thought of it abstractly—as breaking a law, as getting caught, as serving time. But when they see the real human being they hurt, when they hear about the nightmares, the fear, the financial hardship, the ongoing trauma—their perspective changes. They begin to understand that their actions had real consequences for real people.

Addressing the pain of the victim(s) is a crucial aspect of the restorative justice process. It allows the offender to confront the impact of their actions, develop empathy and understanding, and take responsibility for their behavior. It also empowers and validates the victim(s) and can contribute to their own healing and recovery.

Offending an Abstraction vs. Offending Human Beings

Research shows that it is much easier to continue to offend an abstraction than it is to re-offend human beings. This insight is at the heart of restorative justice.

The statement that research shows it is much easier to continue to offend an abstraction than it is to re-offend human beings highlights an important aspect of restorative justice. Restorative justice recognizes that crime is not just a violation of the law, but also a violation of human relationships and social bonds. Therefore, it seeks to address the harm caused by crime by restoring those relationships and bonds.

In traditional criminal justice systems, the focus is on punishing the offender and protecting society from further harm. This often involves treating the offender as an abstract criminal, rather than a human being who has caused harm to others. This approach can lead to a cycle of re-offending, as the offender does not fully understand the harm they have caused and may not be motivated to change their behavior.

Think about how this works. In the traditional system, the offender is processed through courts and prisons. They are assigned a number. They are housed in a cell. They are surrounded by other offenders. The victim is absent, an abstraction. The community is absent, an abstraction. The harm caused is reduced to legal categories and sentence lengths. In this environment, it is easy for the offender to remain detached from the reality of what they have done.

Restorative justice, on the other hand, seeks to hold the offender accountable for their actions by making them confront the harm they have caused and take responsibility for it. By engaging with the victim(s) and the community, the offender is able to see the real impact of their actions and to develop empathy and understanding.

Research has shown that this approach is effective in reducing reoffending rates. When offenders are given the opportunity to make amends and to rebuild relationships with their victims and community, they are less likely to reoffend. This is because they have a greater understanding of the harm they have caused and are motivated to change their behavior to prevent future harm.

Restorative justice recognizes that crime is not just a violation of the law, but also a violation of human relationships and social bonds. By focusing on repairing harm and restoring relationships, restorative justice is able to address the underlying causes of offending behavior and reduce reoffending rates. This is because it is much easier to continue to offend an abstraction than it is to re-offend human beings, and by making offenders confront the harm they have caused and take responsibility for it, restorative justice creates an environment in which offenders are motivated to change their behavior and make amends for the harm they have caused.

The Mentor's Role

The mentor's role with the offender is multifaceted and essential. A mentor is called to be a friend, to advise, to help, and to model the Christian life for the offender.

Proverbs 27:17 says, "Iron sharpeneth iron; so a man sharpeneth the countenance of his friend." Personal and spiritual growth is a communal affair, as Scripture reminds us in various ways. In the beginning, God did not make just one human being but two (Genesis 1:26–27).

David had Nathan the prophet, a faithful friend who brought him to repentance (2 Samuel 12:1–15). And Jesus appointed not just one overseer; rather, He has chosen for His church to be governed by a body of elders and deacons (Acts 6:1–7). Not just ex-offenders, but we ALL need others in our lives to sharpen us and encourage us in our daily walk.

Those of us who have at least one friend upon whom we can count for loving, constructive criticism are blessed. If we do not have any such people in our lives, we should be looking for them. We should also be asking the Lord to help develop us into people who can offer such criticism to others and to enable us to persist in love toward our friends and others.

In a restorative justice context, a mentor plays an important role in supporting and guiding the offender as they work to repair the harm caused by their actions and take steps to prevent future offending behavior.

The mentor's role is to act as a positive role model for the offender and to provide guidance, support, and encouragement throughout the restorative justice process. This can involve helping the offender to understand the impact of their actions on others, to take responsibility for their behavior, and to develop strategies for making amends and preventing future harm.

In addition, the mentor may provide practical support to the offender, such as helping them to access education or employment opportunities, or connecting them with other resources in the community. The mentor may also work with the offender's family and community to help create a supportive environment that encourages positive change.

The mentor's role is not to judge or punish the offender, but rather to support them in the harm caused by their actions and to help them become a responsible and productive member of the community. The mentor should be non-judgmental, empathetic, and respectful of the offender's feelings and experiences.

The mentor's role with the offender is to help them to develop the skills and attitudes necessary to make positive changes in their lives and to prevent future harm. By providing guidance, support, and encouragement, the mentor can help the offender to see the potential for positive change and to take concrete steps towards a more positive future.

The Offender's Family as Victims

Which aspect of criminal justice ministry could easily be listed with the victims of crime? The offender's family and loved ones should always be listed with the victims of crime because they too suffer from the offender's criminal behavior. Even the sanctions levied against the offender, as a result of their crime, are felt by their family and loved ones.

One aspect of criminal justice ministry that could easily be listed with the victims of crime is the need for healing and restoration. Crime can cause significant harm to victims, including physical, emotional, and psychological trauma. Victims may experience feelings of fear, anxiety, anger, and hopelessness, and may struggle to trust others or feel safe in their communities.

But the offender's family also suffers. A spouse becomes a prison widow or widower, left to manage household, children, and finances alone. Children become prison orphans, growing up without a parent, facing stigma and shame, struggling in school, and carrying emotional wounds that may last a lifetime. Parents grieve for their child, even as they struggle with the shame and embarrassment of their child's actions.

Criminal justice ministry can play an important role in supporting victims in their journey towards healing and restoration. This can involve providing emotional support, counseling, and other resources to help victims cope with the aftermath of the crime. It can also involve advocating for victims' rights and needs within the criminal justice system, such as ensuring that victims are informed about court proceedings and have the opportunity to share their story in court.

In addition, criminal justice ministry can work to promote a restorative justice approach that emphasizes repairing the harm caused by crime and restoring relationships between victims, offenders, and the community. This approach recognizes that crime is not just a violation of the law, but also a violation of human relationships and social bonds, and seeks to address the underlying causes of offending behavior.

By focusing on healing and restoration, criminal justice ministry can help victims to feel heard, supported, and empowered in the aftermath of a crime. It can also help to prevent future harm by addressing the root causes of offending behavior and promoting a more just and peaceful society.

Prison Widows, Widowers, and Orphans

Incarceration produces what has been dubbed a prison widow or widower, and the prison orphan. These terms capture the reality that incarceration's impact extends far beyond the person behind bars.

Incarceration can have significant negative impacts not only on the individual who is incarcerated, but also on their loved ones and family members. The term "prison widow" or "prison widower" is used to describe the partners of incarcerated individuals who may experience a sense of loneliness, isolation, and loss while their loved one is in prison. These individuals may struggle to maintain relationships, raise children, and manage the responsibilities of daily life while their partner is incarcerated.

Similarly, the term "prison orphan" is used to describe children who have one or both parents incarcerated. These children may experience emotional distress, academic challenges, and financial hardship as a result of their parent's incarceration. They may also face stigma and social exclusion due to their parent's status as an incarcerated individual.

The impact of incarceration on family members and loved ones can be profound and long-lasting, and may contribute to cycles of intergenerational poverty, trauma, and social exclusion. Children of incarcerated parents are at significantly higher risk for involvement in the criminal justice system themselves. The cycle continues.

As a result, criminal justice systems and ministries should consider the needs and experiences of families and loved ones of incarcerated individuals as they work to address the harms caused by crime and promote a more just and equitable society.

Restorative justice approaches that prioritize healing, restoration, and community engagement may offer a more effective and humane response to crime that recognizes the interconnectedness of individuals and families within communities. By addressing the harms caused by crime in a way that involves and supports all members of the community, including families and loved ones of incarcerated individuals, we can work towards a more just and peaceful society for all.

The Family's Needs

As the offender's family waits on them, they need help spiritually, emotionally, and financially. These needs are often overlooked, but they are real and urgent.

When a family member is incarcerated, it can have significant emotional, financial, and spiritual impacts on their loved ones. The experience of having a family member in prison can be stressful, traumatic, and isolating, and can leave family members struggling to cope with a range of challenges.

Spiritually, family members may experience a sense of guilt or shame, as well as a sense of disconnection from their faith community. They may struggle to reconcile their love for their incarcerated family member with their own sense of moral values and beliefs. They may question God, wondering why this has happened to their family. They may feel abandoned by their church community, which may not know how to respond to their situation.

Emotionally, family members may experience a range of negative emotions such as anxiety, depression, anger, and grief. They may feel a sense of loss, isolation, and shame, as well as a sense of responsibility for their loved one's actions. They may worry constantly about the safety and well-being of their incarcerated family member. They may struggle with the stigma and judgment of others.

Financially, incarceration can impose significant costs on families, including legal fees, travel expenses for visits, phone calls, money sent to the inmate's commissary, and loss of income due to the incarceration of a family member. This can lead to economic hardship, debt, and financial insecurity for the family. Some families lose their homes. Some go into deep poverty.

Given these challenges, criminal justice ministries and other support systems can play an important role in helping families of incarcerated individuals. This can include providing emotional and spiritual support, counseling services, and financial assistance. It can also involve working with families to help them stay connected to their incarcerated loved one, such as through visitation programs or letter writing campaigns.

By addressing the spiritual, emotional, and financial needs of families of incarcerated individuals, we can help to mitigate the negative impacts of incarceration and promote healing, restoration, and community engagement. This can also help to prevent future offending behavior and promote a more just and peaceful society for all.

Marriage Seminars for Offender Families

There is a great need for marriage seminars that could save literally hundreds of offender marriages, and, as a result, break the generational cycle of crime and brokenness in these families. The statistics are stark: approximately 90% of all marriages end in divorce when the incarceration period exceeds one year.

Think about what that means. Nine out of ten marriages fail when one partner is incarcerated for more than a year. The stress of separation, the financial strain, the emotional burden, the stigma, the difficulty of maintaining connection—all of these factors combine to destroy relationships.

If the offender can come home to a loving, waiting, Christian family, they have a greater chance of avoiding crime and staying out of prison in the future. A stable family provides accountability, support, encouragement, and a reason to stay on the right path.

Marriage seminars can be a powerful tool for addressing the needs of families affected by incarceration and breaking the cycle of crime and brokenness that can be passed down from generation to generation. When a family member is incarcerated, it can have significant impacts on their relationships, including their marriage or intimate partner relationships. The stress, trauma, and financial strain associated with incarceration can strain these relationships and lead to divorce or separation.

By providing marriage seminars that address the unique needs of families affected by incarceration, criminal justice ministries and other support systems can help to strengthen relationships, promote healthy communication and conflict resolution skills, and provide a sense of hope and healing to families who may be struggling. These seminars can also help to address the specific challenges faced by families of incarcerated individuals, such as financial strain and emotional distress.

By promoting healthy relationships and strengthening families, marriage seminars can also help to break the cycle of crime and brokenness that can be passed down from generation to generation. Research has shown that children of incarcerated parents are at higher risk for involvement in criminal behavior themselves. By addressing the needs of families affected by incarceration, we can help to prevent future offending behavior and promote a more just and peaceful society for all.

In addition to marriage seminars, criminal justice ministries and other support systems can also provide a range of other services to support families affected by incarceration, such as counseling, financial assistance, and job training. By taking a holistic and restorative approach to criminal justice, we can work towards a more just and equitable society that values the needs and well-being of all members of our communities, including families affected by incarceration.

The Most Difficult Aspect of Criminal Justice Ministry

Which aspect of criminal justice ministry is the most difficult? Working with offenders who are resistant to change or who are struggling with addiction, mental health issues, or other challenges that make it difficult for them to fully engage in the restorative justice process.

Criminal justice ministry can be a challenging and complex field, with many different aspects and challenges to consider. However, one of the most difficult aspects of criminal justice ministry is likely working with offenders who are resistant to change or who are struggling with addiction, mental health issues, or other challenges that make it difficult for them to fully engage in the restorative justice process.

When working with offenders, criminal justice ministries may encounter individuals who are deeply entrenched in their patterns of behavior and who may not be receptive to the idea of taking responsibility for their actions or making amends to their victims. This can be challenging, as it requires a great deal of patience, compassion, and persistence to work with these individuals over time and to help them see the value of the restorative justice process.

In addition, many offenders may be struggling with addiction or mental health issues, which can further complicate their ability to fully engage in the restorative justice process. These individuals may require additional support and resources to address these underlying issues and to fully participate in the restorative justice process.

Working with offenders who are resistant to change or who are struggling with addiction or mental health issues requires a great deal of patience, compassion, and perseverance. It can be a difficult and emotionally taxing aspect of criminal justice ministry, but it is also an essential component of promoting healing, restoration, and community engagement. By working with these individuals over time and providing them with the support and resources they need to fully participate in the restorative justice process, we can help to break the cycle of crime and promote a more just and peaceful society for all.

One thing we can do is to recognize and encourage criminal justice professionals who are positively impacting prisoners by their efforts, and inspiring them to become productive members of our community upon release. Theirs is not an easy job. They work in difficult conditions, often with limited resources, facing constant stress and occasional danger. They deserve our support and appreciation.

Ministering to Criminal Justice Professionals

The first step in ministering to a criminal justice professional is the building of relationships. This is essential for several reasons.

The building of relationships is a crucial first step in ministering to criminal justice professionals for several reasons.

Firstly, criminal justice professionals often work in highly stressful and challenging environments that can take a toll on their mental and emotional well-being. By building relationships with these individuals, criminal justice ministries can provide them with a sense of support, connection, and community that can help to mitigate the effects of this stress and promote greater resilience.

Police officers, correctional officers, probation officers, judges, prosecutors, defense attorneys—all of these professionals face daily exposure to human suffering, conflict, and danger. They witness the worst of humanity. They make life-and-death decisions. They carry heavy burdens. Without support, they are at high risk for burnout, compassion fatigue, post-traumatic stress, and other mental health challenges.

Secondly, building relationships with criminal justice professionals can help to break down barriers and build trust between these individuals and the broader community. Many criminal justice professionals may feel isolated or misunderstood by the communities they serve, and building relationships with them can help to bridge this divide and promote greater understanding and collaboration.

In recent years, trust between law enforcement and many communities has eroded. High-profile incidents of police brutality and misconduct have created deep suspicion and anger. Building relationships one person at a time, through genuine friendship and mutual respect, can begin to heal these wounds.

Thirdly, building relationships with criminal justice professionals can help to promote the values of restorative justice and community engagement within the criminal justice system. By demonstrating the importance of building relationships and promoting healing and restoration, criminal justice ministries can help to shift the focus of the criminal justice system away from punitive measures and towards a more restorative and community-centered approach.

Building relationships with criminal justice professionals is a crucial first step in ministering to these individuals and promoting greater healing and restoration within the criminal justice system. By providing these individuals with a sense of support, connection, and community, criminal justice ministries can help to promote greater well-being and resilience among criminal justice professionals and help to shift the focus of the criminal justice system towards a more restorative and community-centered approach.

The Challenge of Building Relationships

Establishing a relationship requires much patience, because the correctional staff in many ways is a closed community that shuns outsiders. This is not because they are unfriendly, but because their work environment has taught them to be cautious.

Establishing relationships with correctional staff can be a challenging and time-consuming process, as these individuals often work in a closed and insular community that can be resistant to outside influence or involvement.

Correctional staff work in a highly stressful and challenging environment, where their safety and the safety of those in their care is a constant concern. This can create a sense of isolation and distrust among correctional staff, who may view outsiders as a potential threat or interference to their work.

To build relationships with correctional staff, it is important to approach them with respect, sensitivity, and an understanding of the challenges they face on a daily basis. This may require a significant amount of patience and persistence, as trust and rapport are built slowly over time.

One way to build relationships with correctional staff is to seek out opportunities for collaboration and partnership. This might involve offering to provide training or support to staff members, or working with them to identify areas where restorative justice principles could be integrated into their work.

It is also important to be mindful of the boundaries and limitations of the correctional setting, and to work within the constraints of the system in order to build relationships with staff members. This may require flexibility and a willingness to adapt to the unique needs and culture of the correctional environment.

Building relationships with correctional staff requires patience, persistence, and a deep commitment to promoting restorative justice principles within the criminal justice system. By approaching staff members with respect and sensitivity, and by seeking out opportunities for collaboration and partnership, criminal justice ministries can help to break down barriers and build trust with those working in the correctional system, ultimately promoting greater healing, restoration, and community engagement for all.

Including Unique Individuals

Because of varying work hours, a church should be willing to schedule special activities and develop programs to include these unique individuals. Criminal justice professionals cannot always attend Sunday morning services at 11:00 AM. Their schedules are irregular, unpredictable, and demanding.

Because of varying work hours, criminal justice professionals may have difficulty participating in traditional church activities and programs. To include these unique individuals, churches should be willing to schedule special activities and develop programs that are tailored to their specific needs and schedules.

One way to do this is to offer flexible scheduling for worship services and other church activities, such as Bible studies or prayer groups. This might involve offering multiple service times or scheduling events on different days of the week to accommodate the varying work schedules of criminal justice professionals.

Some churches have found success offering a Wednesday night service specifically for first responders and shift workers. Others record their services and make them available online for those who cannot attend in person. Still others offer small groups that meet at unconventional times—early morning before a shift begins, or late evening after one ends.

In addition to flexible scheduling, churches can also develop specialized programs that are designed specifically for criminal justice professionals. This might include support groups for those who work in the correctional system or specialized training programs that address the unique challenges of this work.

It is also important for churches to be intentional about creating a welcoming and supportive environment for criminal justice professionals. This might involve developing specialized outreach efforts or partnering with organizations that work directly with criminal justice professionals.

Churches can play an important role in supporting and ministering to criminal justice professionals by offering flexible scheduling, developing specialized programs, and creating a welcoming and supportive environment. By making an effort to include these unique individuals, churches can help to promote greater healing, restoration, and community engagement within the criminal justice system.

Reconciliation of Damages

To the degree possible, offenders should attempt to reconcile the damages they have caused to those affected by their crime. This is not always possible. Some damages cannot be undone. Some victims are not willing to engage. But to the degree possible, the attempt should be made.

Restorative justice emphasizes the importance of offenders taking responsibility for their actions and attempting to make amends for the harm they have caused. One key aspect of this process is the concept of reconciliation, which involves making efforts to repair the harm that has been done to those affected by the crime.

Reconciliation can take many forms, depending on the circumstances of the crime and the needs of the victim(s) and their community. In some cases, it may involve a direct apology or a face-to-face meeting between the offender and the victim, where the offender can express remorse and take steps to make things right.

In other cases, reconciliation may involve the offender making restitution to the victim, such as paying for damages or providing financial support. This can be particularly important in cases where the victim has suffered financial or material losses as a result of the crime.

In addition to making amends to the victim(s), reconciliation can also involve efforts to address the root causes of the offender's behavior and to prevent future offenses. This might include participation in counseling or rehabilitation programs, or making efforts to address the social and environmental factors that contributed to the offender's criminal behavior.

While reconciliation can be a challenging and difficult process, it can be an important step towards healing and restoration for both the offender and the victim(s). By taking responsibility for their actions and making efforts to repair the harm they have caused, offenders can demonstrate their commitment to making things right and to contributing to the well-being of their communities.

Two Prerequisites to Healing

Discover within James 5:16 two prerequisites to healing: confess your faults one to another, and pray one for another, that you may be healed. These two prerequisites to healing move both the victim and offender toward restoration. In many cases lasting friendships are also developed.

James 5:16 states: "Therefore, confess your sins to each other and pray for each other so that you may be healed. The prayer of a righteous person is powerful and effective."

From this verse, we can identify two prerequisites to healing.

Confession of sins is the first. James emphasizes the importance of confessing our sins to each other as a prerequisite to healing. Confession involves acknowledging and taking responsibility for our actions, as well as seeking forgiveness from those we have wronged. This act of humility and repentance can be a powerful step towards healing and reconciliation.

For the offender, confession means owning what they have done, without excuse or minimization. For the victim, confession may mean acknowledging their own anger, bitterness, or desire for revenge, and releasing these to God. Both need to confess.

Prayer for each other is the second. In addition to confession, James also emphasizes the importance of praying for each other as a means of healing. By lifting up one another in prayer, we demonstrate our care and concern for each other's well-being, and we invite God's healing power into our lives.

When offenders and victims pray for each other, something profound happens. The walls between them begin to crumble. The bitterness begins to dissolve. The possibility of genuine reconciliation emerges.

Taken together, these two prerequisites to healing suggest that the process of healing involves both personal responsibility and communal support. We must be willing to confess our sins and seek forgiveness, while also relying on the prayers and support of our fellow believers to help us in our journey towards healing and restoration.

Understanding the Crime's Impact on Community

An offender also needs to understand how his/her crime has affected the community. Once the offender understands how their crime has affected the community, they will begin to see how they contribute to its stability. As a result, they will take measures to change.

When an offender commits a crime, the harm caused is not limited to just the victim(s). The wider community can also be affected by the crime, either directly or indirectly. For example, a violent crime may cause fear and anxiety in the community, leading to a sense of insecurity and distrust.

Understanding the impact of the crime on the community is an important aspect of restorative justice. It helps the offender to see the wider consequences of their actions beyond the immediate victim(s), and to take responsibility for their role in causing harm.

By understanding the impact of their crime on the community, the offender can begin to see the need for repairing the harm and making amends. This might involve participating in community service or restitution programs, or taking steps to address the root causes of their behavior, such as addiction or mental health issues.

In addition, by engaging with the community and taking steps towards making amends, the offender can also begin to rebuild trust and restore their relationships with others. This can be an important step towards reintegrating back into society and moving forward in a positive direction.

Understanding the impact of their crime on the community is an important aspect of the offender's journey towards restoration and rehabilitation, and is an important component of the restorative justice process.

Crime's Effect on Trust and Fear

Every time an offense occurs in a community, the trust level between people decreases and the element of fear increases. Fearing crime is a common and prevalent issue in modern society. The level or extent of the fear of crime depends on various factors like age, gender, and past experiences.

When an offense occurs in a community, it can have a significant impact on the level of trust between individuals. This is particularly true when the offense is violent or involves a breach of trust, such as theft or fraud. When people feel like they cannot trust those around them, it can lead to a breakdown in community cohesion and a sense of isolation.

In addition to the impact on trust, offenses can also increase the level of fear within a community. This is particularly true for violent crimes or crimes that are perceived as a threat to public safety, such as gang activity or drug trafficking. When people are afraid, they may avoid certain areas or activities, leading to a further breakdown in community cohesion and a sense of isolation.

Both the decrease in trust and the increase in fear can have negative consequences for a community. When people do not trust each other, it can be difficult to build strong relationships or work together to address community issues. When people are afraid, they may be less likely to engage with their community or to participate in activities that promote social cohesion and well-being.

Restorative justice can help to address these issues by promoting healing, reconciliation, and forgiveness. By bringing together victims, offenders, and community members to discuss the impact of the offense and to work towards repairing the harm caused, restorative justice can help to rebuild trust and promote a sense of community. By addressing the root causes of crime and taking steps towards preventing future offenses, restorative justice can also help to reduce fear and increase feelings of safety within the community.

Offenses can have a significant impact on community trust and fear, but restorative justice offers a promising approach for addressing these issues and promoting healing and reconciliation.

How Suspicion Alters Behavior

As people become increasingly suspicious of others, they may begin to do things that further isolate them from community.

They may secure their homes with extra lights, locks, and sturdier fences. Others may even go to the extreme of purchasing a firearm.

As people become increasingly suspicious of others, they may begin to do the following:

Avoiding interactions: They may avoid interacting with others, fearing that they may be harmed or betrayed. This leads to isolation and loneliness.

Checking up on people: They may become obsessive about monitoring other people's actions and whereabouts, creating tension in relationships.

Questioning others' motives: They may start to question the motives of others, even those close to them, and suspect that they are up to no good. This destroys trust.

Secrecy: They may become more secretive themselves, guarding their own actions and thoughts, believing that others might use this information against them.

Isolation: They may choose to isolate themselves, withdrawing from social situations and avoiding interactions with others altogether.

Guarding their possessions: They may become overly protective of their belongings and property, thinking that someone might steal or damage them.

Increased vigilance: They may become more vigilant, always watching out for potential threats or suspicious behavior in others.

Paranoia: In severe cases, they may experience paranoia, believing that everyone is out to get them or harm them in some way.

Taken to the extreme, "scelerophobia" is the fear of burglars, bad men, or crime in general. For those with this phobia, many normal things become difficult. For example, a person might go to great lengths to prevent crime, such as locking one's home or constantly checking and rechecking locks to an extent that it becomes an obsession. Many refuse to step out of their home after dark or travel to lonely places for the fear of being attacked or robbed. Their phobia leads to constant fatigue as it causes them to believe that they need to be vigilant all the time.

I recall a young lady who wanted to be counseled by email. She had not left the house in thirty years. She was afraid of everything and actually collected disability for her anxiety issues. She kept roosters, hens, and dogs in the yard for protection. The roosters and hens were there to alert her to someone approaching, in case the dogs fell asleep.

Her first email to me was full of initials for all the diagnoses she had received from doctors over the years. I told her that may be the way the world sees her and what the doctors see in her, but this is NOT the way the Lord sees her. I began to write a series of devotionals for her to begin her day, highlighting what the Lord says she is. She made index cards with the verses and left them all over the house.

However, the email therapy did NOT work. The day she got a letter of inquiry from Social Security about her disability payments, she went into the fetal position in bed for three days, paralyzed by fear. She went back on her meds and decided to discontinue her email counseling. But at the end, she agreed to allow me to convert these personalized devotionals into a course. I deleted personal comments, and she even edited the final product for me. She did an AMAZING job of finding errors or better ways to say the same thing. She excelled because she was in her comfort zone—at home.

This story illustrates the profound impact that fear can have on a person's life. Restorative justice, by addressing the root causes of crime and promoting healing and reconciliation, can help to break the cycle of fear and isolation that plagues so many individuals and communities.

Offenders Seeing the Wider Impact

When offenders are encouraged to address the harm that results from their crime, they can begin to see that their actions are not isolated, and that their families, as well as friends and neighbors, suffer from their crime. This realization can be transformative.

When offenders are encouraged to address the harm that results from their crime, they are given an opportunity to see the impact of their actions on others beyond just themselves. This can be a powerful experience that can help offenders to take responsibility for their behavior and work towards making amends.

One of the key ways in which offenders can begin to see the wider impact of their actions is through restorative justice programs. These programs aim to bring together the offender, the victim, and other affected parties to discuss the harm caused by the crime and work towards repairing it. By hearing from those directly affected by their actions, offenders can start to understand the full extent of the damage they have caused.

In particular, when offenders see how their crime has impacted their families, friends, and neighbors, they can begin to recognize that their actions do not just affect themselves, but have a ripple effect throughout the community. They may see that their loved ones have been hurt by their behavior, and that their relationships with others have been damaged as a result.

This realization can be a powerful motivator for offenders to make changes in their lives and work towards making amends for the harm they have caused. They may become more invested in repairing relationships with those they have hurt, and in taking steps to prevent future harm.

Encouraging offenders to address the harm caused by their crime can be a valuable tool in helping them to take responsibility for their actions and work towards repairing the damage they have caused. By seeing the wider impact of their behavior, offenders can start to recognize the importance of making amends and working towards a better future for themselves and their communities.

Focusing on the Wrong Things

What happens when the offender focuses on the ills of the prison system, rather than address the harm that resulted from his crime? The offender is not held accountable for the damage they have caused through their offense.

When an offender focuses solely on the ills of the prison system and neglects to address the harm they caused, it can be a form of denial and avoidance of responsibility. This can be problematic for several reasons.

Failure to take responsibility: By deflecting attention away from their own behavior and onto the prison system, offenders may fail to take responsibility for their actions and the harm they have caused. This can hinder the healing process for victims and the community.

Lack of accountability: If offenders do not address the harm they caused, they may not be held accountable for their actions. This can lead to a sense of injustice for victims and can undermine the legitimacy of the justice system.

Failure to address root causes: By focusing solely on the prison system, offenders may fail to address the root causes of their behavior. It is important for offenders to understand the underlying factors that contributed to their actions, so that they can take steps to address them and prevent future harm.

Lack of rehabilitation: If offenders do not take responsibility for their actions and work towards making amends, they may miss out on opportunities for rehabilitation and growth. This can make it more difficult for them to successfully reintegrate into society after their release.

While it is important to acknowledge and address issues within the prison system, it is also important for offenders to take responsibility for their own behavior and the harm they have caused. By doing so, they can begin the process of healing and growth, both for themselves and for the community.

They forget that what they have done harmed others, and also avoid feeling accountable for the harm they have caused through their actions.

Confronting Pain and Rebuilding Trust

A Christian offender needs to be willing to confront the pain he has caused, and discover a way to rebuild the trust that was destroyed by his actions. This is not optional for the follower of Jesus.

As a Christian, an offender must take responsibility for their actions and be willing to confront the pain they have caused to others. This requires a willingness to face the consequences of their behavior and work towards making amends.

To rebuild trust, the offender must first acknowledge the harm they have caused and express genuine remorse for their actions. This involves taking responsibility for their behavior and recognizing the impact it has had on others. The offender must be willing to listen to the victim and other affected parties, and take their feelings and needs into account.

In addition, the offender must be committed to making things right. This may involve making restitution, participating in restorative justice programs, and taking steps to prevent future harm. The offender may also need to seek counseling or therapy to address any underlying issues that contributed to their behavior.

Ultimately, rebuilding trust is a process that requires patience, persistence, and a genuine desire to change. It may take time for the victim and others to forgive the offender, and it is important for the offender to be respectful of this process and continue to take responsibility for their behavior.

As a Christian, the offender may also seek guidance and support from their faith community. This can provide a source of strength and encouragement as they work towards rebuilding trust and making amends.

The Goal: Restoration of Both Victim and Offender

Ministry, using the restorative justice paradigm, ends in the restoration of both the victim and the offender back into the community. This is the ultimate goal—not punishment, not revenge, but restoration.

Restorative justice is a paradigm that seeks to repair harm and restore relationships between those who have been affected by crime. This approach involves bringing together the victim, the offender, and the community to work towards a shared goal of healing and reconciliation.

In a ministry context, the use of the restorative justice paradigm can be particularly powerful. By focusing on restoration and reconciliation, this approach aligns with many Christian values, such as forgiveness, compassion, and love.

In a restorative justice ministry context, the goal is to restore both the victim and the offender back into the community. This involves providing support and resources to both parties as they work towards healing and reconciliation. The victim may receive counseling or other forms of support to help them cope with the trauma they have experienced. The offender may receive counseling or other forms of support to help them address the underlying issues that contributed to their behavior.

In addition, restorative justice ministry may involve community involvement, including support groups, mentoring programs, and other forms of community engagement. By involving the broader community in the restoration process, both the victim and the offender can feel supported and valued.

Ultimately, the goal of restorative justice ministry is to promote healing and reconciliation, and to create a sense of community that is based on forgiveness, compassion, and love. Through this approach, both the victim and the offender can be restored back into the community and can move forward in a positive and healthy way.

The Church as an Accepting Community

The Church, as an accepting community, can help with the issues of restoration, and facilitate reintegration for both the victim and the offender back into the community. This is one of the Church's most important roles.

The Church can play a significant role in promoting restoration and facilitating reintegration for both the victim and the offender back into the community. As an accepting and supportive community, the Church can provide a safe and nurturing space for those affected by crime to heal and find support.

For victims of crime, the Church can offer pastoral care, counseling, and other forms of support to help them cope with the trauma they have experienced. The Church can also offer a supportive community where victims can connect with others who have had similar experiences and find comfort and healing.

For offenders, the Church can offer a space for confession, repentance, and redemption. Through pastoral counseling, mentoring, and other forms of support, the Church can help offenders address the underlying issues that contributed to their behavior and find a path towards rehabilitation and restoration.

In addition, the Church can play a role in facilitating reintegration for both the victim and the offender back into the community. Through community outreach programs, support groups, and other forms of community engagement, the Church can help to bridge the gap between those affected by crime and the broader community.

The Church can help to promote healing, reconciliation, and restoration for all those affected by crime. By creating a supportive and accepting community, the Church can provide a space for both the victim and the offender to heal, find redemption, and be welcomed back into the community.

What a Holistic Ministry Requires

What is required of a ministry, in order to be holistic? It must consider both the offender and victim; it attempts to meet the spiritual as well as the physical and emotional needs of those involved; and it addresses the offender in prison, as well as after they are released back to the community. Putting it in simple terms, you must cover all the bases in order to be holistic.

A holistic ministry is one that addresses the needs of the whole person—body, mind, and spirit. This approach recognizes that people have complex and interconnected needs, and that addressing one area of need can have a positive impact on other areas of their life.

To be holistic, a ministry must take into account the diverse needs of the people it serves. This may involve providing support and resources in a variety of areas.

Spiritual: A holistic ministry should provide opportunities for people to connect with God and deepen their faith. This may involve offering worship services, Bible studies, or prayer groups.

Emotional: A holistic ministry should provide support and resources to help people cope with emotional challenges such as anxiety, depression, or trauma. This may involve offering counseling services, support groups, or other forms of emotional support.

Physical: A holistic ministry should provide resources and support to help people maintain physical health and well-being. This may involve offering health education, exercise classes, or access to medical care.

Social: A holistic ministry should provide opportunities for people to connect with others and build relationships. This may involve offering social events, community service projects, or other forms of social support.

Financial: A holistic ministry should provide resources and support to help people meet their basic needs and achieve financial stability. This may involve offering job training, financial counseling, or emergency assistance.

By addressing the diverse needs of the people it serves, a holistic ministry can help to promote healing, growth, and transformation in the lives of those it serves. This approach recognizes the interconnectedness of our physical, emotional, and spiritual needs and provides a framework for supporting the whole person.

For restorative justice ministry, this means addressing the needs of offenders, victims, families, and communities. It means providing spiritual support for repentance and reconciliation, emotional support for healing from trauma, practical support for reentry and reintegration, and social support for building new relationships and communities. It means being present in prisons and after release, with victims and with families, in times of crisis and in times of ordinary life.

This is the restorative justice ministry paradigm. It is not simple. It is not easy. But it is the calling of the Church, and it is the path to genuine healing and restoration for all those affected by crime.

CHAPTER 08

HOW THE CHURCH CAN IMPACT CORRECTIONS

We have journeyed together through seven chapters, each building upon the last. We have examined the traditional view of justice and found it wanting. We have explored why the system must be restructured. We have considered a different view of justice—restorative justice—and examined its principles, practices, and conceptual frameworks. We have looked at promising practices from around the world. We have explored the biblical foundations for restorative justice and considered whether the Church should be involved. And in the previous chapter, we examined the restorative justice ministry paradigm—a framework for how the Church can actually do this work.

Now, in this chapter, we turn to a practical and pressing question: how can the Church impact corrections? Not just prisons, but the entire corrections system—jails, probation, parole, reentry, and all the agencies and professionals that make up this complex world. How can the body of Christ make a difference in a system that touches millions of lives?

The answer is that the Church can impact corrections in many ways, and it must. The mandate is clear. The need is urgent. And the opportunities are abundant. In this chapter, we will explore the specific ways the Church can minister to victims, offenders, families, and criminal justice professionals. We will consider the power of presence, the importance of relationship, and the practical steps that churches can take to fulfill their calling. And we will see that when the Church shows up, lives are changed, communities are strengthened, and the kingdom of God is advanced.

The Mandate from Matthew 25

Let us begin with the clearest statement in all of Scripture regarding the Church's mandate to do criminal justice ministry. In Matthew 25:35-36, Jesus said:

"For I was hungry and you gave Me food; I was thirsty and you gave Me drink; I was a stranger and you took Me in; I was naked and you clothed Me; I was sick and you visited Me; I was in prison and you came to Me."

Think about what Jesus is saying here. He is not giving suggestions. He is not offering options. He is describing the criteria by which the nations will be judged. The righteous are those who fed the hungry, gave drink to the thirsty, welcomed the stranger, clothed the naked, cared for the sick, and visited the prisoner. The unrighteous are those who did not.

And here is the most astonishing part: when we do these things for "the least of these," we are doing them for Jesus Himself. He identifies with the hungry, the thirsty, the stranger, the naked, the sick, and the prisoner. To minister to them is to minister to Him. To neglect them is to neglect Him.

Notice the progression in Jesus' words. The hungry, thirsty, stranger, naked, and sick are obvious concerns for ministry. Most churches would agree that caring for these groups is part of their calling. But Jesus goes beyond these groups to point out the outcast prisoner's need for love and compassion. Prisoners are included in "the least of these." They are not forgotten. They are not beyond the reach of Christ's concern.

This passage provides a clear and unmistakable mandate for the Church to engage in criminal justice ministry. It means visiting those in prison. It means offering counseling and mentoring to offenders. It means providing support to the families of those who are incarcerated. It means advocating for policies that reflect God's heart for justice and mercy.

In addition, this passage highlights the importance of viewing those impacted by the criminal justice system as individuals who are in need of care and support, rather than simply as criminals. When we see prisoners through Jesus' eyes, we see people made in God's image, people for whom Christ died, people capable of change and worthy of dignity. By offering compassion and support to those impacted by crime and the criminal justice system, the Church can help to promote healing, restoration, and reconciliation.

The mandate is clear. The question is not whether the Church should be involved, but how.

Four Categories of Criminal Justice Ministry

The broad spectrum of criminal justice ministries that the Church can bring to corrections can be divided into four categories: victims, offenders, family, and criminal justice professionals. Each of these groups has unique needs, and each presents unique opportunities for ministry.

Victims are the first category. The Church can bring its resources to bear to support and minister to victims of crime. This could include offering counseling, pastoral care, and other forms of support to help them recover from the trauma of their experience. Victims often feel forgotten by a system that focuses on the offender. The Church can remind them that they are seen, they are valued, and they are not alone.

The Church can also work to advocate for the rights of victims and promote awareness of the impact of crime on individuals, families, and communities. This might mean speaking out when victims are ignored by the system, or providing resources to help victims navigate the complex aftermath of crime. It might mean creating support groups where victims can share their experiences and find healing together.

Offenders are the second category. The Church has a unique perspective on the issue of crime and punishment. It can offer pastoral care, counseling, and spiritual guidance to offenders, helping them to find a path towards repentance, restoration, and healing. The Church can also advocate for restorative justice approaches that seek to address the harm caused by the offender and work towards repairing the relationships that have been broken.

This ministry with offenders is not about excusing their actions or minimizing the harm they have caused. It is about offering hope and a way forward. It is about helping them take responsibility, make amends, and become different people. It is about believing that change is possible because the gospel says it is.

Family is the third category. The Church can provide support and care to the families of offenders and victims alike. It can help them to navigate the criminal justice system and provide a range of pastoral and practical services to help them cope with the challenges they face.

Families of offenders often suffer in silence. They carry shame and stigma. They struggle financially. They worry about their loved one and about their own future. Families of victims also struggle, carrying trauma and grief while trying to hold their lives together. Both need the support of a caring community.

Criminal justice professionals are the fourth category. The Church can play an important role in supporting the work of police officers, prosecutors, judges, and corrections staff. This could include offering pastoral care, counseling, and spiritual support to help these professionals deal with the stresses and challenges of their work. The Church can also work to promote a greater understanding of the issues and challenges facing those who work in the criminal justice system.

These professionals are often overlooked in ministry. They are seen as part of the system, not as people with their own needs and struggles. But they carry heavy burdens. They witness the worst of humanity. They make life-and-death decisions. They need support, encouragement, and spiritual care.

The Church can bring a broad range of criminal justice ministries to the corrections system. By ministering to victims, offenders, families, and criminal justice professionals alike, the Church can help to promote healing, restoration, and reconciliation in our communities.

A Mission to Suffering People

Criminal justice ministry is a mission to suffering people, clearly needing the love and compassion of Christ and His Church. This understanding is essential for several reasons.

First, **criminal justice involves harm and brokenness**. Crime and the criminal justice system often involve harm and brokenness, including victims of crime, families affected by the actions of offenders, and offenders who have committed harm. These individuals are often in need of the love and compassion of Christ and His Church, which can offer healing, restoration, and hope.

Victims suffer. Offenders suffer. Families suffer. Communities suffer. The entire system is saturated with pain. Where there is suffering, the Church must be present. This is not optional; it is essential to our identity as followers of Jesus, who came to heal the brokenhearted and set at liberty those who are oppressed.

Second, **criminal justice ministry is a calling to serve**. For many Christians, criminal justice ministry is a calling to serve those who are often overlooked or forgotten. It is an opportunity to live out the gospel message of love, mercy, and justice, and to share the hope of Christ with those who are in need.

When we serve the hungry, the thirsty, the stranger, the naked, the sick, and the prisoner, we are serving Jesus Himself. This is not just a nice idea; it is the teaching of our Lord. Criminal justice ministry is not a side project for the especially committed; it is a central expression of what it means to follow Christ.

Third, **the criminal justice system can be dehumanizing**. The system can be dehumanizing, both for offenders and for those who work within it. People are reduced to numbers, to case files, to categories. Their humanity is forgotten in the machinery of justice. Criminal justice ministry offers an alternative perspective that values the dignity and worth of every person, regardless of their actions or circumstances.

The Church must be a voice that says, "You are more than your worst action. You are made in the image of God. You have inherent worth and dignity. You are loved." This message is counter-cultural in a system that often treats people as problems to be managed.

Fourth, **the Church has a unique role to play**. The Church offers spiritual care, pastoral support, and a community of faith that can help to sustain individuals as they navigate the criminal justice system. Through its ministries, the Church can bring the hope and compassion of Christ to those who are suffering.

No other institution can do what the Church does. Government agencies provide services. Nonprofits provide programs. But the Church provides community—a family of faith where people can belong, be loved, and find their way back to God and to each other.

Criminal justice ministry is a mission to suffering people who are in need of the love and compassion of Christ and His Church. Through its ministries, the Church can offer healing, hope, and a sense of purpose to those who are affected by crime and the criminal justice system.

The Ministry of Presence

One of the greatest ways the Church can impact the victims of crime is the ministry of presence. Remember the popular cliché "actions speak louder than words" as you minister in silence to victims of crime.

The ministry of presence is a powerful way in which the Church can impact the victims of crime. It involves being present with those who have experienced harm, listening to their stories, and offering emotional and spiritual support. It is not about having the right words or the perfect advice. It is about showing up and staying.

When a person experiences the trauma of crime, they may feel isolated, alone, and overwhelmed. They may struggle with feelings of fear, anger, sadness, and confusion. The ministry of presence involves showing up in these moments, being willing to sit with the person, and offering comfort, care, and compassion.

Sometimes the most powerful thing we can do is simply be there. We don't need to explain why this happened. We don't need to offer solutions. We don't need to quote scripture or pray elaborate prayers. We just need to be present, to listen, to care.

The ministry of presence can take many forms.

Visiting victims in hospitals or homes is one form. The Church can offer practical assistance by visiting victims in hospitals or their homes. This could involve offering prayer, bringing meals, providing transportation, or simply being present to listen and offer comfort. A meal, a ride, a listening ear—these simple acts communicate love in ways that words cannot.

Providing counseling and pastoral care is another form. The Church can offer professional counseling and pastoral care to victims of crime, helping them to process their emotions, cope with trauma, and find hope and healing. Some churches have trained counselors on staff. Others partner with Christian counseling centers. Whatever the method, the goal is to provide skilled, compassionate care to those who are hurting.

Offering support groups and peer counseling is a third form. The Church can offer support groups and peer counseling for victims of crime, providing a safe and supportive environment for people to share their experiences, connect with others who have gone through similar experiences, and find hope and healing. There is something powerful about meeting with others who understand because they have been there too.

Advocating for victims' rights is a fourth form. The Church can advocate for victims' rights by raising awareness of the impact of crime, promoting policies that prioritize victim support, and providing resources for victims to access legal and other support services. The Church has a voice, and that voice can be used to speak up for those who are often overlooked.

In all these ways, the ministry of presence offers a powerful way for the Church to impact the victims of crime. By showing up, listening, and offering care and compassion, the Church can help victims to feel less alone, more supported, and more hopeful as they navigate the difficult aftermath of crime.

Walking with Victims Through Crisis

As Christians, we should be able to refrain from giving reasons, advice, or asking questions, and simply walk with the victims through their period of crisis. This is counter-cultural in a world that always wants to fix things, to offer solutions, to make it better. But sometimes the best thing we can do is nothing—except be present.

As Christians, one of the most important ways we can support victims of crime is by being present with them in their time of crisis. This means being willing to walk alongside them, without judgment or the need to offer reasons, advice, or questions.

Why is this so important?

It shows respect for the victim's experience. When we listen without judgment, we show respect for the victim's experience and validate their feelings. By not trying to explain away their pain or offer quick solutions, we demonstrate our willingness to be present with them in their suffering. We communicate that their experience matters, that their feelings are valid, that they are not alone.

It creates a safe space for the victim to process their emotions. Victims of crime may experience a wide range of emotions, including fear, anger, and sadness. By creating a safe space where they can express themselves without fear of judgment or criticism, we allow them to process their emotions in a healthy way. They need to feel what they feel. They need to say what they need to say. Our role is to receive it with compassion.

It allows the victim to take ownership of their healing. By refraining from giving advice or solutions, we allow the victim to take ownership of their own healing process. They can choose the pace and direction of their healing journey, and we can support them by simply being present. Healing cannot be forced or rushed. It must happen in its own time and in its own way. Our job is to be there while it does.

It reflects the love and compassion of Christ. When we walk with victims without judgment or the need to offer advice or solutions, we reflect the love and compassion of Christ. We show them that they are not alone in their suffering and that God is present with them in their pain. Jesus did not always offer solutions. Sometimes He just wept with those who were weeping. We are called to do the same.

As Christians, our role in supporting victims of crime is to be present with them in their time of crisis. By refraining from giving reasons, advice, or asking questions, we can create a safe space for victims to process their emotions, take ownership of their healing, and experience the love and compassion of Christ.

Why Offenders Are a Receptive Audience

There are two reasons why offenders seem to be the easiest group to which you can minister. First, they are a captive audience with plenty of time on their hands. Second, they usually understand their need for help.

Ministering to offenders can be a unique and fulfilling experience for several reasons.

They are a captive audience with plenty of time on their hands. Offenders are often incarcerated and have a lot of time on their hands. This means that they may be more open and receptive to spiritual and personal growth than those who are not incarcerated. They may also have a greater desire to connect with others and build community.

In prison, the distractions of the outside world are removed. There are no jobs to go to, no errands to run, no social engagements to attend. There is time—lots of time. Time to think. Time to reflect. Time to read. Time to pray. For many offenders, this is the first time in their lives they have had the space to consider deeper questions about meaning, purpose, and their own lives.

They usually understand their need for help. Offenders often have a deep understanding of their own struggles and shortcomings. This awareness can create a sense of humility and openness to receiving help and guidance from others. They may be more willing to seek out and engage with resources that can help them address their issues and grow as individuals.

When you are sitting in a prison cell, it is hard to pretend that everything is fine. The consequences of your choices are all around you. The walls, the bars, the uniform—all of it is a constant reminder that something went wrong. This can create a openness to change that is harder to find in the outside world, where distractions and denial are easier to maintain.

These two factors can make offenders a receptive audience for ministry and personal growth. However, it is important to note that not all offenders will be open to or interested in spiritual growth, and there may be significant barriers to engaging with this population, such as security concerns and limited resources. Additionally, ministering to offenders can be complex and may require specialized training and support.

The ministry of presence could also be effectively used with the offender. This approach could be carried out through correspondence and visits to the prison. A letter, a visit, a listening ear—these simple acts can communicate love and hope to someone who feels forgotten and abandoned.

While offenders may be a unique and potentially receptive group to minister to, it is important to approach this work with humility, sensitivity, and careful consideration of the needs and challenges involved.

The Power of Forgiveness and New Beginnings

Christianity is so powerful because it offers these individuals the opportunity for forgiveness and the ability to start their lives over. This is the heart of the gospel, and it speaks directly to the deepest needs of those caught up in the criminal justice system.

Christianity is a faith that is centered around forgiveness and redemption. The core message of the Christian faith is that Jesus Christ died on the cross to forgive the sins of humanity, and through His resurrection, He offers the promise of eternal life. This message of forgiveness and redemption is particularly powerful for individuals who have been involved in the criminal justice system.

One of the most significant challenges that offenders face is the stigma and shame associated with their past actions. This can lead to feelings of hopelessness, isolation, and despair. They may feel that they are defined forever by their worst moment, that there is no way back, no chance for a different future.

But the Christian message of forgiveness offers these individuals a way to move beyond their past mistakes and start over with a renewed sense of purpose and hope. It says that no one is beyond the reach of God's grace. It says that the past does not have to determine the future. It says that new beginnings are possible.

Through the teachings of Jesus Christ, offenders can find a path to forgiveness and healing. This can involve seeking forgiveness from God, as well as from those who have been impacted by their actions. By taking responsibility for their past mistakes and working towards making amends, offenders can begin the process of healing and transformation.

Christianity also offers a sense of community and support that can be vital for offenders who are trying to rebuild their lives. Through church communities and other Christian organizations, offenders can connect with others who share their faith and their struggles. This can provide a sense of belonging and accountability that can help them stay on track and avoid falling back into old patterns of behavior.

The Christian message of forgiveness and redemption can be a powerful tool for individuals who have been involved in the criminal justice system. By offering the opportunity for forgiveness and the ability to start over, Christianity can provide a path towards healing, transformation, and a renewed sense of purpose.

The Imperative of Relationship

Establishing a relationship with an offender is imperative. This cannot be overstated. Without relationship, there is no trust. Without trust, there is no influence. Without influence, there is no transformation.

Many will shy away from establishing a relationship with an offender because of fear. This is understandable. Offenders have committed crimes, sometimes serious ones. They may be unpredictable. They may be manipulative. There are legitimate concerns about safety.

But fear should not prevent us from fulfilling our calling. Precautionary measures should be taken before making contact. For instance, if your method of establishing a relationship is through correspondence, use your church's address or a post office box instead of your home address. If you are visiting a prison, follow all the rules and protocols. Be wise as serpents and innocent as doves.

Establishing a relationship with an offender is imperative for several reasons.

Building trust is the first reason. Offenders may be wary of people in authority, including those who work in the criminal justice system. By establishing a relationship with an offender, you can build trust and create an environment in which they feel comfortable sharing their thoughts, feelings, and struggles. Trust is the foundation of any meaningful relationship, and it must be earned over time.

Providing support is the second reason. Offenders often feel isolated and alone, particularly if they have few friends or family members who are able or willing to support them. By establishing a relationship with an offender, you can provide them with emotional support and guidance. This can be particularly important during times of crisis or when the offender is feeling overwhelmed. Knowing that someone cares can make all the difference.

Encouraging personal growth is the third reason. Offenders may have deep-seated issues that have contributed to their involvement in the criminal justice system. By establishing a relationship with an offender, you can encourage them to reflect on their past actions, take responsibility for their mistakes, and work towards personal growth and development. A trusted friend can speak truth that would be rejected from anyone else.

Offering hope is the fourth reason. For many offenders, the future may seem bleak and hopeless. By establishing a relationship with an offender, you can offer them a sense of hope for the future. This can involve helping them set realistic goals, connecting them with resources and support, and encouraging them to believe in their ability to change and grow. Hope is a powerful motivator.

Reducing recidivism is the fifth reason. Studies have shown that establishing a positive relationship with an offender can reduce the likelihood that they will reoffend. By building a relationship with an offender, you can help them feel valued and supported, which can decrease the likelihood that they will return to criminal behavior. Relationships change people in ways that programs alone cannot.

Establishing a relationship with an offender is essential for providing support, encouraging personal growth, and reducing recidivism. By building trust, providing emotional support, offering hope, and encouraging personal growth, you can make a positive impact on the lives of offenders and help them to find a path towards healing and transformation.

One of the Best Things Prison Ministers Can Do

What is one of the best things that prison ministers can do? Arrive early to fellowship or sit with the offenders. This simple act communicates more than words ever could.

One of the best things that prison ministers can do is to provide ongoing support and follow-up care to offenders after they are released from prison. Many offenders face significant challenges when reintegrating into society, including finding employment, securing housing, and rebuilding relationships with family and friends. By providing ongoing support and follow-up care, prison ministers can help offenders navigate these challenges and stay on track towards a successful reintegration.

This can involve connecting offenders with community resources, providing emotional support, and offering guidance and encouragement. It might mean helping them find a job, a place to live, a church to attend. It might mean being available for late-night phone calls when they are struggling. It might mean celebrating their successes and encouraging them through their setbacks.

Ultimately, by providing ongoing support, prison ministers can help to reduce recidivism and improve the overall well-being of offenders as they transition back into society.

In addition, the simple gesture of memorizing the offenders' names speaks volumes to these individuals. In prison they are known only by an identification number, a string of digits that reduces them to a case file. When you speak their name, you make them feel like real people. You acknowledge their humanity. You communicate that they matter.

A name is a powerful thing. It says, "I see you. I know you. You are not just a number to me." In a place designed to strip away identity and individuality, the simple act of using someone's name is an act of resistance and love.

Elements of an Effective Criminal Justice Ministry Program

An effective criminal justice ministry program will include a variety of outreach, nurturing, and educational activities using Church volunteers. Church volunteers are the heart of this work, bringing their time, talents, and compassion to bear on the needs of those impacted by the criminal justice system.

An effective criminal justice ministry program is one that includes a variety of outreach, nurturing, and educational activities that engage both offenders and the broader community. Church volunteers play a crucial role in these efforts, as they can offer a range of skills, experiences, and perspectives that can help to make these programs more effective.

Here are a few examples of the types of activities that an effective criminal justice ministry program might include.

Outreach is one of the most important aspects. This might involve visiting prisons or jails, organizing letter-writing campaigns, or connecting with families of offenders. Church volunteers can play a key role in these efforts by providing emotional support, offering encouragement, and connecting offenders with resources and support. Outreach is about making contact, building bridges, letting people know they are not forgotten.

Nurturing is another critical component. Many offenders have experienced trauma, abuse, or neglect in their lives. A criminal justice ministry program can provide a nurturing environment that promotes healing and growth. This might involve offering counseling or therapy services, providing mentorship and role modeling, or creating opportunities for spiritual growth and reflection. Nurturing is about creating safe spaces where healing can happen.

Education is a third component. This might involve offering vocational training, educational classes, or life skills workshops. Church volunteers can help to facilitate these activities by providing instruction, mentorship, or support services. Education empowers people with the knowledge and skills they need to build different lives.

Community engagement is a fourth component. A criminal justice ministry program should also engage the broader community in efforts to reduce recidivism and support offender reentry. This might involve organizing community events, partnering with local businesses and organizations, or creating opportunities for community members to volunteer or offer support. When the whole community is involved, the whole community benefits.

An effective criminal justice ministry program will include a variety of outreach, nurturing, and educational activities that engage both offenders and the broader community. Church volunteers can play a critical role in these efforts by providing emotional support, mentorship, instruction, and other support services. By working together, we can create a more just and compassionate society that supports the needs of all its members, including those who have been involved in the criminal justice system.

The Mentor's Role Revisited

We have discussed the mentor's role before, but it bears repeating. A mentor's role with the offender is to be a friend, to advise, to help, and to model the Christian life for the offender. This is a sacred calling.

A mentor's role with an offender is to provide guidance, support, and accountability as the offender works to reintegrate into society and lead a more positive and productive life. A mentor can be an invaluable resource for offenders, offering them a positive role model, someone to talk to, and someone to hold them accountable for their actions.

Here are some specific ways that a mentor can help an offender.

Providing emotional support is fundamental. Mentors can offer offenders emotional support and encouragement as they work to overcome the challenges they face. This might involve listening to the offender's concerns, offering guidance and advice, and providing a sounding board for their ideas. Sometimes people just need to know that someone is in their corner.

Setting goals is another important function. A mentor can help an offender set goals and work towards achieving them. This might involve developing a plan for finding a job, securing housing, or building healthy relationships. Goals give direction and hope. They turn vague aspirations into concrete steps.

Offering guidance is a third function. A mentor can offer guidance and advice on a range of issues, from managing finances to dealing with legal problems. They can also help offenders navigate the complexities of the criminal justice system and connect them with resources and support services. Mentors who have been through similar experiences can be especially helpful, offering wisdom gained from their own journeys.

Providing accountability is a fourth function. A mentor can hold an offender accountable for their actions, helping them stay on track towards their goals and avoid negative behaviors that might lead to recidivism. Accountability is not about judgment or punishment; it is about loving someone enough to tell them the truth and help them stay true to their commitments.

Ultimately, a mentor's role is to be a positive influence in an offender's life, helping them to build the skills, relationships, and support networks they need to succeed. By providing guidance, support, and accountability, a mentor can help an offender navigate the challenges of reentry and build a brighter future for themselves and their families.

Proverbs 27:17 says, "Iron sharpeneth iron; so a man sharpeneth the countenance of his friend." Personal and spiritual growth is a communal affair, as Scripture reminds us in various ways. In the beginning, God did not make just one human being but two (Genesis 1:26–27).

David had Nathan the prophet, a faithful friend who brought him to repentance (2 Samuel 12:1–15). And Jesus appointed not just one overseer; rather, He has chosen for His church to be governed by a body of elders and deacons (Acts 6:1–7). Not just ex-offenders, but we ALL need others in our lives to sharpen us and encourage us in our daily walk.

Those of us who have at least one friend upon whom we can count for loving, constructive criticism are blessed. If we do not have any such people in our lives, we should be looking for them. We should also be asking the Lord to help develop us into people who can offer such criticism to others and to enable us to persist in love toward our friends and others.

Families as Hidden Victims

Which aspect of criminal justice ministry could easily be listed with the victims of crime? Because they too suffer from the actions of the offender. The offender's family and loved ones should always be listed with the victims of crime because they too suffer from the offender's criminal behavior. Even the sanctions levied against the offender, as a result of their crime, are felt by their family and loved ones.

The aspect of criminal justice ministry that could easily be listed with the victims of crime is the ministry of presence. This is because victims of crime often experience emotional trauma, pain, and isolation, and may feel that no one understands what they are going through. The ministry of presence involves simply being there for the victim, listening to their concerns, and offering emotional support and encouragement. This can be a powerful way to help victims feel seen, heard, and valued, and to remind them that they are not alone in their struggle.

Additionally, the ministry of presence can help victims to begin the process of healing and recovery, as they feel supported and encouraged to move forward with their lives. Therefore, the ministry of presence is a crucial aspect of criminal justice ministry that can be listed with the victims of crime.

But the families of offenders are also victims in their own way. They did not commit the crime, but they bear its consequences. They are stigmatized by association. They are separated from their loved one. They struggle financially and emotionally. They need the Church's ministry of presence as much as anyone.

Prison Widows, Widowers, and Orphans

We have discussed this before, but it bears repeating in this context. Incarceration produces what has been dubbed a prison widow or widower, and the prison orphan. These terms capture the reality that incarceration's impact extends far beyond the person behind bars.

Incarceration can have far-reaching effects on the families of those who are incarcerated. The term "prison widow" or "prison widower" is used to describe the partners of incarcerated individuals who must endure the hardships of separation and often struggle to maintain the relationship while their loved one is in prison. The term "prison orphan" is used to describe children who have a parent in prison and may face a range of emotional, social, and economic challenges as a result.

The impact of incarceration on families can be significant and long-lasting. Here are some of the ways that incarceration can produce a prison widow or widower and a prison orphan.

Emotional trauma is perhaps the most obvious. Families of incarcerated individuals often experience emotional trauma as a result of the separation. Partners may feel abandoned, betrayed, or hopeless, while children may feel confused, anxious, or depressed. These emotional challenges can be difficult to overcome and may have lasting effects on the family.

Economic challenges are also common. Incarceration can have significant economic impacts on families. Partners of incarcerated individuals may struggle to make ends meet without the support of their loved one, while children may experience financial hardship and be forced to rely on social services for support. The costs of incarceration—legal fees, phone calls, visits, commissary money—can drain family resources.

Social isolation is another challenge. Families of incarcerated individuals may also experience social isolation, as they may feel stigmatized or ashamed of their loved one's incarceration. This can lead to a sense of isolation and loneliness, which can further exacerbate the emotional challenges they face. Friends may drift away. Church members may not know what to say. The family suffers alone.

Difficulty maintaining relationships is a fourth challenge. Maintaining relationships with incarcerated individuals can be challenging, as families must navigate the logistics of prison visits, phone calls, and correspondence. This can be especially difficult for children, who may struggle to understand why their parent is not with them and may feel disconnected from them as a result.

The impact of incarceration on families can be significant and long-lasting. Partners of incarcerated individuals can become prison widows or widowers, while children can become prison orphans. The emotional trauma, economic challenges, social isolation, and difficulty maintaining relationships that families of incarcerated individuals face can be difficult to overcome, but with support and resources, they can work towards healing and rebuilding their lives.

Holistic Support for Families

As the offender's family waits on them, they need help spiritually, emotionally, and financially. This is a holistic need that requires a holistic response from the Church.

When an offender is incarcerated, it can be a challenging time for their family members who are left behind. They may experience a range of difficulties, including spiritual, emotional, and financial challenges.

Spiritual Support is essential. The family of an incarcerated person may experience a crisis of faith or struggle to understand why this has happened to their loved one. They may also feel isolated from their church community, as they may be reluctant to share their situation with others. Therefore, they need spiritual support, such as prayer, scripture, and counseling, to help them find peace and comfort in their faith.

They need to know that God has not abandoned them, that their situation is not beyond God's concern, that there is hope even in the midst of this trial. They need a faith community that will welcome them, not judge them, and walk with them through this difficult time.

Emotional Support is equally important. The family members of incarcerated persons may feel a range of emotions, such as shame, guilt, anger, frustration, sadness, and anxiety. They may worry about the welfare of their loved one, and the uncertainty of their situation can cause stress and anxiety. Therefore, they need emotional support, such as counseling and therapy, to help them cope with the challenges they face.

They need someone to listen without judgment, to validate their feelings, to help them process the complex emotions that come with having a loved one in prison. They need to know that it is okay to feel angry, sad, confused, and hopeful all at once.

Financial Support is also crucial. Incarceration can have significant financial impacts on families. They may struggle to make ends meet without the support of their loved one's income, and they may also have to pay for legal fees or other expenses related to the incarceration. Therefore, they need financial support, such as government assistance programs or support from community organizations, to help them maintain their financial stability.

The Church can help by providing emergency assistance, helping with job searches, connecting families with resources, and coming alongside them in practical ways. Sometimes the most spiritual thing we can do is help pay a bill or provide a meal.

The family of an incarcerated person may need help spiritually, emotionally, and financially as they wait for their loved one to be released. They need spiritual support to find comfort in their faith, emotional support to help them cope with their feelings, and financial support to help them maintain their financial stability. Therefore, it is important for criminal justice ministries to provide holistic support to the families of incarcerated persons, in addition to supporting the offenders themselves.

The Critical Need for Marriage Seminars

There is a great need for marriage seminars that could save literally hundreds of offender marriages, and, as a result, break the generational cycle of crime and brokenness in these families. The statistics are sobering: approximately 90% of all marriages end in divorce when the incarceration period exceeds one year.

Think about what that means. Nine out of ten marriages fail when one partner is incarcerated for more than a year. The stress of separation, the financial strain, the emotional burden, the stigma, the difficulty of maintaining connection—all of these factors combine to destroy relationships.

If the offender can come home to a loving, waiting, Christian family, they have a greater chance of avoiding crime and staying out of prison in the future. A stable family provides accountability, support, encouragement, and a reason to stay on the right path. When offenders know that someone is waiting for them, that someone believes in them, that someone is counting on them, they are more motivated to make the changes necessary to succeed.

Marriage seminars are an essential component of criminal justice ministry because they offer support and guidance to offenders and their families. Offender marriages often face unique challenges, such as separation, financial difficulties, and communication issues, which can put a significant strain on their relationship. Without proper support and guidance, these marriages are at risk of failing, which can lead to a cycle of brokenness and crime in the family.

Marriage seminars can provide essential resources and tools for offender couples to help them build strong and healthy relationships. These seminars can offer guidance on topics such as communication, conflict resolution, financial management, and parenting, which can help couples address the challenges they face and build stronger relationships. The seminars can also provide an opportunity for couples to connect with other couples facing similar challenges and to share experiences and support.

By helping to save offender marriages, these seminars can break the cycle of generational crime and brokenness in these families. When offender couples have strong and healthy relationships, they are better equipped to provide a stable and supportive home environment for their children, which can help to break the cycle of criminal behavior and incarceration.

Moreover, research has shown that strong family connections and support can reduce recidivism rates among offenders. Offenders who have positive relationships with their families and receive support and guidance are more likely to successfully reintegrate into society and avoid returning to a life of crime.

Marriage seminars are an essential component of criminal justice ministry as they offer support and guidance to offender couples and help to break the cycle of generational crime and brokenness in families. By providing essential resources and tools, these seminars can help to save hundreds of offender marriages and reduce recidivism rates. Therefore, it is crucial to incorporate marriage seminars into criminal justice ministry programs.

The Most Difficult Aspect

Which aspect of criminal justice ministry is the most difficult? The answer is criminal justice professionals—the officers and officials who work in the system day in and day out.

One thing we can do is to recognize and encourage criminal justice professionals who are positively impacting prisoners by their efforts, and inspiring them to become productive members of our community upon release. Theirs is not an easy job.

It is challenging to identify one specific aspect of criminal justice ministry as the most difficult since each component of the ministry presents unique challenges. However, working with offenders, especially those who have committed heinous crimes, can be one of the most challenging aspects of criminal justice ministry.

Ministering to offenders can be emotionally and mentally challenging for many reasons. Firstly, offenders may be hostile, manipulative, or resistant to change, which can make it challenging to establish a relationship of trust and empathy. Secondly, ministers may have to confront their own biases and preconceptions about offenders, which can interfere with their ability to minister effectively. Thirdly, offenders may have experienced trauma, abuse, or addiction, which can make it challenging to address their spiritual and emotional needs effectively.

Moreover, working with offenders can be challenging because ministers may face opposition from others who believe that offenders do not deserve compassion or forgiveness. There may be negative attitudes toward offenders from the public or even from within the Church, which can make it challenging to advocate for the needs of offenders and to promote restorative justice principles.

While each component of criminal justice ministry presents unique challenges, working with offenders can be one of the most challenging aspects of the ministry due to various factors such as resistance to change, the need for emotional and mental support, addressing spiritual and emotional needs, confronting one's own biases, and negative attitudes from others towards offenders.

Ministering to Criminal Justice Professionals

The first step in ministering to a criminal justice professional is the building of relationships. This cannot be rushed or forced. It must happen organically, over time, through genuine interaction and care.

The first step in ministering to a criminal justice professional is building a relationship because it allows the minister to understand the unique challenges and stressors faced by those working in the criminal justice system.

Criminal justice professionals, such as police officers, correctional officers, and judges, often face high levels of stress, trauma, and burnout due to the nature of their work. They are exposed to violence, crime scenes, and the suffering of victims and offenders on a daily basis. They may also face challenges in balancing their personal and professional lives and may feel isolated or unsupported in their work environment.

By building a relationship, the minister can demonstrate empathy and understanding of the challenges faced by criminal justice professionals. This can help to establish trust and rapport, which are essential for effective ministry. It can also provide an opportunity for the minister to listen and offer emotional and spiritual support, as well as practical resources and referrals to professional services if needed.

Furthermore, building a relationship with a criminal justice professional can help to break down barriers between the Church and the criminal justice system. Criminal justice professionals may have negative attitudes toward the Church or religion, or they may be skeptical of outside influences in their work environment. Building a relationship based on mutual respect and understanding can help to overcome these barriers and promote positive change in the criminal justice system.

Building a relationship is the first step in ministering to a criminal justice professional because it allows the minister to understand the unique challenges faced by these individuals, demonstrate empathy and support, offer practical resources and referrals, and break down barriers between the Church and the criminal justice system.

Patience with a Closed Community

Establishing a relationship requires much patience, because the correctional staff in many ways is a closed community that shuns outsiders. This is not personal; it is protective. They have learned to be cautious.

Establishing a relationship with correctional staff can be a challenging task because they often work in a closed community that may be suspicious or unwelcoming of outsiders. This is particularly true in correctional facilities, where staff members are responsible for maintaining the safety and security of the institution and its inmates.

In order to establish a relationship with correctional staff, it is important to approach them with sensitivity, understanding, and patience. It is important to recognize that these individuals are under a great deal of stress and may be skeptical of outsiders, particularly those who are affiliated with a religious organization.

One effective approach is to start by simply being present in the correctional facility and offering to assist with any needs or concerns that staff members may have. This could include offering to lead a Bible study or prayer group, providing resources on topics such as stress management or conflict resolution, or simply being available to listen and offer support.

It is also important to be respectful of the boundaries and protocols established by the correctional facility. This may include obtaining the necessary approvals and clearances to enter the facility, adhering to the rules and regulations established by the institution, and respecting the privacy and confidentiality of staff members and inmates.

Additionally, it is important to recognize the unique challenges and stressors faced by correctional staff members, and to offer support and encouragement in a non-judgmental and compassionate manner. This may involve offering resources and referrals for mental health or addiction services, providing opportunities for staff members to participate in support groups or counseling sessions, or simply being a supportive and empathetic presence.

Establishing a relationship with correctional staff requires patience, sensitivity, and understanding. By being present, offering support and resources, and respecting the boundaries and protocols established by the institution, ministers can build trust and rapport with correctional staff members and promote positive change in the correctional system.

Including Unique Individuals

Because of varying work hours, a church should be willing to schedule special activities and develop programs to include these unique individuals. Criminal justice professionals cannot always attend Sunday morning services at 11:00 AM. Their schedules are irregular, unpredictable, and demanding.

Correctional staff work in a unique and challenging environment that requires them to maintain a high level of alertness and vigilance at all times. As a result, their work schedules can be unpredictable and may involve long hours, irregular shifts, and weekend and holiday work.

In order to minister effectively to correctional staff, it is important for the Church to be flexible and accommodating in scheduling activities and developing programs. This may involve scheduling activities and events at times when correctional staff are more likely to be available, such as early morning, late evening, or weekends. It may also involve developing programs and activities that can be accessed remotely or on a flexible schedule, such as online Bible studies, devotional materials, or prayer groups.

In addition to scheduling activities and programs at convenient times, it is important to create an environment that is welcoming and supportive of correctional staff. This may involve providing resources and support for common challenges faced by correctional staff, such as stress management, self-care, and mental health resources. It may also involve providing opportunities for correctional staff to connect with one another and build community, such as support groups, social events, and networking opportunities.

Some churches have found success offering a Wednesday night service specifically for first responders and shift workers. Others record their services and make them available online for those who cannot attend in person. Still others offer small groups that meet at unconventional times—early morning before a shift begins, or late evening after one ends.

Ultimately, the church must be willing to adapt and be creative in order to minister effectively to correctional staff. By recognizing the unique challenges and needs of this group, and by providing support and resources in a flexible and accommodating manner, the church can build meaningful relationships and promote positive change in the correctional system.

The Church has a vital role to play in impacting corrections. The mandate from Matthew 25 is clear. The needs are urgent. The opportunities are abundant. By ministering to victims, offenders, families, and criminal justice professionals, the Church can bring the love and compassion of Christ to those who are suffering in and around the criminal justice system.

This is not easy work. It requires patience, persistence, and a deep commitment to the principles of restorative justice. It requires building relationships, showing up, and staying present. It requires flexibility and creativity. But it is essential work, and it is work that the Church is uniquely positioned to do.

When the Church shows up in prisons, in courthouses, in probation offices, in the homes of victims and families, lives are changed. Communities are strengthened. The kingdom of God is advanced. And Jesus, who identifies with the least of these, is honored.

The question is not whether the Church can impact corrections. The question is whether we will answer the call.

CHAPTER 09

ORGANIZATIONAL CHANGE

We have journeyed together through eight chapters, each building upon the last. We have examined the traditional view of justice and found it wanting. We have explored why the system must be restructured. We have considered a different view of justice—restorative justice—and examined its principles, practices, and conceptual frameworks. We have looked at promising practices from around the world. We have explored the biblical foundations for restorative justice and considered the Church's mandate to be involved. We have examined the restorative justice ministry paradigm and explored how the Church can impact corrections.

Now, in this chapter, we turn to a practical and often overlooked aspect of this work: organizational change. How do we actually change the systems and institutions that have been doing things the same way for decades, even centuries? How do we convince justice system officials, policymakers, and the public to embrace a new way of thinking about justice? How do we move from vision to reality, from theory to practice?

This chapter is about the hard work of change. It is about the challenges, the strategies, the persistence required to transform a system. It is about assessments, planning, advocacy, and collaboration. And it is about hope—the conviction that no barrier is insurmountable and that with God's help, we can create a more just and merciful world.

The Difficulty of Convincing Officials to Change

Let us begin with an honest acknowledgment: convincing justice system officials to embrace a new justice paradigm is a difficult task. This is not because they are bad people or because they are opposed to justice. It is because change is hard, especially in large, established systems.

There are several reasons why this is so difficult.

Firstly, justice system officials are often trained and experienced in a particular approach to justice that may be deeply ingrained in their thinking and decision-making processes. They have spent years, sometimes decades, learning and working within the traditional punitive system. They have developed expertise in its procedures, its language, its assumptions. To ask them to adopt a new approach is to ask them to unlearn much of what they know and to start over in some ways. This can feel threatening, even impossible.

Imagine a judge who has spent thirty years on the bench, sentencing offenders according to established laws and precedents. They have developed a rhythm, a set of practices, a way of thinking about their role. Now someone comes along and says, "There's a better way. It involves bringing victims and offenders together, listening to their stories, and crafting restorative agreements." This is not just a new technique; it is a new worldview. It requires a fundamental shift in how the judge understands their role and the purpose of justice.

Secondly, justice system officials may be subject to political pressures or constraints that limit their ability to make significant changes. They operate within a complex web of laws, policies, budgets, and political realities. Even if they personally believe in restorative justice, they may face obstacles that make it difficult to implement.

For example, a prosecutor may be sympathetic to restorative justice but is constrained by mandatory minimum sentencing laws that require certain punishments for certain crimes. A police chief may want to implement community policing but faces budget cuts that make it impossible to assign officers to specific neighborhoods. A corrections official may believe in rehabilitation but is hamstrung by overcrowding and underfunding.

These are real constraints, and they cannot simply be ignored. Any effort to change the system must take them into account and work within them, even as it seeks to change them.

Thirdly, justice system officials may be wary of adopting a new justice paradigm if they are not convinced of its effectiveness or if they perceive it as too risky. They have a responsibility to protect public safety and to ensure that justice is done. If they are not confident that restorative justice will achieve these goals, they will be reluctant to embrace it.

This is why research and evidence are so important. When studies show that restorative justice reduces recidivism, increases victim satisfaction, and saves money, these findings can help to overcome skepticism. When officials see programs that are working in other jurisdictions, they become more open to trying them in their own.

Finally, justice system officials may be resistant to change due to a lack of awareness or understanding of alternative justice paradigms. They may not be familiar with the latest research or evidence-based practices. They may not have had the opportunity to learn about restorative justice or to see it in action. Their resistance may be based on ignorance rather than opposition.

This is why education and dialogue are essential. Advocates must be willing to engage with officials, to answer their questions, to address their concerns, and to provide them with the information they need to make informed decisions.

In order to overcome these challenges, advocates for a new justice paradigm must be persistent, strategic, and collaborative in their efforts to engage with justice system officials. They must be able to effectively communicate the benefits and potential risks of the new approach, and they must be able to demonstrate its effectiveness through research and evidence-based practices. They must also be able to build partnerships and coalitions with other stakeholders, such as community leaders, advocacy groups, and policymakers, in order to create a supportive environment for change.

However, it is important to know that no barrier is insurmountable. Change is often met with resistance because of fear of the unknown. The current punitive system has been in place for years and some are convinced that it is the only way to carry out criminal justice. But history shows that systems do change, paradigms do shift, and what seems impossible today can become reality tomorrow.

While there may be challenges and barriers to implementing a new justice paradigm, it is important to remember that no barrier is insurmountable. With dedication, persistence, and creativity, advocates for change can find ways to overcome even the most difficult obstacles.

One way to do this is by building relationships and fostering collaboration among stakeholders. By working together and finding common ground, justice system officials, advocates, and community members can create a shared vision for a more just and equitable system, and develop strategies to bring that vision to life.

Another important approach is to be open to feedback and be willing to adapt and adjust as needed. If initial efforts to implement a new justice paradigm are met with resistance or challenges, it may be necessary to re-evaluate and make changes to the approach in order to achieve success.

Finally, it is important to remain focused on the ultimate goal: creating a justice system that is fair, effective, and compassionate. By keeping this goal in mind and working towards it with persistence and determination, advocates for change can overcome even the most daunting barriers and create a better future for all members of society.

Assessing Benefits and Challenges

In implementing any restorative justice programs and practices, it is necessary to determine what good will come from restorative justice principles, and to identify any possible challenges. This is not just a matter of wishful thinking; it requires careful assessment and planning.

Implementing restorative justice programs and practices can be a complex and challenging process, as it involves a shift in the way the justice system approaches crime and justice. In order to successfully implement restorative justice principles, it is important to determine what benefits can be gained from this approach, as well as any possible challenges that may arise.

One of the key benefits of restorative justice is that it can help to repair harm caused by crime and promote healing for both victims and offenders. By involving all parties in the process and focusing on addressing the root causes of the crime, restorative justice can help to reduce recidivism and create a safer, more just society.

Research has demonstrated these benefits time and again. Restorative justice programs have been shown to reduce repeat offending, increase victim satisfaction, and save money compared to traditional punitive approaches. Victims who participate in restorative processes often report feeling heard, validated, and empowered. Offenders who go through restorative justice are more likely to take responsibility for their actions and less likely to reoffend.

However, implementing restorative justice programs and practices can also present challenges. For example, there may be resistance from justice system officials or the public, who may be more familiar with traditional punitive approaches to justice. People fear what they do not understand. They may worry that restorative justice is "soft on crime" or that it will not hold offenders accountable.

Additionally, it can be challenging to ensure that all parties involved in the process feel heard and respected, particularly if there are power imbalances or unresolved trauma. Victims may feel intimidated by the prospect of meeting with their offender. Offenders may be defensive or manipulative. Facilitators must be skilled in managing these dynamics.

There may also be logistical challenges. Restorative justice processes take time and resources. They require trained facilitators, safe spaces, and ongoing support for participants. In a system that is already overburdened, finding the capacity to implement these programs can be difficult.

To address these challenges, it is important to engage in ongoing education and dialogue with justice system officials, community members, and other stakeholders. By providing information and resources about the benefits of restorative justice and addressing any concerns or questions, advocates for this approach can help to build support and understanding for these programs and practices.

Additionally, it is important to ensure that restorative justice processes are implemented in a way that is culturally responsive and trauma-informed, taking into account the unique needs and experiences of all participants. This means training facilitators to recognize and respond to trauma, to be sensitive to cultural differences, and to create safe spaces for dialogue.

Implementing restorative justice programs and practices requires careful consideration of the benefits and challenges involved. By engaging in ongoing education, dialogue, and culturally responsive and trauma-informed approaches, advocates for restorative justice can help to create a more just and equitable justice system for all.

The Value of Benefit Assessments

How might the results of a "benefit assessment" help in the implementation of restorative justice programs and practices? A benefit assessment is a process used to evaluate the potential benefits and drawbacks of implementing a particular policy or program. In the case of restorative justice programs and practices, a benefit assessment can help identify the specific ways in which these approaches can benefit victims, offenders, and the community as a whole.

The results of a benefit assessment can be useful in several ways in the implementation of restorative justice programs and practices.

First, it can help to build support and understanding for these approaches among justice system officials, community members, and other stakeholders. By highlighting the potential benefits of restorative justice, such as reduced recidivism and increased victim satisfaction, advocates can help to build momentum for the implementation of these programs and practices.

When people see concrete evidence that restorative justice works, they are more likely to support it. A benefit assessment provides that evidence. It answers the question, "What's in it for us?" For justice system officials, the answer might be reduced caseloads and lower costs. For victims, it might be greater satisfaction and healing. For offenders, it might be the opportunity to make amends and move forward. For the community, it might be safer neighborhoods and stronger social bonds.

Developing marketing messages for various constituencies is an important part of this process. Different groups care about different things. Community members may be most interested in safety and cohesion. Offenders and their advocates may care about fairness and rehabilitation. Victims and service providers want healing and support. Justice practitioners want effectiveness and efficiency. Elected officials want to be responsive to their constituents. The news media wants compelling stories. Allied professionals want to know how restorative justice connects to their work. A benefit assessment provides the information needed to craft messages that resonate with each of these groups.

Second, a benefit assessment can help to guide the development and implementation of restorative justice programs and practices. By identifying specific areas where restorative justice can have the greatest impact, such as reducing racial disparities in the justice system or addressing trauma and mental health issues among offenders, advocates can help to ensure that these programs are tailored to the unique needs and circumstances of the community.

This involves comparing existing approaches to justice in the context of a more beneficial approach. How does restorative justice compare to traditional punishment in terms of cost effectiveness? How does it affect victim involvement and satisfaction? Does it help offenders develop competencies that will help them succeed? Does it increase community appreciation of justice practices? By answering these questions, a benefit assessment helps to build programs on perceived strengths and address identified weaknesses.

Third, a benefit assessment can help to measure the effectiveness of restorative justice programs and practices over time. By regularly evaluating the outcomes and impacts of these programs, advocates can make adjustments and improvements to ensure that they are achieving their intended goals. This is especially important when benefits are tangible and can be measured in terms of performance outcomes.

Overall, restorative justice offers many benefits compared to the traditional criminal justice system. It substantially reduces repeat offending for some offenders, although not all. It reduces repeat offending more than prison for adults and at least as well as prison for youth. It helps reduce the costs of criminal justice. It provides both victims and offenders with more satisfaction that justice had been done than did traditional criminal justice. It reduces crime victims' post-traumatic stress symptoms and the related costs. It reduces crime victims' desire for violent revenge against their offenders.

A benefit assessment can provide valuable information and guidance for the implementation of restorative justice programs and practices, helping to build support, guide development, and measure effectiveness over time.

The Value of Barrier Assessments

In what ways can the results of a "barrier assessment" assist in implementing any restorative justice programs and practices? A barrier assessment is a process used to identify and address potential obstacles or barriers to the successful implementation of a particular policy or program. In the case of restorative justice programs and practices, a barrier assessment can help identify specific challenges or obstacles that may need to be addressed in order to implement these approaches effectively.

The results of a barrier assessment can be useful in several ways.

First, it can help to anticipate and address potential challenges before they become major obstacles. By identifying potential barriers, such as resistance from justice system officials or limited funding, advocates can develop strategies to overcome these challenges and ensure that the programs are implemented successfully.

Early identification of potential opponents' arguments against restorative justice approaches is crucial. If advocates know in advance what objections will be raised, they can prepare responses. If they know that certain groups are likely to resist, they can engage with them early, listen to their concerns, and address them constructively.

Second, a barrier assessment can help to ensure that restorative justice programs and practices are tailored to the unique needs and circumstances of the community. By identifying specific challenges or barriers in the local context, advocates can develop programs that are more responsive and effective in meeting the needs of victims, offenders, and the community as a whole.

This involves focusing planning and implementation on reducing or eliminating possible barriers. If the barrier is lack of funding, the plan must include fundraising or grant writing. If the barrier is lack of trained facilitators, the plan must include training programs. If the barrier is resistance from certain stakeholders, the plan must include outreach and education.

Third, a barrier assessment can help to build support and buy-in for restorative justice programs and practices. By openly acknowledging and addressing potential challenges or obstacles, advocates can demonstrate a commitment to implementing these approaches in a thoughtful and effective way, which can help to build trust and support among justice system officials, community members, and other stakeholders.

This also allows for evaluating program effectiveness based upon success in overcoming any barriers. If a program successfully addresses the barriers identified in the assessment, that is a measure of its effectiveness. If barriers remain, the program may need to be adjusted.

A barrier assessment can help to identify potential challenges or obstacles to the successful implementation of restorative justice programs and practices, tailor these approaches to the unique needs and circumstances of the community, and build support and buy-in for these approaches.

The Long-Term Commitment Required

Changing the criminal justice system requires a disciplined long-term commitment with creative leadership and vision. This is not a quick fix or a short-term project. It is a generational effort that requires patience, persistence, and faithfulness.

All efforts to change the current criminal justice system should not include criticism but be informative and suggestive in nature. This is an important point. Criticism can create defensiveness and opposition. Information and suggestion invite dialogue and collaboration.

Changing any established system, including the criminal justice system, is a complex and challenging task that requires a disciplined long-term commitment with creative leadership and vision. This is because the criminal justice system is deeply rooted in the political, social, and cultural fabric of society. It has a long history, and its practices and procedures are often deeply ingrained in the minds of those who work within it.

To bring about meaningful change, a sustained effort is required that involves multiple stakeholders, including policymakers, criminal justice professionals, community members, and those directly impacted by the system. It is important to engage in ongoing dialogue and collaboration with these stakeholders to ensure that their needs and perspectives are taken into account.

This is not a matter of imposing a vision from above. It is a matter of building consensus from below, of finding common ground, of working together toward shared goals. It requires listening as much as speaking, learning as much as teaching.

In addition, change often requires overcoming resistance to new ideas and practices. This can be especially challenging in a system that is highly bureaucratic and hierarchical, where individuals may be resistant to change or may feel threatened by new approaches. It is important to have leaders who can effectively communicate the benefits of restorative justice and build a coalition of support among stakeholders.

Creative leadership is essential. The challenges are too complex for cookie-cutter solutions. Leaders must be able to think outside the box, to adapt strategies to local circumstances, to find innovative ways forward. They must have vision—the ability to see what could be, even when it is not yet visible to others.

Finally, meaningful change requires resources, including funding, time, and expertise. It is important to develop a clear plan for implementing restorative justice programs and practices and to secure the necessary resources to ensure success. This requires both short-term and long-term planning and a commitment to ongoing evaluation and improvement.

Steps to Becoming a Restorative Justice Advocate

What are some steps you can take to prepare yourself in becoming a restorative justice advocate? This is a personal question, but there are common steps that many advocates have taken.

First, read and learn as much as you can about the principles and practices of restorative justice. Knowledge is the foundation of effective advocacy. Read books, articles, and research studies. Attend conferences, seminars, and workshops. Listen to podcasts and watch videos. The more you know, the more confident and effective you will be.

Second, understand the restorative justice paradigm well enough that you can introduce it properly and be able to explain it to those who want to hear about it. This means not just knowing the facts but understanding the philosophy, the values, the worldview that underlies restorative justice. You need to be able to answer questions, address objections, and articulate the vision in a way that inspires others.

Third, recognize that a comprehensive change process will take a long time and that many justice agencies are currently using some restorative practice. This is important for managing expectations. Change does not happen overnight. But it is also encouraging to know that restorative justice is already happening in many places. You are not starting from scratch; you are building on work that is already being done.

Examining and participating in local restorative intervention programs can also help prepare you in becoming a restorative justice advocate. In other words, get some hands-on experience. There is no substitute for actually seeing restorative justice in action, for sitting in on a circle or a conference, for talking with victims and offenders who have been through the process. This experience will inform your advocacy and give you stories to tell.

If you want to become a restorative justice advocate, here are some steps you can take to prepare yourself:

Educate yourself: Learn as much as you can about restorative justice principles, practices, and theories. Read books, articles, and research studies on the subject. Attend conferences, seminars, and workshops related to restorative justice.

Get trained: Take courses and training programs on restorative justice. Many organizations and universities offer training programs on restorative justice. This training will give you the skills you need to facilitate restorative processes and to advocate effectively.

Volunteer: Find a local restorative justice organization and volunteer your time. You can help with community outreach, victim support, or facilitation of restorative justice meetings. This hands-on experience is invaluable.

Build relationships: Connect with individuals and organizations involved in restorative justice work. Attend local meetings, join online groups, and engage with like-minded people. Relationships are the foundation of effective advocacy.

Advocate: Speak out in support of restorative justice. Write letters to your local government officials, attend public hearings, and share information about restorative justice on social media. Use your voice to raise awareness and build support.

Practice: Apply restorative justice principles in your daily life. Practice active listening, empathy, and forgiveness in your personal and professional relationships. Be the change you wish to see.

By taking these steps, you can become a knowledgeable and effective advocate for restorative justice.

Making the System More Restorative Over Time

Your objective is to make the criminal justice system more restorative over time by encouraging the public to examine existing beliefs about the purpose of crime intervention. This is a long-term goal, but it is achievable.

Encouraging the public to examine existing beliefs about the purpose of crime intervention is a crucial step in making the criminal justice system more restorative over time. People's beliefs shape their attitudes, and their attitudes shape their support for policies and programs. If the public believes that the purpose of crime intervention is punishment, they will support punitive policies. If they come to believe that the purpose is restoration, they will support restorative approaches.

Some steps that can be taken to achieve this objective are:

Education: Educate yourself about restorative justice principles and practices, and the ways in which they differ from traditional criminal justice interventions. Read books and articles on the subject, attend workshops and conferences, and connect with other advocates and practitioners. Then use what you have learned to educate others.

Awareness: Raise awareness about the benefits of restorative justice, and the limitations of traditional punitive approaches. Use social media, public speaking, and other platforms to share stories and information about restorative justice, and its potential to create healing and transformation for all parties involved. Stories are particularly powerful. When people hear about a victim who found healing through meeting with the offender, or an offender who turned their life around after participating in a restorative process, they become more open to the approach.

Advocacy: Advocate for restorative justice policies and programs at the local, state, and national levels. Join or support organizations that are working to promote restorative justice, and engage with elected officials and policymakers to express your support for restorative justice initiatives. Let your voice be heard.

Collaboration: Collaborate with other individuals and organizations in your community to promote restorative justice principles and practices. Work with schools, faith-based organizations, and community groups to implement restorative justice programs, and build partnerships with law enforcement agencies and other criminal justice stakeholders to promote restorative justice initiatives. There is strength in numbers.

Self-reflection: Engage in self-reflection and examine your own biases and assumptions about crime, punishment, and justice. Challenge yourself to see individuals who have committed harm as human beings with the capacity for change, and recognize the importance of healing and restoration for all parties involved in the criminal justice system. This inner work is essential for authentic advocacy.

Action Planning for the Community

What are some tips on action planning for the community? Here are several important considerations.

Go to where the energy is (80/20). This principle recognizes that 80% of the results often come from 20% of the effort. Focus on the people and places where there is already interest and energy. Don't waste time trying to convince those who are completely opposed; invest your time in those who are open or curious. Build on existing momentum.

Reclaim their moral authority. Communities have moral authority that outside advocates do not. When community members speak about their own experiences, their own needs, their own vision for justice, they carry weight that outsiders cannot. Empower community members to be the primary advocates for restorative justice in their own communities.

Be guided by shared principles. Before you start planning, clarify the principles that will guide your work. What are your core values? What are your non-negotiables? Having shared principles helps to keep everyone on the same page and provides a framework for decision-making.

Establish collaborative, diverse and multi-disciplinary teams. No one person or organization can do this work alone. Bring together people with different skills, perspectives, and experiences. Include victims, offenders, family members, justice professionals, faith leaders, educators, business owners, and others. The more diverse the team, the more creative and effective it will be.

Here are some additional tips on action planning for the community:

Start with a clear goal: Determine the specific objective you want to achieve with your action plan. Vague goals lead to vague results. Be as specific as possible.

Identify stakeholders: Determine who will be impacted by the plan and who can support the plan's implementation. Engage them early and often.

Develop a timeline: Break down the goal into smaller tasks and set deadlines for each step. This makes the project manageable and helps to maintain momentum.

Assign responsibilities: Determine who will be responsible for each task and ensure that they have the necessary resources and support to complete it. Clear accountability is essential.

Develop a budget: Estimate the costs associated with implementing the plan and identify potential sources of funding. Be realistic about what is possible.

Identify potential challenges: Anticipate potential obstacles and develop contingency plans to address them. Hope for the best, but plan for the worst.

Measure progress: Determine how progress will be measured and establish benchmarks to evaluate success. What gets measured gets done.

Communicate the plan: Share the plan with stakeholders and the community to build support and gain feedback. Communication is not a one-time event but an ongoing process.

Implement the plan: Take action on the plan and continually monitor progress to ensure that it is on track. Be flexible and willing to adjust as needed.

Evaluate the plan: Conduct a formal evaluation of the plan to determine its effectiveness and identify areas for improvement. Learn from both successes and failures.

Action Planning for the Government

What are some tips on action planning for the government? Engaging with government requires a different approach than community organizing.

Delegate power to shape and decide. Government officials are more likely to support initiatives that they have had a hand in shaping. Give them opportunities to participate in the planning process, to offer input, to make decisions. When they feel ownership, they will be more committed.

Be patient and listen. Government moves slowly. Bureaucracy is real. Officials have many competing demands on their time and attention. Be patient. And listen more than you talk. Understand their constraints, their concerns, their priorities. This understanding will make your advocacy more effective.

Developing a credible and diverse coalition for restorative justice requires advocates to draw in leaders in the victims' rights movement, offender-advocates, law enforcement officials, politicians (from both liberal and conservative ideologies), and other opinion makers. The broader the coalition, the more influence it will have.

It is necessary to promote the vision of restorative justice while responding patiently and respecting the position of systemic and political realities. This is a delicate balance. You must be faithful to the vision while also being realistic about what is possible. You must push for change while also respecting the constraints within which officials operate.

Give information. Government officials need good information to make good decisions. Provide them with research, data, case studies, and other resources that demonstrate the effectiveness of restorative justice. Make it easy for them to be informed.

Practice restraint. Don't demand everything at once. Be willing to accept incremental progress. Celebrate small victories. Build trust over time. Restraint now can lead to greater gains later.

Be clear on roles and expectations. When working with government, it is important to be clear about who is responsible for what. Avoid misunderstandings by spelling out roles and expectations from the beginning.

Programs called "restorative" do not always reflect a restorative vision and values. Evaluation using the right criteria will help government programs become more restorative in their treatment of victims, offenders and community members. Advocates must be willing to hold programs accountable to restorative principles.

Here are some tips on action planning for the government to promote restorative justice:

Build relationships with community stakeholders: The government can work to build relationships with community stakeholders to understand their perspectives on restorative justice and involve them in the decision-making process.

Conduct a needs assessment: The government can conduct a needs assessment to identify the gaps and opportunities in the current justice system and develop strategies to address them.

Develop policies and guidelines: The government can develop policies and guidelines that support restorative justice practices and integrate them into existing criminal justice policies and procedures.

Provide training and support: The government can provide training and support to justice professionals, such as judges, prosecutors, and defense attorneys, on restorative justice principles and practices.

Allocate resources: The government can allocate resources to support restorative justice initiatives, such as funding for victim services and community-based programs.

Evaluate and monitor progress: The government can evaluate and monitor the progress of restorative justice initiatives to ensure they are effective and make adjustments as necessary.

Engage in public education and outreach: The government can engage in public education and outreach to raise awareness of restorative justice and its benefits for both victims and offenders.

Addressing Isolating System Features

Which isolating system features should be addressed in action planning? Several features of the current criminal justice system create isolation and distance between the system and the people it serves. These must be addressed.

Data privacy success: While data privacy laws are important and sensible, they can also isolate the public from information about what is happening in the justice system. When people cannot access information, they are left with fear of the unknown. Action planning should find ways to balance privacy with transparency.

Sterilization of information: When information is shared with the public, it is often sterilized—cleaned of identifying details, aggregated, anonymized. While this protects privacy, it also makes it difficult for ordinary citizens to understand what is really happening. Action planning should find ways to make information accessible and meaningful.

Removal of emotion from process: The orderly environment of the justice process is intolerant of emotional expression. But crime is emotionally charged, and those emotions are central to understanding what happened and what should be done. Action planning should create space for emotion in the justice process.

Intimidating and foreign structures: Courthouses are designed to be imposing and intimidating. The language of the law is foreign to most people. Action planning should seek to make the justice system more accessible and less intimidating.

Professionalism: As justice system personnel gain expertise, they develop specialized jargon and procedures that function like a foreign language to outsiders. A closed system emerges that shuns public influence. Action planning should find ways to bridge this gap.

Public service convenience: American society has developed a "911 mentality" where conflicts are referred to professionals rather than resolved by those involved. Action planning should seek to restore the capacity of communities to resolve their own conflicts.

Goals must be carefully delineated and implementation must be deliberate and monitored, re-evaluated and improved upon to establish the legitimacy of a restorative response to crime.

In action planning for restorative justice, the following isolating system features should also be addressed:

Dehumanization: The system often views offenders as less than human, which can lead to further isolation and stigmatization. Addressing this feature involves promoting human dignity and respect for all individuals, including offenders.

Institutionalization: The prison system can become a self-contained world that is isolated from the outside community. Addressing this feature involves finding ways to connect offenders to the outside world, such as through education or vocational training programs.

Powerlessness: Offenders often feel powerless and disempowered within the criminal justice system. Addressing this feature involves giving offenders a sense of agency and empowerment, such as through restorative justice processes where they have a voice in the process.

Normlessness: The prison environment can be devoid of positive social norms, leading to the development of negative behaviors and attitudes. Addressing this feature involves creating a positive and supportive environment within the criminal justice system, including providing opportunities for personal growth and development.

Marginalization: Offenders can be marginalized from society and may have limited social support networks. Addressing this feature involves finding ways to reintegrate offenders into society and provide them with a sense of belonging, such as through community-based programs and support groups.

How Crime Provokes Community Responsibility

How does crime provoke community responsibility? This is an interesting question because crime is usually seen as something that happens to a community, not something that provokes a response from it. But in fact, crime can be a catalyst for community action.

Calling attention to social problems and harmful social conditions. Crime often highlights underlying issues that have been ignored. A rash of burglaries might draw attention to poverty and lack of opportunity in a neighborhood. A hate crime might expose deep-seated prejudices that need to be addressed. Crime can serve as a wake-up call.

Providing opportunity for the community to affirm its values and behavioral norms. When a crime occurs, the community has an opportunity to say, "This is not who we are. This is not what we stand for." Coming together to condemn crime and support victims affirms shared values and strengthens community identity.

Causing a community obligation to provide a process through which this conflict can be resolved. Crime creates a conflict that must be addressed. In the restorative justice paradigm, it is the community's responsibility to provide a process for resolution. This might involve circles, conferences, or other restorative practices.

Crime can provoke a sense of responsibility in the community because it can be seen as a threat to the safety and well-being of everyone in the community, not just the direct victims of the crime. When a crime occurs, it can create a sense of fear and insecurity among community members, leading them to want to take action to prevent similar crimes from happening in the future. This can include working with law enforcement and other community organizations to address the root causes of crime and develop strategies for prevention, as well as providing support to victims and their families.

Additionally, communities may organize neighborhood watch programs, community patrols, or other initiatives aimed at deterring criminal activity and promoting a sense of safety and security. By taking action in response to crime, communities can demonstrate their commitment to creating a safe and healthy environment for all residents.

Sustaining Community Involvement

Give three solutions to sustain community involvement. Community involvement is essential for restorative justice, but it can be difficult to sustain over time.

Must win support of the public. Without public support, community involvement will wither. This means ongoing communication, education, and engagement. It means showing the public that their involvement matters and makes a difference.

Train citizens and practitioners. People need to know what to do and how to do it. Training builds confidence and competence. It also creates a sense of investment and ownership. When people are trained, they are more likely to stay involved.

Get organizations involved. Individual volunteers are important, but organizations provide infrastructure, resources, and continuity. When churches, schools, nonprofits, and businesses get involved, community involvement becomes more sustainable.

Here are three additional solutions to sustain community involvement:

Provide ongoing education and training: It is important to provide the community with ongoing education and training about restorative justice principles and practices. This can be done through workshops, seminars, and community events that promote awareness and understanding of the issues. Education is not a one-time event but an ongoing process.

Foster collaboration: Collaboration among community members and organizations is critical to sustaining involvement. This can be achieved through partnerships and alliances that share resources and expertise, and work together to address community issues. When people work together, they are more likely to stay engaged.

Empower community members: Empowering community members to take ownership of restorative justice initiatives is key to sustaining involvement. This can be done by providing opportunities for community members to lead and participate in projects, and by recognizing and celebrating their contributions to the community. When people feel ownership, they are more committed.

Challenges to Sustaining Community Involvement

What are some of the challenges to sustaining community involvement? These challenges must be acknowledged and addressed.

History of justice system: The justice system has a long history that may include oppression, discrimination, and injustice. Communities that have been harmed by the system may be reluctant to engage with it, even in a restorative context.

Citizen cooperation: Getting citizens to cooperate and stay involved is always a challenge. People are busy. They have competing priorities. Sustaining their engagement requires ongoing effort.

Lack of organizational involvement: Without organizational support, community involvement can be fragile. Organizations provide structure, resources, and continuity. When they are not involved, sustainability is at risk.

Lack of understanding: Many people do not understand restorative justice. They may confuse it with being soft on crime or letting offenders off the hook. This lack of understanding can undermine support and involvement.

Previous victim experience: Individuals who have been victims of crime may be reluctant to participate in restorative justice processes. They may fear re-traumatization or may not believe that restorative justice can address their needs.

Community diversity: Diverse communities have diverse needs and perspectives. What works in one community may not work in another. Sustaining involvement requires adapting approaches to local contexts.

There are several additional challenges to sustaining community involvement in restorative justice efforts, including:

Lack of resources: Restorative justice programs often rely on volunteers, but it can be challenging to recruit and retain volunteers over time. This can be due to limited resources for training, supervision, and support.

Resistance to change: Some community members may be resistant to the idea of restorative justice or may prefer traditional punitive approaches to crime intervention. This resistance can be difficult to overcome.

Limited awareness and understanding: Many people may not be aware of restorative justice or may not fully understand how it works. This can make it difficult to generate community support and engagement.

Lack of political will: Restorative justice programs may require political support and funding to be sustainable, and there may be competing priorities for government resources. Without political will, sustainability is impossible.

Trauma and burnout: Restorative justice work can be emotionally taxing, and community members may experience burnout or vicarious trauma if they are not adequately supported. Self-care and support systems are essential.

Cultural barriers: Restorative justice programs may need to be adapted to meet the needs and cultural norms of diverse communities, which can present additional challenges. One size does not fit all.

Addressing these challenges requires ongoing effort and collaboration between community members, government officials, and other stakeholders.

Principles of Behavioral Change

Give four general principles about behavioral change. These principles are relevant not only for offenders but for all of us as we seek to change our own behavior and the behavior of systems.

Behavior is derived from thoughts. Proverbs 23:7 says, "For as he thinketh in his heart, so is he." People do the things they do because they believe the things they believe. The battlefield really is the mind. If we want to change behavior, we must address the underlying thoughts and beliefs that drive it.

This is true for offenders who need to change their criminal behavior. It is true for justice system officials who need to change their approach to justice. It is true for community members who need to change their attitudes toward offenders and victims. Change begins in the mind.

Relationships count. People do not change in isolation. They change in the context of relationships. A mentor, a friend, a supportive community—these relationships provide the encouragement, accountability, and support that make change possible. Restorative justice recognizes this by involving the community in the change process.

Community accountability counts. When a community holds its members accountable, change is more likely to stick. This is not the formal accountability of the justice system but the informal accountability of people who know each other, care about each other, and expect certain behaviors from each other. Restorative justice seeks to strengthen this kind of community accountability.

Humans do not always follow principles. This is a realistic admission. We know what we should do, but we do not always do it. We have principles, but we do not always follow them. Change is not a straight line; it involves setbacks, failures, and learning. This is why grace and persistence are essential.

Here are four additional general principles about behavioral change:

Behavioral change takes time and requires persistence: Change rarely happens overnight, and it often requires consistent effort over a long period of time. Impatience is the enemy of change.

Behavioral change requires motivation: People are more likely to change their behavior if they are motivated to do so. Motivation can come from a variety of sources, including personal values, social pressure, and external rewards. Finding and sustaining motivation is key.

Behavioral change is most effective when it is tailored to the individual: Different people have different needs, motivations, and obstacles to change. Effective behavioral change programs take these individual differences into account and provide personalized support. One size does not fit all.

Behavioral change requires a supportive environment: People are more likely to change their behavior when they are surrounded by a supportive network of family, friends, and community members. A supportive environment can provide encouragement, accountability, and resources to help individuals achieve their goals. Environment matters.

Organizational change is hard work. It requires patience, persistence, creativity, and collaboration. It requires assessing benefits and barriers, planning carefully, building coalitions, and sustaining involvement over time. It requires addressing the isolating features of the current system and engaging with government in constructive ways. And it requires a deep understanding of how change happens—in individuals, in communities, and in systems.

But it is possible. With God's help, with dedication and perseverance, with the support of like-minded advocates, we can change the system. We can make it more restorative, more just, more compassionate. We can create a world where crime is addressed not with punishment alone but with healing, where victims are heard and supported, where offenders are held accountable and offered a path to restoration, and where communities are empowered to resolve conflicts and build peace.

This is the vision. This is the goal. And it is worth all the effort it will take to achieve it.

CHAPTER 10

CONCLUSION

We have traveled a long and winding road together in this book. We began by examining the traditional view of justice—its ancient roots in the law of retaliation, its psychological appeal, and its troubling consequences. We saw how a system designed to punish has grown into a massive enterprise that incarcerates more of its citizens than any other nation on earth, at enormous cost and with little to show for it.

We explored why this system must be restructured. We looked at the soaring costs, the public's fear and frustration, the isolation of communities, and the way the system steals conflicts from those to whom they belong. We saw how the traditional model fails victims, fails offenders, and fails communities.

We then began to glimpse a different view of justice. We explored restorative justice—what it is, how it differs from the traditional model, and why it offers hope for healing and reconciliation. We considered the principles and practices that make restorative justice unique, and we saw how it centers victims, holds offenders accountable through repair, and involves communities in the process of justice.

We examined the conceptual frameworks that undergird restorative justice—the ideas, theories, and models that give it shape and substance. We saw how thinkers like Nils Christie have helped us understand crime as a catalyst for community empowerment, and how various conceptual models provide frameworks for community-based practice.

We explored the promising practices that have emerged as communities embrace restorative justice. We looked at sentencing circles, victim impact statements, community reparation boards, community service, restitution, victim-offender mediation, family group conferencing, victim impact panels, victim impact classes, and a range of community-based initiatives that connect the justice system with the public.

We considered whether the Church should get involved in restorative justice and saw that God has selected the Church as His primary instrument of restorative justice, giving it a clear mandate to do criminal justice ministry. We explored the biblical foundations of this calling and the questions it raises for those who would answer it.

We examined the restorative justice ministry paradigm—a framework for how the Church can actually do this work. We explored what it means to minister to offenders, to victims, to families, and to communities. We considered the role of repentance, the importance of addressing harm, the necessity of forgiveness, and the goal of restoration for all parties.

We looked at how the Church can impact corrections, ministering to victims, offenders, families, and criminal justice professionals. We considered the power of presence, the importance of relationship, and the practical steps that churches can take to fulfill their calling.

And in the previous chapter, we explored the hard work of organizational change—the challenges, strategies, and persistence required to transform a system. We considered benefit assessments, barrier assessments, action planning, and the principles of behavioral change.

Now, in this final chapter, we bring all of these threads together. We reflect on where we have been and where we are going. We consider the implications of all that we have learned. And we issue a call to action—a call to embrace restorative justice, to embody the ministry of reconciliation, and to work toward a more just and compassionate world.

The Paradox of Freedom and Safety

Our country is becoming less free as Americans call for the passing of new laws, harsher punishment, and longer sentences. This is a paradox that deserves our attention. In our desire for safety, we are sacrificing freedom. In our demand for punishment, we are creating systems that diminish us all.

Laws are created as a result of crime. In many instances they affect everyone. Consider this example: medicines that are sold over the counter but because of abuse, a law is passed mandating that they be prescribed by a doctor. This law affects everyone—the responsible person who now must take time to see a doctor, as well as the potential abuser who is restricted from easy access. Some laws are designed to protect us, but in doing so they rob us of certain freedoms and privileges.

This is the trade-off we constantly make. We trade freedom for security. We trade liberty for safety. And sometimes the trade is worth it. But sometimes we trade too much. Sometimes we give up freedoms that are essential to our humanity, and we do not get the safety we were promised in return.

There is a trend towards more punitive measures in the criminal justice system, which can be seen as a reflection of a broader cultural shift towards a desire for increased safety and security. While it is certainly understandable that people want to feel safe in their communities, there are some potential problems with this approach.

Firstly, the passing of new laws, harsher punishments, and longer sentences may not necessarily lead to a reduction in crime. In fact, research has shown that longer sentences may have little deterrent effect on crime rates and may even contribute to higher rates of recidivism. The certainty of punishment matters more than the severity. When people believe they will be caught, they are deterred. When they believe they can get away with it, harsh sentences do not matter. And our system is far from certain.

Secondly, the increased use of punitive measures can lead to over-incarceration, particularly of people from marginalized communities who are disproportionately impacted by the criminal justice system. This can have long-term negative consequences for individuals, families, and communities, as well as a significant financial cost to taxpayers.

The war on drugs, mandatory minimum sentences, and three-strikes laws have filled our prisons with people from poor communities and communities of color, while doing little to address the underlying problems of addiction and poverty.

Thirdly, there are concerns about the erosion of civil liberties and the expansion of government power that can result from a focus on punitive measures. This can include issues such as the use of invasive surveillance, the erosion of privacy rights, and the militarization of law enforcement. When we give the government more power to keep us safe, we must ask: safe from whom? And at what cost? And who watches the watchers?

Ultimately, while it is important to prioritize public safety, there is a need for a balanced approach that takes into account the potential harms of punitive measures and recognizes the importance of rehabilitation, restorative justice, and addressing the root causes of crime.

The Illusion of "Out of Sight, Out of Mind"

Local governments feel "freed" when they send the offender away for years, but in reality they have only postponed and compounded the problem. Many elected officials seem not to consider the long-term effects of sending the offender away for years or the need to resolve the problems created by criminal behavior. "Out of sight, out of mind" will never serve as an effective measure of intervention.

This statement highlights the issue of mass incarceration and the belief that simply sending offenders to prison does not solve the root causes of crime or address the needs of both victims and offenders. Instead, it perpetuates a cycle of incarceration that disproportionately affects communities of color and low-income individuals, creates a burden on the criminal justice system and taxpayers, and often fails to address issues such as mental health, addiction, and poverty that may have contributed to the criminal behavior in the first place.

Think about what happens when we send someone away for years. We remove them from their community. We separate them from their family. We take away their job, their housing, their relationships. We expose them to violence, trauma, and criminal influences. We provide little education, job training, or mental health treatment. And then, years later, we release them back into the same community, with the same problems, plus new ones acquired in prison. And we wonder why they so often reoffend.

Furthermore, incarceration often strains families, leaving spouses without partners and children without parents, leading to negative long-term effects on their emotional and financial well-being. Children of incarcerated parents are at higher risk for poverty, mental health problems, academic failure, and eventual involvement in the criminal justice system themselves. This can ultimately contribute to intergenerational poverty and perpetuate the cycle of crime.

Simply relying on imprisonment as a solution to crime is not effective and requires a more holistic approach that addresses the underlying causes of criminal behavior, provides support for victims, and offers opportunities for rehabilitation and reintegration of offenders back into society.

The Wisdom of Rehabilitation

The reality is that it is better to help successfully rehabilitate the offender than to deal with their continued criminal behavior. This is not just a matter of compassion; it is a matter of practicality. Rehabilitation works better than punishment alone.

Successful rehabilitation of offenders can have numerous benefits for society. Here are a few reasons why it is better to help rehabilitate offenders.

Reduced Recidivism: Successful rehabilitation helps offenders break the cycle of criminal behavior and reduces the likelihood of reoffending. This can reduce the burden on the criminal justice system and help keep communities safe. When offenders are given the tools they need to change, they are less likely to return to crime.

Improved Public Safety: Rehabilitated offenders are more likely to become law-abiding citizens, leading to improved public safety. A person who has addressed their addiction, learned job skills, and developed healthy relationships is far less dangerous than someone who has simply served time and been released unchanged.

Cost-Effective: It is often more cost-effective to rehabilitate offenders than to incarcerate them. Rehabilitation programs can be tailored to meet the specific needs of each offender and can be less expensive than maintaining a prison population. The cost of a year of prison can fund extensive rehabilitation services.

Humanitarian: Successful rehabilitation can help offenders turn their lives around and lead productive, fulfilling lives. This can have a positive impact on their families and communities. Every person who is restored is a person who can contribute to society rather than being a burden on it.

Restorative Justice: Rehabilitation programs can incorporate restorative justice principles, which focus on repairing harm caused by crime and addressing the needs of both the victim and the offender. This can lead to healing and reconciliation, promoting a more just and peaceful society.

The Ripple Effects of Rehabilitation

How does rehabilitation of the offender reap benefits to many people? The benefits ripple outward from the offender to touch many lives.

The offender benefits because they are able to live a different lifestyle. Instead of a life of crime, addiction, and incarceration, they can experience freedom, purpose, and productivity. They can develop their gifts, contribute to society, and find meaning and satisfaction in legitimate pursuits.

Their families benefit because they are restored to their position in the family as a contributor to the household. A parent who was absent is now present. A spouse who was a burden is now a partner. Children who were ashamed now have a role model. The family is strengthened and stabilized.

Other families, businesses and neighborhoods benefit because there is a reduction in crime. When one person is rehabilitated, the entire community is safer. Fewer burglaries, fewer robberies, fewer acts of violence mean that everyone can live with less fear and more freedom.

The community benefits because the offender no longer is a tax burden but rather a taxpayer. Instead of costing the community money through incarceration and social services, they now contribute through taxes, spending, and economic activity. They become part of the solution rather than part of the problem.

The rehabilitation of an offender can reap benefits to many people in several ways. First and foremost, it benefits the offender themselves by helping them address the underlying issues that led to their criminal behavior and providing them with the necessary tools and skills to lead a productive and law-abiding life. This, in turn, reduces the likelihood of them reoffending, which benefits their families, communities, and society as a whole.

Rehabilitation can also benefit the victims of crime by providing them with a sense of closure and healing. Through restorative justice practices, offenders can take responsibility for their actions and make amends to their victims, which can help the victims feel heard and validated.

Additionally, rehabilitation programs can provide job training, education, and other resources to offenders, which can increase their chances of finding employment and becoming self-sufficient. This, in turn, can reduce the burden on social welfare programs and benefit taxpayers.

Finally, a focus on rehabilitation can help shift the criminal justice system away from a punitive model and towards a more restorative and holistic approach. This can improve public trust in the justice system and reduce the negative impacts of mass incarceration on communities.

The Epidemic of Shifting Responsibility

The shifting of responsibility from community to state is epidemic. This is a phenomenon that has been observed in various aspects of society, including criminal justice. This shift is often due to the increasing complexity of issues and the perceived inability of individuals and local communities to effectively address these problems.

In the criminal justice system, this shift of responsibility is seen in the increased reliance on incarceration and the development of a punitive mindset. The belief is that punishment through incarceration will deter criminal behavior and provide justice for victims, while simultaneously removing the offender from society and shifting the responsibility for their rehabilitation to the state.

However, this approach has proven to be ineffective, as the high rates of recidivism and overcrowding in prisons demonstrate. Moreover, this approach has shifted the responsibility for addressing criminal behavior from the community to the state, leading to a loss of community involvement and empowerment.

Think about what this means. In the past, communities took responsibility for their members. They knew each other. They watched out for each other. They held each other accountable. When someone went wrong, the community was there to correct, to support, to restore. Now, we call 911 and wait for professionals to handle it. We have outsourced our responsibility.

Instead of shifting responsibility to the state, it is important to recognize that the community has a critical role to play in addressing criminal behavior. Communities can provide support and guidance for individuals who have been involved in criminal activity, helping them to turn their lives around and reintegrate into society. Communities can also provide opportunities for education and job training, which can help individuals to avoid criminal behavior in the first place.

Therefore, it is important to focus on rehabilitation and community involvement in addressing criminal behavior. This will require a shift in mindset from punishment and incarceration to support and guidance for offenders, and a renewed focus on empowering communities to take responsibility for the well-being of their members.

The Hospital Analogy

Building more prisons and merely locking people away is doomed to continued failure. Consider this illustration. What would happen if we built more hospitals for the sick and merely gave them rooms without the medical care needed? Would the sick get well? Of course, they would not! Simply building hospitals without providing medical care for the patients would be doomed to failure.

This analogy is powerful because it exposes the flaw in our thinking. We would never treat physical illness this way. When someone is sick, we do not just lock them in a room. We diagnose their condition. We provide treatment. We offer therapy and medication. We give them the care they need to get well.

Why do we treat criminal behavior differently? Crime is often a symptom of deeper problems—addiction, trauma, mental illness, poverty, lack of education and opportunity. If we simply lock people away without addressing these underlying issues, we should not be surprised when they emerge unchanged and reoffend.

The strategy of building more prisons and relying solely on incarceration as a means of addressing crime has been widely criticized by many experts in the criminal justice field. While incarceration may be necessary in certain cases to protect public safety, it is not a sustainable solution for reducing crime rates in the long run. Here are some reasons why.

High Cost: The cost of building and maintaining prisons is extremely high, with taxpayers bearing the brunt of the expense. This puts a strain on government budgets and diverts resources away from other important social services, such as education, healthcare, and housing. Every dollar spent on prisons is a dollar not spent on things that might actually prevent crime.

Overcrowding: The continued focus on incarceration has led to a significant increase in the number of people behind bars, resulting in overcrowded prisons that are often inhumane and unsafe. This not only puts prisoners at risk of harm but also creates a breeding ground for criminal activity and recidivism. Prisons become schools for crime rather than places of rehabilitation.

Lack of Rehabilitation: Prisons are often seen as a place of punishment rather than a place of rehabilitation, with limited opportunities for prisoners to receive education, job training, and mental health services. This makes it difficult for individuals to successfully reintegrate back into society upon release, leading to higher rates of recidivism. We punish them, but we do not help them.

Racial Disparities: The overreliance on incarceration has disproportionately affected communities of color, perpetuating systemic racism and social inequality. This is evidenced by the fact that Black Americans make up only 13% of the U.S. population but account for nearly 40% of the prison population. This is not justice; it is injustice on a massive scale.

Ignoring Root Causes: Incarceration alone does not address the root causes of crime, such as poverty, lack of education, and mental health issues. Focusing solely on punishment ignores the underlying factors that contribute to criminal behavior and fails to provide the necessary support for individuals to make positive changes in their lives.

Building more prisons and relying solely on incarceration is not an effective long-term solution to reducing crime rates. Instead, a more comprehensive approach that focuses on prevention, rehabilitation, and addressing the root causes of crime is needed to create a safer and more just society.

Smart Justice

Smart justice realizes that community-based, restorative justice is what works. This is not just a slogan; it is a conclusion supported by research and experience.

Smart justice recognizes that community-based, restorative justice is a more effective approach than simply locking people away in prisons. Restorative justice focuses on repairing harm caused by the offender and restoring relationships between the offender and the victim, as well as the community.

By involving the community in the process, restorative justice creates a sense of accountability and responsibility for the offender's actions. It allows for a more individualized approach to addressing the underlying issues that led to the criminal behavior, such as substance abuse, mental health issues, or a lack of education and employment opportunities.

Restorative justice also takes into account the needs and perspectives of the victim, providing them with a sense of closure and satisfaction. It allows them to have a voice in the process and to play an active role in the resolution of the situation.

In contrast, a punitive justice system that relies solely on incarceration and punishment often leads to further harm to the offender, the victim, and the community. It can result in a cycle of recidivism, as offenders are released from prison with little support or resources to reintegrate into society.

Therefore, smart justice recognizes that community-based, restorative justice is a more effective and sustainable approach to addressing crime and repairing harm caused by criminal behavior.

Restoration for All

Criminal justice using the restorative justice paradigm ends in the restoration of both the victim and the offender back into the community. This is the ultimate goal—not punishment, not revenge, but restoration for all.

Restorative justice is a paradigm shift from the traditional retributive justice approach, which focuses on punishing the offender for their crime. Restorative justice recognizes that the harm caused by the crime extends beyond the offender and affects the victim, the community, and even the offender themselves. Therefore, it seeks to repair the harm and restore relationships that have been damaged by the crime.

One of the core principles of restorative justice is the involvement of the victim in the process. Victims are given a voice and an opportunity to express their feelings, needs, and expectations. This allows them to participate in the decision-making process regarding the outcome of the case, which can lead to a sense of empowerment and healing.

Offenders are also encouraged to take responsibility for their actions and make amends for the harm they have caused. This could involve apologies, restitution, community service, or other forms of restorative action. The goal is to reintegrate the offender back into the community as a responsible and productive member, reducing the likelihood of future criminal behavior.

Restorative justice also recognizes the importance of the community in the process. Community members may be involved in supporting the victim, holding the offender accountable, or providing opportunities for the offender to make amends. By involving the community in the process, restorative justice promotes a sense of accountability and responsibility for the safety and well-being of the community as a whole.

The restorative justice approach recognizes the interconnectedness of individuals, communities, and the criminal justice system. By focusing on repairing harm, restoring relationships, and reintegrating offenders back into the community, restorative justice can lead to a more just and peaceful society.

The Needs of Victims

A victim loses his/her sense of security and community stability, and desperately needs assistance to go on with their life. This is a truth that must never be forgotten in our discussions of justice.

When someone becomes a victim of a crime, their life can be severely impacted, both physically and emotionally. Victims often experience a loss of sense of security and stability in their community, as they may fear for their safety or the safety of their loved ones. This can lead to feelings of vulnerability and helplessness.

Victims also may suffer from a range of emotional and psychological trauma, such as anxiety, depression, and post-traumatic stress disorder (PTSD). These can have long-lasting effects on their mental health and well-being. The effects of crime do not end when the incident is over; they continue for months, years, sometimes a lifetime.

It is important that victims receive support and assistance in coping with the aftermath of the crime. This may include counseling and therapy, financial assistance, and other resources to help them rebuild their lives. Restorative justice programs can also provide opportunities for victims to have a voice in the criminal justice process and to receive restitution from the offender, which can help them feel a sense of justice and closure.

Community members and organizations can play a crucial role in supporting victims of crime. They can provide emotional support and practical assistance, such as transportation, child care, and help with household chores. They can also advocate for victims' rights and promote restorative justice practices in their communities.

It is important to recognize the needs of victims of crime and to provide them with the support and resources they need to recover and move forward with their lives.

The Transformation of Offenders

The offender needs to become a caring member of the community. This is not just a nice idea; it is essential for public safety and community well-being.

The restorative justice paradigm recognizes that the offender is not just a lawbreaker but also a member of the community who has caused harm. Therefore, the process of restoration involves helping the offender recognize the harm they have caused and take responsibility for their actions. This process also involves helping the offender understand how their actions have impacted the victim and the community as a whole.

Restorative justice seeks to provide the offender with the opportunity to make amends and take actions to repair the harm they have caused. This could include financial compensation, community service, or other forms of restitution. In addition, the offender is encouraged to actively participate in their own rehabilitation and take steps to become a responsible member of society.

Restorative justice recognizes that the offender is not simply a passive recipient of punishment but an active agent in their own rehabilitation and restoration. By involving the offender in the process of repairing the harm they have caused, restorative justice seeks to promote personal growth, accountability, and social responsibility.

The goal of restorative justice is not just to punish the offender but also to help them become a caring member of the community. This approach recognizes that everyone in the community has a stake in preventing crime and promoting healing, and that the best way to achieve this is by working together towards the common goal of restoration.

Restorative Justice Is Smart Justice

Restorative justice is smart justice. This is the conclusion that more and more people are reaching as they see the failures of the punitive system and the promise of the restorative alternative.

Restorative justice was born out of the belief that crime is something more than just breaking a law, and that the role of the criminal justice system should be about more than catching, convicting and punishing the guilty. The expanding and still evolving vision of restorative justice presents new perspectives and new tools that offer the future of an effective paradigm of justice—one focused on accountability, inclusion, problem-solving and healing.

Restorative justice is an approach to justice that emphasizes the restoration of harm caused by criminal behavior. This approach seeks to provide justice by repairing the harm caused by crime, addressing the needs of victims, and helping offenders take responsibility for their actions and make amends. Restorative justice is often contrasted with traditional retributive justice, which emphasizes punishment for wrongdoing rather than repairing harm.

Restorative justice is a smart justice approach for several reasons.

First, it provides a more effective way to prevent future crime. By addressing the underlying causes of criminal behavior, restorative justice programs can help reduce recidivism rates and promote long-term rehabilitation. This is particularly important given the high rates of repeat offending in the criminal justice system.

Second, restorative justice can help improve public safety by promoting stronger, more connected communities. When offenders are held accountable for their actions and take responsibility for repairing the harm they have caused, they become more invested in the community and more likely to act in ways that promote public safety.

Third, restorative justice can help reduce the costs of the criminal justice system. Traditional retributive justice is often expensive and time-consuming, requiring extensive court proceedings, incarceration, and supervision. Restorative justice programs, on the other hand, can be less costly and more efficient, while also providing better outcomes for victims and communities.

Fourth, restorative justice can help address the harms caused by the criminal justice system itself. The traditional criminal justice system can be traumatizing and dehumanizing for both victims and offenders, perpetuating cycles of harm and dysfunction. Restorative justice offers a more humane and healing approach that prioritizes the needs of victims and focuses on repairing harm rather than punishing wrongdoing.

Restorative justice is a smart justice approach that can help reduce crime, promote public safety, reduce costs, and address the harms caused by the criminal justice system itself. By prioritizing the needs of victims, promoting rehabilitation and reintegration of offenders, and strengthening communities, restorative justice offers a more effective, efficient, and compassionate approach to justice.

A Final Word

As we come to the end of this journey, I want to leave you with a few final thoughts.

First, the traditional system of punitive justice has failed. It has failed victims, who are ignored and re-traumatized. It has failed offenders, who are punished but not changed. It has failed communities, which are fragmented and fearful. It has failed taxpayers, who bear an enormous burden for a system that does not work. We must be honest about this failure if we are to move forward.

Second, there is a better way. Restorative justice offers a vision of justice that is more faithful to the Scriptures, more responsive to the needs of victims, more effective at holding offenders accountable, and more empowering for communities. It is not a panacea; it is not easy; it is not always appropriate. But it is a proven approach that works.

Third, the Church has a vital role to play. God has chosen the Church as His primary instrument of restorative justice and has given it a clear mandate to do criminal justice ministry. The

Church can minister to victims, offenders, families, and criminal justice professionals. It can offer the ministry of presence, the power of relationship, and the hope of the gospel. It can be a community of healing and restoration in a broken world.

Fourth, change is possible. Organizational change is hard, but not impossible. With persistence, creativity, collaboration, and faith, we can transform systems and institutions. We can make them more restorative, more just, more compassionate. We can create a world where crime is addressed not with punishment alone but with healing, where victims are heard and supported, where offenders are held accountable and offered a path to restoration, and where communities are empowered to resolve conflicts and build peace.

Finally, this work is ultimately about the kingdom of God. It is about participating in God's mission of reconciliation, healing, and restoration. It is about being agents of God's grace in a world that desperately needs it. It is about living out the gospel in concrete ways that transform lives and communities.

I invite you to join this work. Educate yourself about restorative justice. Get involved in your community. Advocate for change. Build relationships with those who are impacted by crime and the criminal justice system. Pray for wisdom, courage, and perseverance. And trust that God, who began a good work in you, will bring it to completion.

The journey is long, but the destination is worth it. A more just, more compassionate, more restorative world is possible. Let us work together to bring it into being.

www.ingramcontent.com/pod-product-compliance
Lightning Source LLC
LaVergne TN
LVHW052222200926
848481LV00001B/185
9798295654954